Living Rich and Loving It

Your Guide to a Rich, Happy, Healthy, Simple and Balanced Life

Arthur V. Prosper

COPYRIGHT AND TRADEMARK OWNERSHIP

PAPERBACK ISBN: 9781980638360
Imprint: Independently published by:
A-Team, PO Box 153, Pinebrook, NJ 07058
Cover Models: My grandchildren, Cordelia & Lucien
Printed in the United States
Author's Email Address: arthurvprosper@gmail.com

Also by Arthur V. Prosper:

Stop Paying Your Credit Cards: Obtain Credit Card Debt Forgiveness Volume 1

DEBT FORGIVENESS Volume 2 WHEN CREDITORS DECIDE TO SUE

Dynamic Budgeting Techniques: Cut your expenses in half and double your income

The Simplest Path to Wealth: Turn $50,000 into $3.3 Million

The Six Million Dollar Retiree: Your roadmap to a six million dollar retirement nest egg

How Much Federal Income Tax Will I Pay in 2018? The New Tax Law's winners and losers

DISCLAIMER

Notice: The information contained in this book is provided to you "AS IS" and does not constitute legal or financial advice. The advice provided is general advice only and does not take into account your own personal objectives, financial situation or needs. Consult an attorney or a financial professional before acting on any information provided herein. Any companies, enterprises, organizations and products mentioned in this book are for reference only, have no affiliation with the author or publisher and are not specifically endorsed by the author or publisher.

ABOUT THE AUTHOR

Arthur V. Prosper heads the finance department of a privately held manufacturing firm in the great state of New Jersey. Previously, he was the Vice President of Finance of the Kuoni Group and the Accounting Director of Cantel Medical. He was responsible for the financial objectives, retirement and benefit plans, investment goals and capital structures of the companies he worked for.

Arthur V. Prosper predicted the approximate start and end of the great recession of 2007-2009 by using the methods discussed in PART II. In this chapter, the author reveals his investment technique and market timing strategy so as to avoid the typical 30% to 60% loss of value of stocks during the bear market that follows a recession.

Arthur V. Prosper is a freelance writer, author and columnist with 30 years of market experience. He writes articles about the markets and finance under the header "DidoSphere, DidoSpin and Vox Populi". He is the author of several published articles in business, politics, sports and entertainment including: How We Got Here, Market Crash of 2008, Housing Bubble, The Obama Recession, Bank Stress Tests & Other Terms, Scrap Mark to Market Valuation, Recession Over, The Labyrinth of Obamacare, Bush-Obama Recession, No Different From the Rest, A Tale of Two States, NJ & VA, SEC's Case vs. GS&CO., Weak, Most Experts Agree, PIIGS: Too Big to Fail, What Causes Stock Market Fluctuations, Sluggish Recovery, Good for Investors, QE2=Printing Money, Stock Market Investors, Fasten Your Seatbelt, No Double Dip Recession, 10% Unemployment Rate, Not Enough to Derail Recovery

Visit the author's website: http://didosphere.com

Author's email address: arthurvprosper@gmail.com

I. PREFACE

At its core, this book is a compilation of my first three books: **"Dynamic Budgeting Techniques"**, **"The Simplest Path to Wealth" and "The Six Million Dollar Retiree"**. However, it has several distinct differences between those three standalone books. Some of the most fervent feedback I received from readers on my previous three books was that a "manifesto" is necessary to bind together the three previous books. Therefore, I have included a section on the principles I follow which I believe lead to a rich, happy, healthy, simple and balanced life. See Part V. The previous three books are treated as individual sections of this book, as a whole, where together in sequence, they guide you through the three books as a cohesive game plan towards your own path of positive personal change. In addition, I have included a chapter in this book on how to plan for college and how to formulate a strategy to increase your children's chances to receive financial aid offers from top colleges and universities. I believe that my previous three books have already helped hundreds of families who are seeking enlightenment, to put what they have learned into action and to get their financial house in order, but this book should appeal to a broader market, those who are seeking a general reference guide for simple living, simple investing and simple day to day existence.

II. INTRODUCTION

I want to thank you for purchasing this book. If this book is worthy of your praise, your positive review would be much appreciated.

This book strives to develop a vision that being rich is not only about achieving financial independence. It's about living a happy, healthy, simple, balanced and fulfilling life with minimal stress. Aiming high and setting your goal much higher than your peers to build a successful life sounds great but it should not be at the expense of your health and relationships. Doing more than you think is necessary, than just doing enough to get by is admirable but it may take its toll on you. Your mental drive must be balanced with maintaining physical fitness and spending ample leisure time with loved ones. Workaholics and over achievers realize much too late in life that the path they had taken was the wrong one. The road to victory does not have to be the roughest road. Why not make life easy?

Life does not have to be complicated. If you succeed in following the life strategies in this book, your children will end up well, your investments will provide you with a nice retirement nest egg that will last for as long as you live, you will minimize stress in your life, you will not spend much time managing money and you will have more time for leisure and for activities that will keep your mind, body and spirit healthy. This book is not the magic bullet for success but a playbook to improve your odds for achieving success. There will be unexpected twists and turns in your life but the principles and strategies in this book will help lead you back to the correct path to success and keep you on track to achieve all you want in life. If you have goals, dreams and aspirations in life, you have a sense of direction but you still need a road map to take you from here to there. I hope this book will serve as that road map for you.

Learn how to:

- o Find a job you love. If you cannot wait to get up and get to work every morning, then you've found the job you love. Otherwise, you need to read the chapter, "Find a Job You Love" and the chapter, "Increase Your Income with these Ideas".

- o Create a budget so that you will always have a surplus at the end of each month.

- o Maximize contributions to your retirement account and accumulate more than a million dollars for retirement.

- o Determine if converting to a Roth IRA or Roth 401k is right for you. Ed Slott, the IRA guru says converting your IRA to a Roth IRA is tantamount to moving your account from "accounts that are forever taxed to accounts that are never taxed". WRONG! See Chapter, "Your Retirement Plan".

- o Never lose money in the stock market by using "The KISS Principle" and "Auto-Pilot Strategy".

- o Predict the next recession by watching the "yield curve". It is so simple yet so effective.

- o Calculate the amount of life insurance you need. Insurance brokers will hate this chapter. The answer will surprise you.

- o Avoid Veblen Goods – the savings will amaze you.

- o Shop around for everything. If you are struggling to make ends meet, this chapter will show you why. Learn how to save more and spend less.

- Purchase your primary residence – Pros and cons of owning vs. renting. The analysis chart shows the clear winner which will surprise you.

- Distinguish good debt from bad debt---when borrowing makes sense. Analysis table proves that some debts are good.

- Never take unnecessary risks. Don't do anything stupid. This chapter shows that stupidity is the great equalizer in life. Doing any of the things on the list may change your life or worse may end it in the blink of an eye.

- Stay away from rental properties. This chapter tells you why it is not worth being an absentee landlord.

- Handle emergencies without an emergency fund. The analysis chart shows why you should not have an emergency fund. The figures will astound you. This chapter also shows the reader where to get cash for emergencies once you get rid of your emergency fund.

- Never ever listen to Suze Orman that 401k loans are taxed twice. 401k loans are not taxed twice. This chapter proves it.

- Plan for college. How will you pay for your children's college education? Read the many different ideas in this chapter on how to increase your children's chances of getting offers from good colleges and universities. See the 9 simple steps you can take in chapter, "Planning for College".

- Increase your income. Make more money in your spare time with these ideas. When you read the money-making ideas in this chapter, you will scratch your head and say, "why didn't I think of that?"

- Create a document storage and retrieval system. So simple yet so effective. It will free up a lot of your limited living space.

- Implement a stress-free personal time management system. This system will organize your day and free up plenty of your time for use at your leisure.

- Store and safeguard passwords – Simple trick will help you create and remember strong passwords.

- Maximize your Social Security benefits – In light of the elimination of "File and Suspend" and "Restricted Application" strategies, the chart shows claiming strategies for 1) Single never married, 2) currently married, 3) married at least 10 years, divorced at least 2 years, currently single, 4) divorced, has remarried and currently married, 5) widow/widower, 6) surviving divorced spouse, married at least 10 years, currently single or remarried after the age of 60.

- Find the best places for retirement – Some of these retirement communities are surprising. Some viable locations have ½ the cost of living of most U.S. cities.

- Pay for nursing home and long-term care. The cost of nursing home and long term care can wipe out your entire estate. Read this chapter for solutions.

- Qualify for Medicaid benefits for LTC. You may not have to spend down your savings. This chapter explains many different ways other retirees have been dealing with the "spend down" dilemma.

- Establish estate planning. How to protect your estate from estate tax and inheritance tax.

- ○ **Enrich Your Life by Exploring the World – Travel as soon as you can while you are still young. This chapter discusses why the money you spend traveling and exploring the world is money well spent.**

- ○ **Stay Healthy and Fit as You Age – There are a few minor behavior modification changes that you can put into practice that will keep you healthy throughout your retirement years.**

- ○ **Live a Rich, Happy, Healthy, Simple and Balanced Life**

III.   INVESTING WISELY

My financial advisor lost 60% of her savings in the stock market during the great recession of December 2007 to June 2009. I lost nothing because I got out of equities in August 2007. Then my portfolio gained more than 50% in 2009 because I got back into equities in December 2008. The Federal Reserve Bank of St. Louis reported that household wealth plunged $16 trillion from the beginning of the last recession until it ended in June 2009. As of mid-2013, my financial advisor had not yet recovered all the money she lost. If you succeed in following my strategy in PART II, you will never lose money in the stock market. In fact you could make a killing when the next recession hits.

You can be living rich without taking unnecessary risks and without doing anything fancy. The steps are simple but you will need a road map to navigate through the difficult terrain so as to avoid the financial pitfalls which include taxation, debts, lack of income, medical needs, market risks, estate preservation, insurance, cash flow, etc. This book will help you traverse through life's winding roads. You will get to your destination with the help of this book. But the first step is to get rid of all your non-mortgage debts. Pay off all your unsecured consumer debts, or ask your creditors for reduction or forgiveness of your debts. Get more information. Open the following link about debt forgiveness:

https://www.amazon.com/Stop-Paying-Your-Credit-Cards-ebook/dp/B019ZY3D1E?ie=UTF8&*Version*=1&*entries*=0

IV. THIS BOOK IS FOR EVERYONE

My objective for writing this book is to touch and improve the quality of life of everyone who reads it. My hope is for the reader to put the life-changing ideas presented in this book into practice. Whether you have millions of dollars in assets or are struggling to get by, living paycheck to paycheck, this book has something for you. Success means different things to different people. An additional $1000 a month in retirement is considered success for some, but for others protecting a six million dollar estate from taxation is their definition of success.

Dave Ramsey's advice to keep 6 months' worth of living expenses in a checking account to use as an emergency fund is not a good idea. This book will tell you why and show you a better alternative. **Suze Orman's** advice not to borrow money from your 401k plan because you will pay it back in after tax money is not true and this book will prove it. This book will show why you will save thousands of dollars by NOT following Dave Ramsey's advice to pay off your mortgage. **Robert Kiyosaki** says, "A house is a liability…because it costs money to own and run". False. This book will prove that your primary residence is one of the best assets you can own and this book will help you accurately assess the real value of your primary residence. Save money by buying term life insurance instead of whole life and only for 7 times your annual income, not for 10 to 12 times annual income as most personal finance gurus recommend. This book will explain why. **Ed Slott** claims that he will show you how to "move your retirement savings from accounts that are forever taxed to accounts that are never taxed". With due respect to Ed Slott, there is no such thing as "accounts that are never taxed". All money is taxed at least once. This book will explain why there is no advantage to convert your traditional IRA and 401k into a Roth IRA and Roth 401k.

If you need help on budgeting, investing, real estate purchase, personal insurance (health, accident, life, auto, personal liability, homeowner's and disability insurance), retirement planning, how to spend your leisure time wisely, and how to increase your income, this book is for you. Perhaps you are just starting out, just out of college, started your first job, this book will show the beginner basic monthly budgeting, investment strategies and the fundamentals of money management. Many Americans are falling into a pattern of spending more than they take in so they steadily go deeper into debt as a result. Increasing income, getting rid of credit card debts and creating a budget are steps in the right direction. If you are like most people, you dream of the day you can get rid of your debts and boost your savings and retirement accounts. The reality is that many who want to achieve financial freedom are not sure where to start. The life strategies in this book will help strengthen your financial future.

PART I: DYNAMIC BUDGETING TECHNIQUES – CUT YOUR EXPENSES IN HALF & DOUBLE YOUR INCOME

1. Introduction TO BUDGETS

The title of Part I is "Dynamic Budgeting" because it refers to a process that is continuously in motion. It's ongoing and fluid. Budgets are not screen shots but videos of events in perpetual motion. Your budget must become a dynamic budget to help you achieve financial freedom faster. The strategy presented in this section of the book requires active monitoring of your income and expenses which for most of us can be accurately projected. Adjusting your budget throughout the year as your income and expenses change should be part of your strategy. You may have unexpected income but more often you will have unexpected expenses. Any overage at the end of each month must be added to your retirement savings, traditional or Roth 401k and IRA, 403b and 457b. You have to make up for any shortage at the end of the month by reducing any discretionary expenses. This is the way a dynamic budget works.

For some people, creating a budget is plain and simple common sense but it is an overwhelming and an unpleasant undertaking for others. Many people still believe they can spend more than their take home pay and that an interest free credit card balance transfer with a 7% transaction fee is really interest free.

This chapter will make it easy for those who need basic guidance in evaluating their current financial situation. A cash flow worksheet and a sample budget with all the necessary components are shown under the chapter, "Create a Budget". If lack of income is the problem, there are practical suggestions in this book on how to start your own business and how to earn extra money in your spare time by offering tax preparation service, organizing social events and karaoke parties, being a concert promoter, conducting seminars (cooking demonstrations, public speaking, dancing, how to tie a

Windsor knot, fly fishing demo, mixed martial arts, buying your first house, couponing, teaching time management, basic computer skills, basic carpentry and plumbing), writing travel and restaurant reviews, turning yourself into a local tour guide, being a coach/trainer, an Uber or Lyft driver, selling autographed books, Blog writer, being a Court translator, offering products and services to the government (Federal and State), selling advertisements on restaurant placemats, offering dog-sitting and dog walking services, building or buying tiny houses that you can transport and rent or sell, offering baked goods to local bakeries and many other money-making ideas, too many to list. Details on how to start and implement these money-making ideas and how much you can earn from these ventures are shown under the chapter, "Increase Your Income with These Ideas". Know where your money is going and learn how to custom tailor your budget to compensate for the adversities that come with life changes such as marriage, divorce, birth of children, career change, loss of job, bankruptcy, accidents, major illnesses, being a crime victim, death of a relative, depression and mid-life crisis. Sometime in your lifetime you will encounter one or more of these life-changing events. You never know what curve balls life throws at you. Some people experience multiple curve balls simultaneously, a perfect storm of calamities. You may be in the middle of divorce, then lose your job, then go into a deep depression that prevents you from getting another job. In the middle of all this, your retirement account loses 50% due to the recession and your principal residence has lost 30% of its original value because of the housing bubble burst. You must be flexible enough to adjust your lifestyle accordingly. When big changes happen in your life, you must not lose sight of the important things in life such as your health and your relationship with loved ones. If you lose 50% of your income, it's not the end of the world and you can easily adjust to living with less. But you can do irreparable damage to your health and to your relationship with loved ones if you continue to blame yourself and loved ones for the difficult predicament in which you find yourself. If you harbor resentment, it will cause pain, anguish and stress in your life. You will find many tips throughout this book on how to handle stressful situations caused by life changes.

The road to financial freedom starts by creating a budget and taking control of your finances which many people think is easy and "plain and simple commonsense". As for me, the following is the step by step pathway to a budget that always produces a surplus instead of a shortfall at the end of every month:

o   Create a cash flow statement as shown under this chapter
o   Create a budget
o   Get rid of your consumer debts
o   Reduce all your insurance premiums
o   Reduce or eliminate all non-essential expenses
o   Reduce essential expenses
o   Never lease a car and get rid of your auto loans
o   Never buy a new car
o   Avoid Veblen goods
o   Increase your income
o   Fund your children's college education using the techniques shown under this chapter.
o   Maximize contributions to your retirement account
o   Invest wisely so you may preserve your retirement nest egg
o   Buy your principal residence
o   Start early. Think of retirement planning including estate, long term care and nursing home planning
o   Unclutter your life by creating more space and developing an effective time management system

2. Get Rid of All Your Consumer Debts First

As long as you have non-mortgage debts, you will continue to struggle in finding the doorway to financial independence. You should not be paying monthly installments on your credit card debts and other consumer debts such as pay day loans, car loans, department store loans, furniture and home improvement loans. Pay them in full right now from other sources or ask your creditors for a reduction or complete forgiveness of your debts. Refer to my book, "STOP PAYING YOUR CREDIT CARDS" for more information on debt reduction/forgiveness negotiation. https://www.amazon.com/dp/B019ZY3D1E/ref=rdr_kindle_ext_tmb "STOP PAYING YOUR CREDIT CARDS" will show you how to negotiate reduction or forgiveness of your debt so that you will have a fighting chance to start fresh without the heavy baggage of credit card and other consumer debts. Bite the bullet now to get your financial life back on track rather than postpone the inevitable. Do not charge anything on your credit cards if you cannot afford to pay the balance in full when you receive your statement. It is not OK to borrow money from revolving credit accounts and pay only the minimum monthly installment. As long as you keep a balance on your credit card accounts, it will be hard to achieve your financial goals because you are throwing away hard earned cash. Some people think: "If I can afford to pay the monthly minimum payment, I can afford to borrow (even at 25% APR)". NO, it's NOT! If you are constantly borrowing and charging purchases on your credit cards and paying only the minimum each month, chances are your credit card balances will continue to increase and you will never achieve financial independence. Paying 25% APR interest on your credit card debt is a waste of money. Getting rid of your credit card debts is your first step in creating a budget and in controlling your finances. If you cannot afford to pay your credit card debt in full when the statement comes, you cannot afford the purchase. Stop using your credit cards. Plan A is to borrow money from your 401k account or refinance the mortgage on your house if you can to pay off the high interest credit card balances. Stop contributions to your 401k account and send the credit card companies the amount you would have contributed. It does not matter if your employer matches

100% of 10% of your contributions. The money is peanuts compared to what you will save by getting rid of credit card debt bearing 25% or more annual interest rate. Do the math if you can refinance your mortgage loan for a higher amount at a lower interest rate and can afford the new (higher) monthly payment. That way you may get enough money from the bank to pay off high interest bearing credit card debt. A debt-free lifestyle is an integral part of the financial game plan. If you cannot get cash from your 401k or from the equity in your house and there is no available cash from other sources, plan B is to sell any hard assets you may have such as a car, furniture, jewelries, anything of value and drastically reduce your expenses. Plan C is to increase your income. Review the chapter, "Increase Your Income with these Ideas". There are specific strategies in this chapter on how to make extra money in your in your spare time. Plan D is to stop paying your credits cards and beg the creditors for a reduction or forgiveness of your debt. This is the last resort. This move will negatively affect your credit and your FICO scores will tumble. This can set you back several years and may prevent you from obtaining a home mortgage loan. Click on the link that follows to get more information on how I mollified the effect of the negative information on my credit report. See the Chapter, **"How to Mitigate Negative Credit Report"**: https://www.amazon.com.au/DEBT-FORGIVENESS-Chapter-CREDITORS-DECIDE-ebook/dp/B01ACTBTIU

3. Find a Job You Love

It is such a common phrase but it's easier said than done. If you live in an industrialized country there is no reason why you cannot pursue and land a job you love. It is a different story if you live in a third world country where your choices are limited. So why in the world would you stay in a job that you don't love? You should be excited to get up every morning and get to work.

If you are in high school and thinking about college or perhaps as an alternative vocational or trade school, contemplating on your career path, ask yourself these questions: "What do I enjoy doing the most? What am I good at? What subjects do I excel in?" If you just started your first job, ask yourself this question, "Will I be happy getting up every morning doing this type of work for the rest of my working life?" The answers to the questions will help you find yourself. God gave us gifts when we were born and the natural talents God gave us are meant to be used to our full advantage. God made each and every one of us good at something. It is enjoyable and fun for us when we are doing something that we are good at. Our mind is powerful it can work wonders for us. It can dictate our future, our well-being, our hopes and dreams and it can take us to places we never even imagined. Carl Jung said, "I am not what happened to me, I am what I choose to become." If you are not in a job you love, snap out of it and move forward and condition your mind to see the unlimited possibilities for your life. But this does not mean you should march to your boss's office tomorrow and tell him to, "take this job and shove it." Any move especially a change in careers requires a lot of planning. Any wrong move can set you back many months or even years. You may have to go back to school and learn additional skills if the job you are in now is not the job you foresee yourself doing for the rest of your working life. This is where a good and realistic budget comes in. It will help you plan for the future and project what your life will be if you succeed with your goal of finding the job you love. Review the chapter, "Increase Your Income with these Ideas" for realistic ways to increase your income by doing what you love.

If finding the job you love means changing careers and going back to school, it is all the more important to create a budget to project your financial position during and after the change. Be cautious. Do not make a decision based solely on financial considerations. Your personal satisfaction and mental well-being can more than offset any financial short fall that comes with changing careers to pursue what you love. Happiness has an intrinsic value that cannot be measured by dollars and cents.

If finding the job you love simply means leaving the company you currently work for to get a better job in the same line of work, do not quit your job until someone else hires you. It is easier to find another job while you are still employed. Just like millions of other employees, you can look for another job while still employed and not neglect your duties in your current position. For more information about job interviews, see the Chapter, "Increase Your Income with these Ideas" under the topic, "Mock Interviewer".

One last parting comment on this chapter. Oftentimes, it is human nature to be afraid and wary whenever we try something new. When an opportunity that we are not familiar with presents itself, most of us freeze and inaction takes over, so the opportunity passes. We will not know if we are good at something and that we will enjoy doing something unless we give it a try. Condition yourself, your mind to try something new. Give it a chance and whatever it is may just prove to be the job you would love doing for the rest of your working life.

4. Reduce Term Life Insurance

Term life insurance is the best and the most cost effective way to protect your family when you die. Whole life insurance is very expensive and will take a bigger bite off of your budget over the years. The biggest argument for advocates of whole life is that term insurance pays only death benefits and therefore should be called "death insurance". My argument is that insurance should not be a tax shelter or savings for retirement. Insurance is insurance for loved ones that you leave behind. Although it may be true that perhaps after a fixed period of time (e.g. 20 years), the premium may substantially go up, you may not need as much insurance or may not need the insurance at all when that time comes. One thing to consider is that, the surviving spouse and children of the deceased are entitled to social security survivors' benefits. The amount of benefits is based on the earnings of the deceased. As you grow older your social security wages will increase. Your survivors' benefits will increase as well. That is why you may not need as much insurance. Click on the link below to find out more about survivors' benefits: https://www.ssa.gov/planners/survivors/#&sb=2

This is an important component that should be considered when buying term life insurance.

In the event of your untimely demise if your death occurred while performing your duty as an employee, your beneficiaries will be compensated in accordance with Worker's Compensation Laws. So my recommendation is to get coverage for only 7 times annual household income instead of 10 to 12 times as many financial planners recommend. You can get term life premium quotes from Zander Insurance Group and Select Quote.

The purpose of insurance is to provide income replacement for your survivors for at least 10 years after you die. The following chart shows that your beneficiaries will have more than enough money to live on for at least 10 years even if you buy insurance for only 7 times your annual salary:

ANNUAL SALARY $65,000 x 7 TIMES	= $455,000
SS SURVIVORS' BENEFITS	
$2,000 PER MONTH x 12 MOS. x 10 YEARS	= $240,000
COMPANY PROVIDED LIFE INSURANCE	= $65,000
TOTAL = Greater Than 10 x ANNUAL SALARY	$760,000

As time goes by your assets grow, such as the equity in your house and your 401k account. Your survivors will be the beneficiaries of these assets that will increase in value over the years. After 10 years it is likely that your spouse and your children will be able to financially take care of themselves or at least contribute to the family income. So to summarize my advice: do not over insure.

5. Reduce Medical, Dental & Disability Insurance

Medical and Dental Insurance

If you live in the USA where there is no socialized health care, your number one priority is to make sure you, your spouse and your children have medical and dental coverage to avoid getting financially wiped out in case of large medical bills. According to labor statistics, 80% of employers provide some type of insurance coverage. The Affordable Care Act (ACA or Obamacare) can cover the uninsured. If you are one of them go to this website and obtain coverage, http://www.obamacareusa.org/get-quotes.

Most states offer some type of assistance for health insurance coverage for households with minor children if an employee cannot get insurance coverage elsewhere, or if the worker's employer requires a big contribution from the employee. In NJ as shown on the following chart, a husband and wife with two minor children and with an income of $60,756 a year qualify for a state subsidized health insurance coverage and will pay only a monthly premium of $43. Check with your state if they have a similar program.

NJ**FAMILYCARE**
Affordable health coverage. Quality care.

Income Chart effective 2016

1-800-701-0710
TTY: 1-800-701-0720
www.njfamilycare.org

FAMILY SIZE *	Adult(s) (Age 19-64)	Pregnant Women (Any Age)	Children (Under Age 19)					
	Federal Poverty Level % (FPL)							
	0 - 138%	0 - 205%	0 - 147%	> 147 - 150%	> 150 - 200%	> 200 - 250%	> 250 - 300%	> 300 - 355%
	Maximum Monthly Income							
1	$1,367	N/A	$1,456	$1,485	$1,980	$2,475	$2,970	$3,515
2	$1,843	$2,737	$1,963	$2,003	$2,670	$3,338	$4,005	$4,740
3	$2,319	$3,444	$2,470	$2,520	$3,360	$4,200	$5,040	$5,964
4	$2,795	$4,152	$2,977	$3,038	$4,050	$5,063	$6,075	$7,189
5	$3,271	$4,859	$3,484	$3,555	$4,740	$5,925	$7,110	$8,414
6	$3,747	$5,566	$3,992	$4,073	$5,430	$6,788	$8,145	$9,639
Each Additional	$479	$711	$510	$520	$694	$867	$1,040	$1,231
Monthly Premium	No premium	No premium	No premium	No premium	No premium	$43.00 per family	$86.00 per family	$144.50 per family
Copayments	No copay	No copay	No copay	No copay	$5 - $10	$5 - $35	$5 - $35	$5 - $35

* The size of your family may be determined by the **total number** of parent(s) or caretaker(s), and all blood-related children under the age of 21 **who are tax dependent, as well as any other tax dependent** residing in the home.

NJFC-INCOME-E-2016 rev 02/16

Disability Insurance

You need short term disability or Temporary Disability insurance (STD/TDI) coverage which usually pays a percentage of employees' salaries for the period of disability up to 6 months if they are ill, injured or pregnant and cannot perform their job. Coverage usually starts from one to 14 days after an employee suffers disability. A typical policy pays a benefit of 60% of an employee's gross salary. At the time of writing, only California, Hawaii, New Jersey, New York and Rhode Island are known as "mandatory states" which requires employers to provide coverage for disability benefits to employees either through the state or through a private plan. The premiums are usually shared by the employer and the employee. In some states where there is no mandatory requirement for STD/TDI, many employers offer the coverage at the expense of employees. The premium is really not that expensive. So check with your employer first, then shop around for other insurance providers if your company does not offer it. Many large and medium size companies in non-mandatory states offer paid maternity leave as a company benefit.

You need long term disability coverage (LTD). This coverage begins when STD/TDI ends. Most policies pay benefits for as long as the employee is disabled until the age of 65. Some policies have a defined period of time for payment of benefits, e.g. 10, 15 or 20 years. The most common policies pay 60% of an employee's total income which means total earnings from all sources. Review each policy to make sure it meets your needs. Various policies have different payout conditions such as diseases or pre-existing conditions that may be excluded and other conditions that may be unfavorable to you. Some policies will pay out the benefits if the claimant can no longer work in his or her current profession because of the disability but other policies expect the claimant to accept any job that he or she is capable of performing, so the disability claim may be rejected. The cost of LTD through your employer is surprisingly inexpensive. An annual benefit of $40,000 may only cost $400 a year through a company provided plan. The cost can be double that amount if you purchase the policy on your own. A medical underwriting may be required to determine risk vs. benefit for the insurance company. Your age will be a factor and if you drink and smoke and have pre-existing conditions, your premium will be more. If you have to buy an individual plan, start by contacting your credit union, AAA, AARP and other professional organizations that you can be a member of. Check out the following Social Security Administration's website on how to qualify for disability under the government program www.socialsecurity.gov/disability.

LTD premiums are not expensive because if you become disabled due to an automobile accident or injury in the workplace, your LTD coverage is usually subordinate to your auto insurance and worker's compensation insurance. ERISA (Employee Retirement Income Security Act) neither requires a plan to contain a subrogation clause nor does it bar such a clause, most LTD insurance companies have an "offset clause" allowing them to deduct the amounts received by the claimant from other sources such as the insurance payments from auto insurance and worker's compensation insurance. Even SSDI (social security disability) benefits may be deducted from benefits paid by the insurance carrier. So the insurance company's payout for LTD may not be that much. See, "Maddox v.

LifeIns. Co., 536 F.Supp.2d 1307, 1327 (N.D. Ga. 2008)". Consider this further. In accordance with the Tort Laws, if you become disabled because of a wrongful act, whether intentional or accidental, caused by another person or business entity, in theory you can claim disability payments from the wrongdoer's insurance provider.

6. Reduce Auto & Homeowner's Insurance

Automobile Insurance

By law everyone who drives needs **liability** automobile insurance. This coverage pays for accidental bodily injury and property damage that you may accidentally cause to others. Injury damages include medical expenses, pain and suffering and lost wages. Property damage includes damage to property and automobiles. The coverage also pays defense and court costs. Some states require the driver to purchase a minimum coverage and the insurance brokers are familiar with the requirements.

Collision insurance covers damages to your vehicle caused by collision with another vehicle or object if you caused the accident. This coverage is not mandated by law.

Comprehensive insurance covers losses or damages to the insured vehicle that does not occur in an auto accident. Examples are damages from fire, wind, hail, flood, vandalism or theft. This coverage is not required by law.

Uninsured and Underinsured Motorist insurance covers your car's damages if the other driver who causes the accident does not have liability insurance or has insufficient liability insurance. This coverage is mandatory in some states.

Medical Coverage covers your medical expenses resulting from an auto accident regardless of fault. This coverage is not mandatory.

PIP (Personal Injury Protection) covers medical expenses and loss of income of the insured and passengers regardless of fault. This coverage is mandatory in some states.

The following factors are used by insurance companies to determine the premium they will charge you: Gender, age, marital status, address, type of car, year, make, model, security system, overnight parking (street, driveway, garage), primary use (commuting, business, pleasure, school), annual mileage, education, occupation, credit rating, number of tickets and moving violations in last 3 years, amount of deductible, number of claims in the last 3 years.

With the cost of auto insurance always on the rise, the following has been my strategy for the past 30 years: If my car is less than 5 years old, I purchase the mandatory minimum coverages, and collision and comprehensive with a $1000 deductible. After 5 years, I drop the collision and comprehensive coverages. The premiums for collision and comprehensive are expensive. I do not spend the money I save. Instead I dump it into my 401k account. I sort of self-insure. Here is my thinking. I think I am a good and defensive driver. I am confident that I myself will not cause a major accident. If I do, I only have myself to blame and I deserve to pay the cost for fixing or replacing my 5 year old car. Yes I know, no one knows and I'm taking an awful chance, but please follow my line of thinking. If I cause the accident, my liability coverage should cover the other driver's damages. The damage to my car will not be covered by insurance. Let's say my car is damaged to the tune of $7000, this is a deductible casualty expense on my tax return in our current tax system, even if I caused the accident, as long as it was not a willful act on my part. In my tax bracket, I will realize approximately $1500 in tax benefit. If another driver causes the accident, then his liability insurance coverage should cover any damages I've suffered. The bottom line is that I will not get reimbursed for damages to my vehicle unless the damages were caused by another driver who has insurance. If my 5 year old car is stolen or vandalized, I will be responsible for the casualty loss which will generate a tax deduction. If you are not comfortable with this strategy, by all means continue to pay the premiums for collision and comprehensive insurance coverages.

Home Owner's Insurance
This coverage is not required by the state but mortgage providers will require you to have it. But even if no one requires you to have it, only foolish people do not have homeowner's insurance. If you have a home, you need it. The insurance includes **liability** coverage if you are sued for damages or injuries to someone else. For example, if someone slipped on a patch of ice on the sidewalk in front of your house or fell off the stairs of your house. Homeowner's insurance also includes coverage for damages to **dwelling and contents**. Typical coverage includes damage from fire, lightning,

windstorm, hail, smoke damage, water damage due to faulty plumbing, burst pipes, etc. Damage from flooding, earthquakes and tornados are generally not covered and a separate natural disaster coverage must be purchased. If you live in one of the most expensive states for homeowner's insurance such as Florida, Texas, Louisiana, Oklahoma and Washington DC, you may opt for a high deductible, say $2000 to $5000 to reduce the premiums if your mortgage provider has no objections. My reason for this is that you can afford to pay for minor damages and not even report the incident to the insurance company. If you have a low deductible, say $500, it is logical that you will have more claims to report which will just increase your premiums.

7. Create a Cash Flow Statement

A cash flow statement will show where you are and a budget is where you want to be. Before you can move on to creating a budget, you have to know where you are. That is why a cash flow projection is an integral part of this process. Net cash flow is simply Cash Receipts less Cash Disbursements. Your cash receipts from all sources should always be more than your expenditures. Otherwise, you have a negative cash flow which spells trouble. You cannot offset the negative cash flow by borrowing from your credit cards. The remedy for a negative cash flow is to reduce your expenses or increase your cash receipts (take home pay) or both. The continuous cash flow projection that follows will show you where you are now and where you will be at any given time in the future. You can keep projecting your cash flow as far in the future as you want as long as you have an accurate projection of your receipts and disbursements. Your running cash balance should keep increasing. If the excel table you will create shows that the running balance is starting to flatten or become negative at a certain date, you must immediately take action to increase income and reduce expenses long before that date comes or you will find yourself in financial trouble. If you have difficulty keeping track of your expenses, there is a simple and fool proof way of accomplishing this. Avoid paying for anything in cash. Use your credit card for all purchases and for expenses you cannot charge, use the "bill pay" option from your bank if available. Most banks nowadays provide this "bill pay" service for free. You will have a more accurate projection if you follow this advice because you will have a record of all your expenses. Step 1, start by creating an excel spreadsheet with 3 columns and enter the titles of the columns as shown. Enter your take home pay first as shown on the following table and make sure you enter the actual dates you will receive the income:

CASH FLOW		AMOUNT
DUE DATE	DESCRIPTION	
4/11/2015	BI-WEEKLY NET PAY After Taxes & 401K	2,400
4/25/2015	BI-WEEKLY NET PAY After Taxes & 401K	2,400
5/9/2015	BI-WEEKLY NET PAY After Taxes & 401K	2,400
5/23/2015	BI-WEEKLY NET PAY After Taxes & 401K	2,400
6/6/2015	BI-WEEKLY NET PAY After Taxes & 401K	2,400
6/20/2015	BI-WEEKLY NET PAY After Taxes & 401K	2,400
7/4/2015	BI-WEEKLY NET PAY After Taxes & 401K	2,400
7/18/2015	BI-WEEKLY NET PAY After Taxes & 401K	2,400
8/1/2015	BI-WEEKLY NET PAY After Taxes & 401K	2,400
8/15/2015	BI-WEEKLY NET PAY After Taxes & 401K	2,400
8/29/2015	BI-WEEKLY NET PAY After Taxes & 401K	2,400
9/12/2015	BI-WEEKLY NET PAY After Taxes & 401K	2,400
9/26/2015	BI-WEEKLY NET PAY After Taxes & 401K	2,400
10/10/2015	BI-WEEKLY NET PAY After Taxes & 401K	2,400
10/24/2015	BI-WEEKLY NET PAY After Taxes & 401K	2,400
11/7/2015	BI-WEEKLY NET PAY After Taxes & 401K	2,400
11/21/2015	BI-WEEKLY NET PAY After Taxes & 401K	2,400
12/5/2015	BI-WEEKLY NET PAY After Taxes & 401K	2,400
12/19/2015	BI-WEEKLY NET PAY After Taxes & 401K	2,400
1/2/2016	BI-WEEKLY NET PAY After Taxes & 401K	2,400
1/16/2016	BI-WEEKLY NET PAY After Taxes & 401K	2,400
1/30/2016	BI-WEEKLY NET PAY After Taxes & 401K	2,400
2/13/2016	BI-WEEKLY NET PAY After Taxes & 401K	2,400
2/27/2016	BI-WEEKLY NET PAY After Taxes & 401K	2,400
3/12/2016	BI-WEEKLY NET PAY After Taxes & 401K	2,400
3/26/2016	BI-WEEKLY NET PAY After Taxes & 401K	2,400

Step 2, on the same spreadsheet, enter all fixed expenses and due dates and estimate the average expenses for non-fixed expenses as shown on the following chart. Make sure that any anticipated increase in those expenses are taken into consideration. Enter all your expenses as negative numbers as shown. It is important to enter the correct due dates of all the expenses to get an accurate cash flow statement:

CASH FLOW DUE DATE	DESCRIPTION	AMOUNT
7/15/2015	AUTO REPAIR & MAINT	-500
10/15/2015	AUTO REPAIR & MAINT	-500
12/15/2015	AUTO REPAIR & MAINT	-500
3/14/2016	AUTO REPAIR & MAINT	-500
4/15/2015	CABLE, INTERNET, PHONES	-250
5/15/2015	CABLE, INTERNET, PHONES	-250
6/15/2015	CABLE, INTERNET, PHONES	-250
7/15/2015	CABLE, INTERNET, PHONES	-250
8/15/2015	CABLE, INTERNET, PHONES	-250
9/15/2015	CABLE, INTERNET, PHONES	-250
10/15/2015	CABLE, INTERNET, PHONES	-250
11/15/2015	CABLE, INTERNET, PHONES	-250
12/15/2015	CABLE, INTERNET, PHONES	-250
1/15/2016	CABLE, INTERNET, PHONES	-250
2/15/2016	CABLE, INTERNET, PHONES	-250
3/14/2016	CABLE, INTERNET, PHONES	-250
9/1/2015	CAR REGISTRATION	-90
9/1/2015	CAR REGISTRATION	-90
4/15/2015	CO-PAY DOCTOR	-30
6/15/2015	CO-PAY DOCTOR	-50
8/15/2015	CO-PAY DOCTOR	-30
10/15/2015	CO-PAY DOCTOR	-50
11/15/2015	CO-PAY DOCTOR	-30
1/15/2016	CO-PAY DOCTOR	-50
3/14/2016	CO-PAY DOCTOR	-30

4/11/2015	FOOD & TOILETRIES	-443
4/25/2015	FOOD & TOILETRIES	-443
5/9/2015	FOOD & TOILETRIES	-443
5/23/2015	FOOD & TOILETRIES	-443
6/6/2015	FOOD & TOILETRIES	-443
6/20/2015	FOOD & TOILETRIES	-443
7/4/2015	FOOD & TOILETRIES	-443
7/18/2015	FOOD & TOILETRIES	-443
8/1/2015	FOOD & TOILETRIES	-443
8/15/2015	FOOD & TOILETRIES	-443
8/29/2015	FOOD & TOILETRIES	-443
9/12/2015	FOOD & TOILETRIES	-443
9/26/2015	FOOD & TOILETRIES	-443
10/10/2015	FOOD & TOILETRIES	-443
10/24/2015	FOOD & TOILETRIES	-443
11/7/2015	FOOD & TOILETRIES	-443
11/21/2015	FOOD & TOILETRIES	-443
12/5/2015	FOOD & TOILETRIES	-443
12/19/2015	FOOD & TOILETRIES	-443
1/2/2016	FOOD & TOILETRIES	-443
1/16/2016	FOOD & TOILETRIES	-443
1/30/2016	FOOD & TOILETRIES	-443
2/13/2016	FOOD & TOILETRIES	-443
2/27/2016	FOOD & TOILETRIES	-443
3/12/2016	FOOD & TOILETRIES	-443
3/26/2016	FOOD & TOILETRIES	-443

4/15/2015	GAS & ELECTRIC	-220
5/15/2015	GAS & ELECTRIC	-220
6/15/2015	GAS & ELECTRIC	-220
7/15/2015	GAS & ELECTRIC	-220
8/15/2015	GAS & ELECTRIC	-220
9/15/2015	GAS & ELECTRIC	-220
10/15/2015	GAS & ELECTRIC	-220
11/15/2015	GAS & ELECTRIC	-220
12/15/2015	GAS & ELECTRIC	-220
1/15/2016	GAS & ELECTRIC	-220
2/15/2016	GAS & ELECTRIC	-220
3/14/2016	GAS & ELECTRIC	-220
4/11/2015	GAS & TOLLS	-46
4/25/2015	GAS & TOLLS	-46
5/9/2015	GAS & TOLLS	-46
5/23/2015	GAS & TOLLS	-46
6/6/2015	GAS & TOLLS	-46
6/20/2015	GAS & TOLLS	-46
7/4/2015	GAS & TOLLS	-46
7/18/2015	GAS & TOLLS	-46
8/1/2015	GAS & TOLLS	-46
8/15/2015	GAS & TOLLS	-46
8/29/2015	GAS & TOLLS	-46
9/12/2015	GAS & TOLLS	-46
9/26/2015	GAS & TOLLS	-46
10/10/2015	GAS & TOLLS	-46
10/24/2015	GAS & TOLLS	-46
11/7/2015	GAS & TOLLS	-46
11/21/2015	GAS & TOLLS	-46
12/5/2015	GAS & TOLLS	-46
12/19/2015	GAS & TOLLS	-46

1/2/2016	GAS & TOLLS	-46
1/16/2016	GAS & TOLLS	-46
1/30/2016	GAS & TOLLS	-46
2/13/2016	GAS & TOLLS	-46
2/27/2016	GAS & TOLLS	-46
3/12/2016	GAS & TOLLS	-46
3/26/2016	GAS & TOLLS	-46
8/15/2015	GYM	-1,000
6/15/2015	INSURANCE-auto	-450
9/30/2015	INSURANCE-auto	-450
12/30/2015	INSURANCE-auto	-450
3/14/2016	INSURANCE-auto	-450
4/30/2015	LAWN MAINT	-123
5/15/2015	LAWN MAINT	-123
6/15/2015	LAWN MAINT	-123
7/15/2015	LAWN MAINT	-123
8/15/2015	LAWN MAINT	-123
9/15/2015	LAWN MAINT	-123
10/15/2015	LAWN MAINT	-123
11/15/2015	LAWN MAINT	-123
4/15/2015	LIQUOR	-50
5/15/2015	LIQUOR	-50
6/15/2015	LIQUOR	-50
7/15/2015	LIQUOR	-50
8/15/2015	LIQUOR	-50
9/15/2015	LIQUOR	-50
10/15/2015	LIQUOR	-50
11/15/2015	LIQUOR	-50
12/15/2015	LIQUOR	-50
1/15/2016	LIQUOR	-50
2/15/2016	LIQUOR	-50
3/14/2016	LIQUOR	-50

4/7/2015	MORTGAGE (PITI)	-1,800
5/7/2015	MORTGAGE (PITI)	-1,800
6/7/2015	MORTGAGE (PITI)	-1,800
7/7/2015	MORTGAGE (PITI)	-1,800
8/7/2015	MORTGAGE (PITI)	-1,800
9/7/2015	MORTGAGE (PITI)	-1,800
10/7/2015	MORTGAGE (PITI)	-1,800
11/7/2015	MORTGAGE (PITI)	-1,800
12/7/2015	MORTGAGE (PITI)	-1,800
1/7/2016	MORTGAGE (PITI)	-1,800
2/7/2016	MORTGAGE (PITI)	-1,800
3/6/2016	MORTGAGE (PITI)	-1,800
4/30/2015	T&E	-300
5/30/2015	T&E	-300
6/30/2015	T&E	-300
7/30/2015	T&E	-300
8/30/2015	T&E	-300
9/30/2015	T&E	-300
10/30/2015	T&E	-300
11/30/2015	T&E	-300
12/30/2015	T&E	-300

4/6/2015	TERM INSURANCE	-80
5/6/2015	TERM INSURANCE	-80
6/6/2015	TERM INSURANCE	-80
7/6/2015	TERM INSURANCE	-80
8/6/2015	TERM INSURANCE	-80
9/6/2015	TERM INSURANCE	-80
10/6/2015	TERM INSURANCE	-80
11/6/2015	TERM INSURANCE	-80
12/6/2015	TERM INSURANCE	-80
1/6/2016	TERM INSURANCE	-80
2/6/2016	TERM INSURANCE	-80
3/5/2016	TERM INSURANCE	-80
4/15/2015	WATER & SEWER	-220
7/15/2015	WATER & SEWER	-80
10/15/2015	WATER & SEWER	-80

Step 3, sort all the rows by "DUE DATE", income and expenses combined. Insert a couple of rows just below the header and describe them as "BANK 1 – BALANCE" and "BANK 2 – BALANCE" if you have a checking and a savings accounts. Add more rows if you have other bank accounts. Enter the amount of cash that is currently available to you. Add a new column "D" entitled "RUNNING BALANCE" as shown. On cell D3, enter this formula, +C3. It should return a result of 2,000. On cell D4, enter this formula, +C4+D3. It should return a result of $4,000. Copy this formula all the way to the bottom of the column. The table that follows should be the final result:

CASH FLOW DUE DATE	DESCRIPTION	AMOUNT	RUNNING BALANCE
3/31/2015	BANK 1 - BALANCE	2,000	2,000
3/31/2015	BANK 2 - BALANCE	2,000	4,000
4/6/2015	TERM INSURANCE	-80	3,920
4/7/2015	MORTGAGE (PITI)	-1,800	2,120
4/11/2015	BI-WEEKLY NET PAY After Taxes & 401K	2,400	4,520
4/11/2015	FOOD & TOILETRIES	-443	4,077
4/11/2015	GAS & TOLLS	-46	4,031
4/15/2015	CABLE, INTERNET, PHONES	-250	3,781
4/15/2015	CO-PAY DOCTOR	-30	3,751
4/15/2015	GAS & ELECTRIC	-220	3,531
4/15/2015	LIQUOR	-50	3,481
4/15/2015	WATER & SEWER	-220	3,261
4/25/2015	BI-WEEKLY NET PAY After Taxes & 401K	2,400	5,661
4/25/2015	FOOD & TOILETRIES	-443	5,218
4/25/2015	GAS & TOLLS	-46	5,172
4/30/2015	LAWN MAINT	-123	5,049
4/30/2015	SAVINGS - ADD TO 401K CONTRIB	-1,000	4,049
4/30/2015	T&E	-300	3,749
5/6/2015	TERM INSURANCE	-80	3,669
5/7/2015	MORTGAGE (PITI)	-1,800	1,869
5/9/2015	BI-WEEKLY NET PAY After Taxes & 401K	2,400	4,269
5/9/2015	FOOD & TOILETRIES	-443	3,826
5/9/2015	GAS & TOLLS	-46	3,780
5/15/2015	CABLE, INTERNET, PHONES	-250	3,530
5/15/2015	GAS & ELECTRIC	-220	3,310
5/15/2015	LAWN MAINT	-123	3,187
5/15/2015	LIQUOR	-50	3,137
5/23/2015	BI-WEEKLY NET PAY After Taxes & 401K	2,400	5,537
5/23/2015	FOOD & TOILETRIES	-443	5,094
5/23/2015	GAS & TOLLS	-46	5,048
5/30/2015	T&E	-300	4,748
5/31/2015	SAVINGS - ADD TO 401K CONTRIB	-	4,748

Date	Description	Amount	Balance
6/6/2015	BI-WEEKLY NET PAY After Taxes & 401K	2,400	7,148
6/6/2015	FOOD & TOILETRIES	-443	6,705
6/6/2015	GAS & TOLLS	-46	6,659
6/6/2015	TERM INSURANCE	-80	6,579
6/7/2015	MORTGAGE (PITI)	-1,800	4,779
6/15/2015	CABLE, INTERNET, PHONES	-250	4,529
6/15/2015	CO-PAY DOCTOR	-50	4,479
6/15/2015	GAS & ELECTRIC	-220	4,259
6/15/2015	INSURANCE-auto	-450	3,809
6/15/2015	LAWN MAINT	-123	3,686
6/15/2015	LIQUOR	-50	3,636
6/20/2015	BI-WEEKLY NET PAY After Taxes & 401K	2,400	6,036
6/20/2015	FOOD & TOILETRIES	-443	5,593
6/20/2015	GAS & TOLLS	-46	5,547
6/30/2015	SAVINGS - ADD TO 401K CONTRIB	-1,000	4,547
6/30/2015	T&E	-300	4,247
7/4/2015	BI-WEEKLY NET PAY After Taxes & 401K	2,400	6,647
7/4/2015	FOOD & TOILETRIES	-443	6,204
7/4/2015	GAS & TOLLS	-46	6,158
7/6/2015	TERM INSURANCE	-80	6,078
7/7/2015	MORTGAGE (PITI)	-1,800	4,278
7/15/2015	AUTO REPAIR & MAINT	-500	3,778
7/15/2015	CABLE, INTERNET, PHONES	-250	3,528
7/15/2015	GAS & ELECTRIC	-220	3,308
7/15/2015	LAWN MAINT	-123	3,185
7/15/2015	LIQUOR	-50	3,135
7/15/2015	WATER & SEWER	-80	3,055
7/18/2015	BI-WEEKLY NET PAY After Taxes & 401K	2,400	5,455
7/18/2015	FOOD & TOILETRIES	-443	5,012
7/18/2015	GAS & TOLLS	-46	4,966
7/30/2015	T&E	-300	4,666
7/31/2015	SAVINGS - ADD TO 401K CONTRIB	-	4,666

8/1/2015	BI-WEEKLY NET PAY After Taxes & 401K	2,400	7,066
8/1/2015	FOOD & TOILETRIES	-443	6,623
8/1/2015	GAS & TOLLS	-46	6,577
8/6/2015	TERM INSURANCE	-80	6,497
8/7/2015	MORTGAGE (PITI)	-1,800	4,697
8/15/2015	BI-WEEKLY NET PAY After Taxes & 401K	2,400	7,097
8/15/2015	CABLE, INTERNET, PHONES	-250	6,847
8/15/2015	CO-PAY DOCTOR	-30	6,817
8/15/2015	FOOD & TOILETRIES	-443	6,374
8/15/2015	GAS & ELECTRIC	-220	6,154
8/15/2015	GAS & TOLLS	-46	6,108
8/15/2015	GYM	-1,000	5,108
8/15/2015	LAWN MAINT	-123	4,985
8/15/2015	LIQUOR	-50	4,935
8/29/2015	BI-WEEKLY NET PAY After Taxes & 401K	2,400	7,335
8/29/2015	FOOD & TOILETRIES	-443	6,892
8/29/2015	GAS & TOLLS	-46	6,846
8/30/2015	T&E	-300	6,546
8/31/2015	SAVINGS - ADD TO 401K CONTRIB	-2,000	4,546
9/1/2015	CAR REGISTRATION	-90	4,456
9/1/2015	CAR REGISTRATION	-90	4,366
9/6/2015	TERM INSURANCE	-80	4,286
9/7/2015	MORTGAGE (PITI)	-1,800	2,486
9/12/2015	BI-WEEKLY NET PAY After Taxes & 401K	2,400	4,886
9/12/2015	FOOD & TOILETRIES	-443	4,443
9/12/2015	GAS & TOLLS	-46	4,397
9/15/2015	CABLE, INTERNET, PHONES	-250	4,147
9/15/2015	GAS & ELECTRIC	-220	3,927
9/15/2015	LAWN MAINT	-123	3,804
9/15/2015	LIQUOR	-50	3,754

9/26/2015	BI-WEEKLY NET PAY After Taxes & 401K	2,400	6,154
9/26/2015	FOOD & TOILETRIES	-443	5,711
9/26/2015	GAS & TOLLS	-46	5,665
9/30/2015	INSURANCE-auto	-450	5,215
9/30/2015	SAVINGS - ADD TO 401K CONTRIB	-1,000	4,215
9/30/2015	T&E	-300	3,915
10/6/2015	TERM INSURANCE	-80	3,835
10/7/2015	MORTGAGE (PITI)	-1,800	2,035
10/10/2015	BI-WEEKLY NET PAY After Taxes & 401K	2,400	4,435
10/10/2015	FOOD & TOILETRIES	-443	3,992
10/10/2015	GAS & TOLLS	-46	3,946
10/15/2015	AUTO REPAIR & MAINT	-500	3,446
10/15/2015	CABLE, INTERNET, PHONES	-250	3,196
10/15/2015	CO-PAY DOCTOR	-50	3,146
10/15/2015	GAS & ELECTRIC	-220	2,926
10/15/2015	LAWN MAINT	-123	2,803
10/15/2015	LIQUOR	-50	2,753
10/15/2015	WATER & SEWER	-80	2,673
10/24/2015	BI-WEEKLY NET PAY After Taxes & 401K	2,400	5,073
10/24/2015	FOOD & TOILETRIES	-443	4,630
10/24/2015	GAS & TOLLS	-46	4,584
10/30/2015	T&E	-300	4,284
10/31/2015	SAVINGS - ADD TO 401K CONTRIB	-	4,284
11/6/2015	TERM INSURANCE	-80	4,204
11/7/2015	BI-WEEKLY NET PAY After Taxes & 401K	2,400	6,604
11/7/2015	FOOD & TOILETRIES	-443	6,161
11/7/2015	GAS & TOLLS	-46	6,115
11/7/2015	MORTGAGE (PITI)	-1,800	4,315

11/15/2015	CABLE, INTERNET, PHONES	-250	4,065
11/15/2015	CO-PAY DOCTOR	-30	4,035
11/15/2015	GAS & ELECTRIC	-220	3,815
11/15/2015	LAWN MAINT	-123	3,692
11/15/2015	LIQUOR	-50	3,642
11/21/2015	BI-WEEKLY NET PAY After Taxes & 401K	2,400	6,042
11/21/2015	FOOD & TOILETRIES	-443	5,599
11/21/2015	GAS & TOLLS	-46	5,553
11/30/2015	SAVINGS - ADD TO 401K CONTRIB	-1,000	4,553
11/30/2015	T&E	-300	4,253
12/5/2015	BI-WEEKLY NET PAY After Taxes & 401K	2,400	6,653
12/5/2015	FOOD & TOILETRIES	-443	6,210
12/5/2015	GAS & TOLLS	-46	6,164
12/6/2015	TERM INSURANCE	-80	6,084
12/7/2015	MORTGAGE (PITI)	-1,800	4,284
12/15/2015	AUTO REPAIR & MAINT	-500	3,784
12/15/2015	CABLE, INTERNET, PHONES	-250	3,534
12/15/2015	GAS & ELECTRIC	-220	3,314
12/15/2015	LIQUOR	-50	3,264
12/19/2015	BI-WEEKLY NET PAY After Taxes & 401K	2,400	5,664
12/19/2015	FOOD & TOILETRIES	-443	5,221
12/19/2015	GAS & TOLLS	-46	5,175
12/30/2015	INSURANCE-auto	-450	4,725
12/30/2015	T&E	-300	4,425
12/31/2015	SAVINGS - ADD TO 401K CONTRIB	-	4,425
1/2/2016	BI-WEEKLY NET PAY After Taxes & 401K	2,400	6,825
1/2/2016	FOOD & TOILETRIES	-443	6,382
1/2/2016	GAS & TOLLS	-46	6,336
1/6/2016	TERM INSURANCE	-80	6,256
1/7/2016	MORTGAGE (PITI)	-1,800	4,456

1/15/2016	CABLE, INTERNET, PHONES	-250	4,206
1/15/2016	CO-PAY DOCTOR	-50	4,156
1/15/2016	GAS & ELECTRIC	-220	3,936
1/15/2016	LIQUOR	-50	3,886
1/15/2016	WATER & SEWER	-80	3,806
1/16/2016	BI-WEEKLY NET PAY After Taxes & 401K	2,400	6,206
1/16/2016	FOOD & TOILETRIES	-443	5,763
1/16/2016	GAS & TOLLS	-46	5,717
1/30/2016	BI-WEEKLY NET PAY After Taxes & 401K	2,400	8,117
1/30/2016	FOOD & TOILETRIES	-443	7,674
1/30/2016	GAS & TOLLS	-46	7,628
1/31/2016	SAVINGS - ADD TO 401K CONTRIB	-3,000	4,628
2/6/2016	TERM INSURANCE	-80	4,548
2/7/2016	MORTGAGE (PITI)	-1,800	2,748
2/13/2016	BI-WEEKLY NET PAY After Taxes & 401K	2,400	5,148
2/13/2016	FOOD & TOILETRIES	-443	4,705
2/13/2016	GAS & TOLLS	-46	4,659
2/15/2016	CABLE, INTERNET, PHONES	-250	4,409
2/15/2016	GAS & ELECTRIC	-220	4,189
2/15/2016	LIQUOR	-50	4,139
2/27/2016	BI-WEEKLY NET PAY After Taxes & 401K	2,400	6,539
2/27/2016	FOOD & TOILETRIES	-443	6,096
2/27/2016	GAS & TOLLS	-46	6,050
2/29/2016	SAVINGS - ADD TO 401K CONTRIB	-2,000	4,050
3/5/2016	TERM INSURANCE	-80	3,970
3/6/2016	MORTGAGE (PITI)	-1,800	2,170
3/12/2016	BI-WEEKLY NET PAY After Taxes & 401K	2,400	4,570
3/12/2016	FOOD & TOILETRIES	-443	4,127
3/12/2016	GAS & TOLLS	-46	4,081
3/14/2016	AUTO REPAIR & MAINT	-500	3,581
3/14/2016	CABLE, INTERNET, PHONES	-250	3,331
3/14/2016	CO-PAY DOCTOR	-30	3,301
3/14/2016	GAS & ELECTRIC	-220	3,081
3/14/2016	INSURANCE-auto	-450	2,631
3/14/2016	LIQUOR	-50	2,581
3/14/2016	WATER & SEWER	-80	2,501
3/26/2016	BI-WEEKLY NET PAY After Taxes & 401K	2,400	4,901
3/26/2016	FOOD & TOILETRIES	-443	4,458
3/26/2016	GAS & TOLLS	-46	4,412

In this budget strategy, it is the goal of the subject individual to maintain a minimum of $4,000 cash in his bank account for emergencies and non-recurring expenses and a maximum of $5,000. Whenever the balance is over $5,000 at the end of each month, he will reduce the running balance in increments of $1000 as long as the balance does not dip below $4000. The money is added to his 401k contribution. Most 401k plans allow additional contributions every pay period by either allowing you to write a check to the plan or by increasing your contribution just for that payroll period up to your total net pay. Speak with your plan administrator on how to accomplish this. In the preceding cash flow example, the subject had a balance of $5049 on 04/30/2015. So he wrote a check for $1000 as additional contribution. As an alternative, he can ask the payroll manager to deduct an additional $1000 from his pay as additional 401k contribution. On 05/31/2015, the subject's running balance was $4748, so he took no action. On 01/31/2016, his balance was $7628, so he reduced his cash balance by $3000. In reality, there will be unexpected, non-recurring expenses that are not shown on this cash flow such as unplanned travel, gifts, auto and home repairs, parties and educational expenses. You should keep updating this cash flow statement by adding income and subtracting expenses that have not been accounted for. You should not face any surprises if you spend a couple of hours each month to update the cash flow statement. There are no provisions for savings and children's college education in this cash flow statement. Instead, any excess cash is added to the subject's 401k contribution. This strategy is designed to maximize the subject individual's 401k contribution while minimizing the current tax liability. This strategy is further explained under Chapter, *"Planning for College"*.

8. Create a Budget – Sample Budget

Now that you know where you are, where do you want to go? The sample budget that follows came from the U.S. Bureau of Labor Statistics (USBLS) and is the most reliable budget I have seen. The figures were compiled from statistics received by the bureau for the year 2014. The consumer price index (rate of inflation) has not changed much since then, so the numbers are as reliable at the time of writing as they were when they were compiled. The sample is based on nationwide averages. The first table showing a gross income before taxes and 401k contribution in the amount of $78,407 is the average income for a family of 3 according to the USBLS. The expenses that follow are the average expenses in relation to that income.

To start, you have to go through the exercise of comparing your actual expenses to the averages according to the USBLS website. First, create your own personal budget by entering your figures on the **"Household Budget Worksheet"** ("HBW") link below:

http://www.kiplinger.com/tool/spending/T007-S001-budgeting-worksheet-a-household-budget-for-today-a/index.php

The top number should be your take home pay. For this purpose, your take home pay is your gross pay less taxes and 401k contribution, shown on the sample budget as "NET AFTER TAXES AND 401K". There is no need to enter your 401k contribution under "Retirement (IRA)" in the Savings and Investments section of the HBW. Let us ignore the 401k or IRA contribution for now. The reason for this is so we can try to maximize contributions to your retirement account by dumping all your savings, i.e. college fund, emergency fund and miscellaneous savings as additional contributions to your 401k plan. In subsequent chapters, you will see how this strategy will work out nicely by the time you are ready to retire. Just to recap, gross pay less taxes less 401k contribution = NET. Do not deduct medical deductions from gross. Healthcare is listed as a separate expense on the budget that is why any healthcare contribution deducted from your paycheck should be entered under

"Health" in the Insurance Premiums section of the HBW. The NET is your starting number from which your expenses and savings will be deducted. The sample budget shows expenses and savings as a percent of the take home pay. Your actual expenses from the HBW should not deviate too much from the percentages shown on the sample budget. To figure out the average approximate monthly income and expenses from this sample budget, just copy the amounts on an excel file and divide the income and expenses by 12. How is your actual monthly food expense compared to the sample budget? Ideally, your actual expenses should be less than the averages shown on the sample. If any expense is more than the percent shown on the budget, you have to look at that expense very carefully and find a way to reduce it. Although the expenses will vary based on the region you live in (for example, NYC will have a higher housing cost than Kansas City) you will still be able to create a good sensible budget based on the sample.

Nationwide Averages from: http://www.bls.gov/			
Annual Gross Income before taxes (G.I.)		78,407	
Taxes, 15%	15%	-11,761	15.00%
401K, 5%	5%	-3,920	5.00%
NET AFTER TAXES AND 401K	80%	62,726	80.00%
			as % of
EXPENSES:	Category	Amount	Net Income
Food	4	8,029	12.80%
Housing	4	20,950	33.40%
Alcoholic beverages	1	565	0.90%
Apparel and services	1	2,007	3.20%
Entertainment	1	3,136	5.00%
Miscellaneous, Savings, Emergency, etc.	1	815	1.30%
Personal care products and services	1	753	1.20%
Subscription & Dues	1	125	0.20%
Tobacco products and smoking supplies	1	376	0.60%
Cash contributions	2	2,195	3.50%
Healthcare	2	4,704	7.50%
Personal insurance and pensions	2	6,774	10.80%
Transportation	2	10,852	17.30%
Education, "Saving for College":	3	1,443	2.30%
Average annual expenditures		62,726	100.00%

I have added my comments on the following charts. You will notice that any reduction of expense is added to the contribution to the retirement fund (401k Account, 403b or IRA). This move is an integral part of the financial game plan.

When starting a budget, it is important to account for every dollar you spend and to categorize each dollar that you spend. That is the only way you can figure out how much you are spending for each expense category. If you are spending more in one category when you compare it as a percent with that shown on the budget, you should find a way to reduce that expense. You have a lot of flexibility on expenses labeled 1. Most of them are discretionary expenses. Expenses labeled 2 can also be reduced if you scrutinize them carefully.

Note 1 - Expenses you can reduce by 50%. If you are able to reduce these expenses, put the money you save into your 401k account:		
Alcoholic beverages	1	565
Apparel and services	1	2,007
Entertainment	1	3,136
Personal care products and services	1	815
Subscription & Dues	1	753
Tobacco products and smoking supplies	1	125
Miscellaneous, Savings, Emergency, etc.	1	376
Total		7,778
Note 2 - Expenses you may reduce. If you can reduce these expenses, add the money you save into your 401k account:		
Cash contributions	2	2,195
Healthcare	2	4,704
Personal insurance and pensions	2	6,774
Transportation	2	10,852
Total		24,526
Note 3 - Do not save money for college education. Instead, put this budgeted amount into your 401k account. This strategy is explained under the chapter:		
Education, "Saving for College":	3	1,443
Note 4 - Food and housing are the expenses that are usually fixed. Any savings from these categories are usually minimal. If you can reduce these expenses, contribute whatever savings you realize into your 401k account.		

Although my note on the preceding chart states that food and housing are pretty much fixed expenses, you can reduce your housing expenses drastically if you have to. If you are renting an $1800 per month apartment, you can move to a smaller one and possibly reduce your rent to $1200. A $600 a month savings is serious money that you can use to pay off credit card debt, student loans or add to your contribution for your retirement fund.

If your company offers a 401k plan, and most companies do, you should strive to contribute the maximum allowable contribution every year. It is important to follow your budget and carefully and proactively monitor your spending. Many people who have a surplus at the end of the month go crazy trying to find ways to spend it. Deposit that surplus into your retirement fund. You will realize in the following chapters that your retirement fund can be used as a catch all for all extra income and expenses. If you still have a big overage at the end of every month even after maximizing your 401k contributions, then you may be in a good position to buy your own house, thereby making your extra cash build wealth for you.

9. Dealing with any monthly surplus:

1.   Use the full amount of the surplus to pay off your credit card and non-mortgage debts.

2.   If there is a remaining amount after No. 1, put the remaining surplus into your 401k acct

3.   If there is a remaining amount after No.1 and 2, put the remaining surplus into a savings account targeted for buying your primary residence. See the chapter, "Buy Your Principal Residence".

If you do not follow the above instructions in dealing with the surplus, you will find a way to squander it. Spending your monthly surplus instead of saving it will delay your achievement of the goals outlined in this book.

10. Dealing with any monthly shortage:

1. Negative cash flow means you are spending more than you take in. What a surprise! In many cases they are due to monthly installments on credit card debts or other high interest consumer loans. Get rid of these debts and don't borrow anymore. If possible borrow from your 401k, relatives or the bank at a lower rate to payoff high interest installment loans. If this is not possible and your budget reveals that you will continue to struggle to pay off non-mortgage loans, you may want to consider asking your creditors for full or partial forgiveness of your loans. Click on the link below for more information,
    https://www.amazon.com/Stop-Paying-Your-Credit-Cards-ebook/dp/B019ZY3D1E/ref=sr_1_3?s=digital-text&ie=UTF8&qid=1469652606&sr=1-3&keywords=Arthur V. Prosper#navbar
    If there is a light at the end of the tunnel, i.e. your budget shows you can pay off the balances within a year or so, then bite the bullet and continue to pay your credit cards, more than the minimum if possible (see #6), then go on to steps 3 and 4. There is a price to pay if creditors agree to reduce your debts or forgive them in full. "Charge Off" will show up on your credit report which will bring down your FICO scores and make it harder for you to obtain a mortgage loan.

2. Sell any hard assets such as jewelry, clothing, appliances, artwork, collectibles, vehicles, gadgets and anything of value that you can sell to pay off high interest debts.

3. Reduce all your expenses. The expenses marked #1 can be cut in half. Drastically reduce expenses marked #2. Try to reduce expenses marked # 4.

4. Watch every dollar that goes out of your pocket. Do not compound your problem by borrowing more on your credit cards to make up for the monthly deficit. This will only lead you down a slippery slope.

5.	Increase your income. See the chapter, "Increase Your Income with these Ideas". These are realistic and doable ideas that most people can implement if they want to earn extra income in their spare time.

6.	If your budget review shows that there is a light at the end of the tunnel with regard to your credit card debt, temporarily stop any contributions to your 401k plan. Add the amount you would have contributed to your monthly credit card payment. The savings, interest and company match you will lose is small change compared to the savings you will realize by paying off credit card debt that carries a 25% APR. Do not make any contributions to your 401k plan until your credit card debt is paid off.

Negative cash flow at the end of each month means you are overspending. This phenomenon is generally caused by the availability of credit. If no one will advance you the money and you have to pay for everything in cash, you will find a way to make ends meet and make that dollar last until the next pay check. If you cannot pay for your monthly purchases in full as soon as you receive the statement, you cannot afford the purchase. Stop using your credit cards and pay cash for everything until you get your spending under control and your budget in order. Sometimes I just don't understand some people's attitude when it comes to money. For example, in my office there is a group of co-workers, that is perhaps the biggest bunch of complainers for, "not having enough money", "always having difficulty trying to make ends meet", "living pay check to pay check" that has developed a daily routine of planning what to order for lunch every day at 11:30 AM on the dot. The excitement starts when one of them yells out, "What are we ordering for lunch today, Chinese, Italian, sushi, pizza, deli?" Granted that this group enjoys the camaraderie, planning lunch and eating together, $8 to $12 a day for lunch is just too much…for me anyway, that is, if you constantly complain that you are flat broke by month-end and cannot make any contributions to your 401k plan because there is no money left. Why not make a sandwich or salad or bring a yogurt or ramen for lunch? Better still why not bring some left-overs from dinner? Part of having a sound financial plan is being able to go on a financial diet too. It's practical, sensible and necessary. You don't really need to buy the NY Daily News everyday do you? Can't you get through the day without that $2 can of soda from the vending machine or that $5 latte from Starbucks? These small-change expenses can add up. But you can really do without them, can't you? I mean, c'mon!

11. Dealing with life changes and unexpected problems:

There are no guarantees in life. You will encounter many unexpected problems and major changes in your life. The most common are divorce, catastrophic illnesses and job loss. You must be flexible enough to bend and go with the flow so as not to lose track of your life goals. Being flexible sometimes means temporarily suspending your belief system and moral principles in order to sidestep the fatal blow and fight again another day. You may look down at people who declare bankruptcy but be open to that option as a last resort if you qualify for it. No one likes being dubbed a deadbeat, but if you owe so much in credit card debt because you had some set-backs such as huge medical bills and loss of income, don't hesitate to ask the credit card companies for reduction or forgiveness of your debt if you do not see the light at the end of the tunnel. Your family's welfare comes first. Get more information about debt forgiveness. Download the book, **"Stop Paying Your Credit Cards",**

https://www.amazon.com/dp/B019ZY3D1E/ref=rdr_kindle_ext_tmb

If you got divorced, be prepared to cut your expenses in half even if you have to move into a studio apartment in a marginal neighborhood. If you lost your job, do not hesitate to check with your state if you qualify for food stamps. You may not like the idea of stooping down so low but it's a jungle out there. It's survival of the fittest. It's a dog eat dog world and in a period of financial and emotional distress, you must do everything that is lawful and within your power to take care of yourself and your family. The sooner you can make the necessary adjustments in your lifestyle the quicker you can get back on track towards your financial goals.

12. Reduce or Eliminate Non-Essential Expenses

I have identified the following expenses as non-essential because you can really do without them if you have to. These expenses are marked "No. 1" on the sample budget:

Alcoholic beverages

Apparel and services

Entertainment

Personal care products and services

Subscription & Dues

Tobacco products and smoking supplies

Miscellaneous

If you have to, you can literally spend zero dollars on the above-mentioned expenses but for most people, reducing the above expenses by 50% can be accomplished without batting an eye. According to the sample budget the total of these expenses is $7,778 per annum which represents 12.4% of total expenses and which translates to $648 a month for a family of 3. This is a significant amount you can use towards payment of high interest credit card debt.

13. Reduce Essential Expenses

I have identified the following expenses as essential. These expenses are marked "No. 2" on the sample budget:

Cash contributions

Healthcare

Personal insurance and pensions

Transportation

Even if these are essential expenses, they may be drastically reduced. Charitable contributions may be reduced or temporarily stopped until you are able to take control of your budget and finish paying off credit card debt if any. Refer to the previous chapters on personal insurance about ideas for reducing premiums. Commuting expenses, fuel and transportation are difficult expenses to reduce so we will leave them alone for now.

14. Never Lease a Car and Get Rid of Your Auto Loans

Never leasing a car is part of the financial game plan. You will spend extra money unnecessarily each time you lease a car. First, you will drown in the mumbo jumbo that car dealers use to confuse you into thinking you are getting a good deal because of the lower monthly payment compared to a loan for the same period. You will be deluged with terms such as capitalized cost reduction, money factor, adjusted cap cost, depreciation fee, lease fee, residual, finance fee on rent charge, purchase option, gap insurance, close ended, open ended, etc., etc., etc. Second, it is the same as renting a car. You are paying only for the car's depreciation for the period of time you will keep it plus interest, appropriately called "rent charge". Here again some people say: "If you can afford the monthly lease, you can afford the car." NOT! But what if you need a car? See my strategy under the chapter, "Avoid Conspicuous Consumption".

No one ever needs a new car. People drive new cars because they want to, to make them happy, to boost their ego or simply because a brand new car smells good and it's great to drive. Get over it! In my 35 plus years as a driver, I've only bought 3 brand new cars and that was only to keep the peace with my partner. I consider buying a new car a financial mistake because it's true, a car depreciates 20% to 30% as soon as you drive it out of the car dealer's parking lot. The money you can save by never buying a new car is a significant amount. If you are a recent graduate and just got your first job, resist buying a new car unless you need a new car for your job. Do not start your career by taking on a new car loan. But what if you need a car? See my strategy in the next chapter.

15. Avoid Conspicuous Consumption

I avoid buying products that have these labels associated with them: status symbol, brand name, upscale, designer, exclusive, limited edition, signature collection, luxury, prime, high society, etc. etc. etc. First, I am not willing to pay a premium for products for their "Veblen Good" value. These are goods that cost more than other products because of their snob appeal. They are bought by status-conscious consumers. Second, I do not think I gain the respect of others by using Veblen Goods. Third, I know the difference between "necessity and luxury". Finally, I know what to do with my budget surplus, and that is to put it into my retirement account instead of throwing it into a luxury car. Why would I buy a Mercedes Benz S-Class for $100,000 when a $35,000 Consumer Reports highly rated Chevy Impala would do? A snobbish reader will scoff at this statement but no amount of interior comfort and luxury or amazing handling, performance and technology can convince me to shell out an extra $65,000 for a car. I am street smart and "Living Rich" in my books does not have to include driving a $100,000 luxury car. Perhaps a luxury car to some people represents power and success, not to me. And I don't have to keep up with the Joneses. Perhaps a luxury car makes up for deficiencies some people have. I will be quite content with a Chevy Impala, Buick Regal, a Toyota Camry or Honda Accord. And if I don't have $35,000, I will buy a 2 to 4 year old low mileage reliable used car for $12,000 such as a small Toyota, Kia or Hyundai. If I only have $2000 cash, that is the price of a used car I am going to look for. Not having a monthly car payment will pay off in the long run. The huge monthly car loan installment would go instead towards paying high interest credit card debt and student loans or add to your contributions to your retirement account. The lifetime savings you will realize by never buying luxury cars is life-changing, and you aren't impressing anybody worth impressing anyway by driving a Mercedes or BMW. Yes, I partake in life's pleasures but sans brand name products, designer jeans, luxury vehicles and limited edition Rolex watches. I find ways to spend less money and achieve greater pleasure at the same time. In summary, if you need a car, buy a 2 to

5 year old low mileage car. You will pay less in insurance premiums, worry less about nicks, dings and dents when you park and with the technology advancement nowadays, you will not spend that much more in maintaining an older car.

Once you get used to it, you will realize that you can enjoy life's pleasures on a shoestring. This may sound like skimping to some people, but some status-symbol material things just do not matter to me. I am just not that materialistic. I do not live by some standard other people live by. You just have to learn to shop around and select the best value for everything. I have all the stuff I need to be happy. Although I am low maintenance, it does not mean that I do not partake in the finer things in life. I can afford steaks and lobsters and I always drink wine with my dinner. I don't pay $50 per bottle. Not even $20. Not even $10. For my palate there is no big difference in the taste of wines that cost $50 and the ones that cost $8.99. Some snooty reader will probably say, "of course there is". I used to think so too in my younger days until I got a job in a company which is a subsidiary of a European company. When I worked for them, I visited Italy, Germany, France and Switzerland regularly. My European colleagues paid our U.S. branch a visit regularly also. These Swiss, Italian, German and French associates grew up on wine and beer. Most of them started drinking wine and beer with their dinners at the age of 12. They did not find any big difference in the quality and taste of the wines between the one priced at $49 and the one priced at $8.99. I like living like the rich and famous but I cannot bear throwing money away on a bottle of Dom Perignon for $400 when a Gruet for under $20 tastes just the same. A boastful scotch drinker neighbor told me once that all he drinks is the $200+ a bottle Johnny Walker Blue Label Scotch because he "cannot stand the taste of cheap scotch". He agreed when I challenged him to a taste test to see if he can really tell the difference between the red label (the cheapest), black, green and blue labels. I laughed out loud when he chose the red label thinking it was the blue label. So unless there is a method to your madness, i.e. the Veblen Good you want to acquire will perhaps earn you extra money, increase your prestige so you can earn extra money or cure your depression so you can earn extra money, avoid spending money that you don't have to spend. Put that extra money into your retirement fund if you don't know what to do with it. Don't waste your money trying to impress people. If you still have a surplus after contributing the maximum to your 401k and saving for a house, then spend it travelling to broaden your world view. Travel opens your mind and provides unique experiences to include in your "back in my day" stories to tell your grandkids.

16. Shop around for everything

If you do not realize that you should not spend money that you don't have to spend, your journey towards financial independence is going to be much harder. You must control spending and always find ways to reduce expenses. You must comparison shop and bargain for everything. Everything means food, gasoline, health care, airline tickets, hotel accommodations, appliances, insurance, college education, gym membership, services, all expenses and all products great and small. Do not hesitate to choose store brands and generic brands over brand name products whenever possible. In most cases generic brands have the same ingredients as brand name products. An extra dollar saved here and there will accumulate over time with little notice. Comparison shopping and bargaining for everything does not necessarily mean I am being stingy. It just means I do not want to spend more than I have to, and in so doing I am on the fast track to financial independence. When I get there, I will have plenty of money to buy the things that matter to me. For now, I do not need any jewelry, expensive perfume and brand name anything. Sure designer jeans, brand name, expensive material things are nice to have, but you can really do without them at this point in your life, can't you?

Be a wise shopper not a bargain hunter. Always assess cost vs. benefit. The cheapest goods are not necessarily "the best buy". Neither are the most expensive products. If you buy a product that does not work the way it is supposed to work or the way you expected it to work; and does not last as long as it is supposed to last or as long as you expected it to last, then its cost (no matter how minuscule) outweighs its benefit.

17. Increase Your Income with These Ideas

If you can spare 5 to 20 hours a week, why not make extra money doing what you love? If you like driving maybe you can sign up to be an Uber and Lyft driver. If you are handy, advertise in your local newspaper for your services as a "handyman for hire". Do you enjoy yard work? Part time landscapers and gardeners are in demand and there aren't enough of them. If you don't mind doing a little dirty work, there are many offices that need cleaning after office hours. It is hard to get workers to do these odd jobs. Here are other money making ideas that you can do in your spare time:

1. Computer Repair Technician – If you are good with fixing problems relating to software and hardware of desktop and laptop computers, you can offer your services through word of mouth or advertise your services in your local newspaper. You can easily make $50 an hour.

2. Teach Computer Skills – Most office workers in any capacity are now required to possess computer skills in programs such as MS Outlook, Word and Excel. You can easily make $50 an hour offering private lessons and a lot more if you set up a computer training service in your basement or garage. You will need an initial investment of cheap desks or tables, office chairs, several workstations, a training projector, giant monitor or TV screen that can be connected to the workstations. You can buy additional workstations as this part time venture grows. Tip: Specialize in something. For example, if you are well versed in Excel, teach only courses in advanced excel, Vlookup, Pivot, VBA and Macros. In my neck of the woods, instructors for advanced excel are hard to come by and there is no shortage of students who are willing to pay the price to acquire these skills. Start by visiting your state unemployment office. Tell them that you are offering your services to provide additional training to the unemployed to improve their skills. Chances are your state's department of labor will refer many unemployed clients to you. In some cases, the state may even pay you for training them if they have tax-payer subsidized career

development and self-improvement programs for the unemployed.

3. Tax Preparation Service – Although this job is seasonal, you can make a lot of money in just a few months. Besides, many taxpayers are willing to file an extension which will extend the tax season for a tax preparer like you. All you have to do is buy a Tax software program such as H & R Block (Tax Cut), Turbo Tax, Tax Act, etc. Advertise in your local papers or contact local CPA offices and offer your services. You can easily make $130 for a basic tax return, to $400 for more complicated ones. There is no special skill or formal training needed. The tax soft wares are user friendly and menu driven, relying on interview questions that you only need to answer for your client. This type of work will be even easier if you are good with numbers and are already performing related work in your day job. To familiarize yourself with this part time money making venture, contact senior citizens' centers and offer your services for free. You will gain experience and the time you spend in assisting the elderly is a tax deductible expense on your income tax return. Most importantly, you will receive appreciation from senior citizens for your time, generosity and kindness.

4. Social Events Organizer – If you are outgoing and enjoy mingling with people, this is something you will enjoy. Many people like partying on weekends and do not mind paying an entrance fee to mingle. Start by locating the venue then check the venue, type, cost and availability. Obviously you want a venue that has no restrictions on dancing and that offers food and alcoholic beverages. The best deal is to locate a night club, restaurant or a dance hall that will sell food and liquor to your guests. All you do is sell tickets, hire a DJ who can play the tunes and teach a little line dancing as well. You will need a door attendant to let your paying guests in. These social clubs are very popular to the Hispanic population and to Latin music lovers, Reggae, country music, disco music lovers and oldies party goers. It is not surprising for the

host/hostess to make $1000 a night clear profit. After your success in organizing your first, you will only need word of mouth as the advertising outlet for subsequent parties. The trick is to invite beautiful and interesting people to your parties to attract other guests. You can negotiate with the nightclub owner to let you have 5% to 7% of the liquor profits. Proper scheduling is very important. For example, do not schedule your event on Super Bowl Sunday, on a long weekend or on a weekend when there are popular sporting events or concerts taking place that could affect attendance.

5. Seminar and Workshop Organizer/Presenter – If you are personable, possess good verbal communications skills and there is a subject matter you are good at that is worth sharing with others, you will find this undertaking rewarding and fulfilling. First, you should approach your state to find out if they have a business training program whereby they pay instructors to train company employees at the state's expense. Many states offer these training grants and they will pay you as a trainer. Oftentimes, if you have a good resume, all you have to do is sign up as an instructor in a certain subject such as basic computer training, telephone manners, communications, management, salesmanship, behavior modification, clerical skills, role playing, conflict management, etc., etc. If you succeed with your first few seminars, you may find that you want to do it full time. You can conduct seminars and workshops on subjects and topics that you are familiar with, but preparation and planning is always important for the success of this venture. Define the following: Subject matter, presenter and organizer (you), target group, number of participants, venue, duration, technical equipment (mike, amplifier, TV monitor, slide show equipment, props, etc.), brochures, refreshments, name tags and advertising scheme. If you conduct training for your state, the venue of the training will be at the business location of the company they will assign to you. If you will do this on your own, you have to secure a venue for

your seminar. Try churches, local elementary or high school, your house, a friend's house, public park, reception hall, YMCA, VFW, Knights of Columbus, American Legion, Police Athletic League, Senior Citizens' Centers, etc. etc. etc. Subject matter? Every person is good at something. There is something you know that can enrich other people's lives or at least entertain them.

a. Sports - Is there a particular sports that you excel in? Conduct a seminar or workshop to teach others your skill. Can you teach others a unique trick for shooting a basketball into the hoop, soccer ball dribbling, fast ball pitch, bowling technique and fly fishing? As an example, in my younger days when I was still active in martial arts I held a seminar on a basketball court of a local high school. I advertised that the seminar would take 2 hours and I would be teaching only two martial arts techniques, "a spinning back kick" and the "sweep" and that I would charge $30 per person for the 2 hour session. After I received 10 calls, I set the time and date and secured the venue. To my surprise, 28 paying customers showed up. The lessons were interactive. So the entire session took almost 4 hours and I charged everyone who wanted to participate. Needless to say, it was one of the most personally satisfying seminars I've ever conducted.

b. Cooking and Baking – Do you love cooking and baking? Do you have a special cooking technique? Do you have a secret recipe that you want to share with others? You may not think that you can make money doing this because of the availability of many you tube instructional videos, but believe me you will be pleasantly surprised. Reading about it or watching the demo on a computer monitor can never be as good and as fun as a personal demonstration. You can conduct the demo in your own house, at a friend's house or at your church's bingo hall. You can serve the food that you and the participants cook. At the start, make sure you do not overcharge. Your space in your house is limited. You will only have a handful of people in the beginning. You can charge $25 an hour each, $35 for an hour and a half session. Tip: Pre-cook the dish that you are going to concoct to save time and to make sure it is done right. The dish that you are going to make in front of an audience may not turn out as good. Some of the more popular dishes conducive to personal demonstration are Mexican Tamales, fondue, sushi, Spanish paella and any flambé recipes.

c. Dance Lessons – Michael Jackson said, "You were either born with it or without it". He is talking about natural rhythm which is what you need for this next part time venture. If you were born with "it", you can conduct dance lessons and workshops. You have to know the steps and dance moves or you can learn them. You can make extra money teaching salsa, cha-cha, tango, waltz, rumba, samba, jive, quickstep, reggae, bolero, disco, swing and hip-hop in your spare time. If only I was born with "it", I imagine that I can make a lot of money teaching only Michael Jackson's dance moves. I would specialize and teach only his dance moves in 3 of his music videos, "Bad", "Billie Jean" and "Thriller". I assume that many people would enroll and I would make a lot money and also have fun at the same time in my spare time. I am saying this because I have been looking in vain for someone to teach me those dance numbers. I am willing to pay a dance instructor $500 to teach me the step by step dance moves, footwork and numerous variations of the MJ pelvic thrust.

d. There are many other skills that you can conduct "how to" seminars on. There are some things you must be good at that you can demo and teach others such as tying a Windsor Knot, cigar-rolling, magic tricks, self-defense for women, public speaking, computer skills, makeup demo and instruction, couponing, time management, carpentry, painting, drawing and designing, flower arrangement, bonsai planting, teaching etiquette, casino gambling strategy, interior design, conducting IQ Tests, teaching a musical instrument, positive thinking, theological discussions, political discussions, poetry reading, how to hula hoop, skiing lessons, surfing lessons, chanting, memory enhancement, swimming lessons, voice lessons, chess strategy, karaoke parties, stand-up comedy, acting lessons, breathing technique, fitness tricks, diet and nutrition, resume writing, etc. etc. etc. As a postscript, I've mentioned tying a Windsor knot several times because I have actually conducted this seminar. Now that casual office attire is the norm, teaching men how to form a perfectly balanced knot may not draw as many participants as it did in the early nineties. But I made money showing men how to tie this knot because many men do not know how to. Watch the news and the Sunday morning political round table shows and you will notice that many of the "talking heads" and "suits" have uneven and lopsided ties. The Windsor knot is as close to perfect as you can get when it comes to tying a tie. For this seminar, I bought cheap ties as props for the demo then gave them to the participants after the seminar. I made an average of $200 profit for an hour's work each time I conducted this seminar. What else can you think of that is as simple as this?

Tip: I attended a real estate seminar once which was held at a popular hotel in Manhattan. It started at 9am right after the continental breakfast. I don't know if it was the effect of the donuts, bagels, pastries, croissants and muffins that made everyone languid. No one was paying attention to the speakers and everyone seemed half asleep. There was almost no sign of life in the audience…that was until the next speaker took over the mike. This energetic speaker pulled out a $20 bill from his pocket and walked along the front row asking, "Who wants this?" The audience came to life with many yelling out their answer, "ME, ME". He continued walking close to the attendees dangling the $20 bill in front of everyone's face and kept asking the question in a voice that grew louder and louder with each repetition of the question, "WHO WANTS THIS, WHO WANTS THIS?" Then he started stomping his feet. This took a while until somebody got up and grabbed the bill from his outstretched hand. "There you go my friends…" he continued, "you cannot make money unless you get off your ass and grab every opportunity that is being offered to you". Then the attendee who got the money proceeded to return the $20 bill to the speaker, at which point the speaker said, "My friend it's yours. You worked for it". Then everybody was paying attention to the speakers for the rest of the seminar. I've copied this trick in some of my seminars. You're welcome to use it too because you purchased this book.

6. Dog Walking, Dog Sitting - If you live in a city like NYC and love dogs and can control them, you can make good money with this task while enjoying yourself. A couple of hours in the morning before starting your day job is all it

takes. Start by offering your service to a neighbor. If you are good, word will spread like wildfire and you will be walking ten dogs in no time. You can make $15 to $20 per dog for a half hour walk.

7. Walking Tour Guide – How well do you know your community? Are there some hidden gems off the beaten path that tourists may be interested in seeing? Tourists have money to spend, are looking for something to do and would be delighted to spend several hours with a local guide such as yourself. Some tourists are eager to leave behind the popular attractions to explore the areas that tourists don't often get to see. Here are just a few examples of actual walking tours from the viator.com website:

New York City:

Step back in time to Prohibition-era New York with a tour of some of the Big Apple's hidden speakeasies. During this 3-hour walking tour, a local guide will lead you to four tucked-away watering holes where patrons defied the national ban on liquor during the 1920s. Enjoy three vintage-inspired drinks and a bar snack while discovering the clandestine history of these rule-breaking East Village establishments. Minimum age is 21 yrs. due to licensing regulations.   ID   required.

Read more about New York City Speakeasy Tour - New York City | Viator at: http://www.viator.com/tours/New-York-City/New-York-City-Speakeasy-Tour/d687-6390PROHIBITION?aid=vcps

Amsterdam:

Enjoy an insider's perspective on this 2.5-hour afternoon food walking tour in Amsterdam. A knowledgeable guide takes a small group, limited to just 12 foodies, around town to taste popular local dishes like salty fries and fresh herring. At a much-loved cheese shop sample pungent artisan cheeses, and kick back a house spirit at a 17th-century distillery. Along the way, gain insight into Amsterdam's gastronomic roots and the historic Dutch spice trade.

Read more about Amsterdam Food Tour - Amsterdam | Viator at: http://www.viator.com/tours/Amsterdam/Amsterdam-Food-Tour/d525-5923NLUF?aid=vcps

New Orleans:

During this two our walking tour you will discover the haunted streets and supernatural legends of the French Quarter. This tour is led by a local professional guide. During this tour an EMF Meter, Ghost/ Paranormal Detector will be used. Guests (Adults & Youth) will   be   allowed   to   use   the   equipment.

Read more about New Orleans Supernatural Tour - New Orleans | Viator at: http://www.viator.com/tours/New-Orleans/New-Orleans-Supernatural-Tour/d675-9349P15?aid=vcps

Brooklyn, NY:

Get a taste for local food culture of Brooklyn as you visit some of its many tasty eateries and small food shops during this 3-hour, small-group walking tour of borough's Carroll Gardens neighborhood with a local guide. Come hungry as your walking expedition stops for tastings at an eclectic range of ethnic and local food shops available to residents. During your walk you'll have the chance to sample everything from artisanal cooking spots and longstanding Middle Eastern markets.

Read more about Local Flavors of Brooklyn Small-Group Walking Tour - Brooklyn | Viator at: http://www.viator.com/tours/Brooklyn/Local-Flavors-of-Brooklyn-Small-Group-Walking-Tour/d22371-5403LOCAL?aid=vcps

You can easily apply these same walking tour ideas to your own community in your spare time. First, decide what type of walking tour you will create, outline the tour, itinerary and highlights. Figure out the duration of the tour, and then offer your services to tour companies such as Viator, Grayline Tours, Orbitz, Travelocity and others. If you are good at this, you can create your own walking tour company too and advertise your services on social media but check with your city's small business assistance center for any legal requirements. Tip: there are interesting places, sceneries, streets, malls, buildings, bridges, houses, churches, restaurants, breweries, wineries and neighborhoods in your community that you know as well as anybody. You can select some of these attractions as the highlights of a tour that you are going to create. Write a script and memorize it to use as your itinerary for the tour.

Tour guides who are fluent in Spanish, French, Mandarin and Japanese are even in more demand. And if you are good, cheerful and polite, you can make more money in tips than the hourly salary from the tour company.

8. Part Time Personal Coach/Trainer – If you love physical fitness and want to help others become physically fit too, you will enjoy being a personal coach and trainer. It is easy and inexpensive to obtain a certificate/license from the Personal Training Institute of America (PTIA). Many colleges and universities charge approximately $600 for this 20 hour course and the certificate is good for 2 years. In addition there is a 10-hour internship/shadowing requirement for final certification so you can see how other trainers work and interact with their clients. After that, continuing education credits of 10 hours must be earned per two year period to maintain your certification. Contact your nearest college or university to find out if they offer this course. Tip: Personal hygiene is very important. Although the main reason for going to a gym is to sweat it out, many people, men and women alike are offended by bad odors particularly if it's emanating from their coach. Make sure to take care of this. You may think this is a trivial issue for you, but may not be for your clients. Also encourage your clients to maintain hygiene by asking them to bring towels and exercise mats. Keep enough tissues and paper towels for your clients to use for wiping gym equipment after use.

9. GSA Contractor – Make the U.S. Government your best

and most loyal customer. Become a Government Services Administration (GSA) contractor. Open the link below to get more information. https://www.fbo.gov/index?s=opportunity&mode=list&tab=list&pageID=7 & https://vsc.gsa.gov/stepstosuccess.pdf

There are many products and services that the government buys. Following simple procedures and attending a couple of seminars may enable you to obtain a GSA Contract. Once you obtain your GSA contract number, you can apply to be listed as a bidder with the federal government and with various states and you may be awarded a contract. You can sell anything to the government that the government needs. You don't even have to stock any products yourself. You don't need money to buy the products ahead of time. You can simply locate the products or services that the government is looking for. The government is always looking for supplies such as infrastructure and transportation equipment, office furniture, computers, military and medical equipment, building materials and toilet seats. The government will issue a purchase order and you and the supplier will get paid. Your income will come from the supplier in the form of a commission or sub-contractor fee. If you establish your business as a small business, minority business, woman owned or veteran owned, do not be surprised if you receive more business than you can handle. Although the government does not officially follow an affirmative action program for awarding government contracts, the Office of Federal Contract Compliance Programs (OFCCP), the enforcer of GSA laws, often looks for statistically significant disparities based on the type of businesses contractors and sub-contractors partner with. To avoid deviations, government purchasers often seek out GSA contractors and sub-contractors whose businesses are listed as small businesses, minority owned, woman owned and veteran owned. Yes, you can do all this while holding another full time job, but you may end up being so successful and find yourself making so much money with this endeavor that you may decide to leave your regular job and do this full time.

10. Selling Autographed Books – You can make a lot of money acquiring and selling autographed books. This is a money making undertaking that is so much fun and so rewarding that it will make you wonder why very few people are doing it. 1) Locate a famous person's address. For example, President Barack Obama, White House, 1600 Pennsylvania Avenue NW, Washington, DC 20500. 2) Buy his book, **Dreams from My Father**   3) Mail the book with a cover letter that says:

Dear President Obama:
I very much enjoyed reading your book. You will always have my support. It would be a great honor if you can autograph your book and return it to me in the enclosed self-addressed, stamped envelope. I wish you continued success, good health and blessings.

Very truly yours,

I was surprised that 99% of the celebrities I sent their books to returned their book with an autograph. 4) Sell the book on EBay or Amazon. Somehow, I have had more success with books than with pictures. When I sent out a picture for a celebrity's autograph, I only received a return rate of 20%, 2 out of 10. The remaining 80% kept their picture and did not even give me the courtesy of a reply.

11. Court Interpreter – If you are fluent in both English and another foreign language, you can get certified as a Court interpreter. Spanish language interpreters currently make $282 a day in a California Court. Not too shabby.

12. Home Brewery – This is more of a hobby than a money-making enterprise. But if you love beer and you find out you have a knack for it, this will appeal to you and you can make money with this nevertheless. Surprisingly,

making beer is not that hard to do. There will be an initial investment. If you succeed, the potential for personal and monetary rewards are great. First, get all the information on the internet about the equipment you will need. After you are set up, spend some time experimenting on the taste by using different combination of ingredients and flavors, then have your friends try different batches. This will be a labor of love so it will take a while to realize the fruits of your labor. In the beginning, you can serve your home brews at family gatherings and friends' parties. If you regularly receive complements on certain flavors, think big and seriously contemplate on going into business. Start by checking this website:

http://growlermag.com/so-you-want-to-start-your-own-brewery/

13. Tiny House Movement – Tiny houses are quickly gaining in popularity. Tiny house communities are appearing all over the nation. For readers who are not familiar with a tiny house, these are houses ranging between a compact 100 square feet to the more spacious 600 square feet unit. Tiny houses are very popular with Millennials. What we used to call "starter houses" are now called "tiny houses". A tiny house costs anywhere between $10,000 and $50,000 to build and can be built on a relative's backyard or on a rented lot. Most buyers of tiny houses buy their houses for cash with no mortgage. This is where you come in. You can do this as a money-making part time project if it appeals to you. Locate a builder and ask if you can get appointed as an exclusive representative in your area. This means that if the builder receives a lead in your area of responsibility, the potential buyer will contact you so you can arrange for them to see a model. You will get a commission if they buy. Many of these tiny houses are portable, i.e. they can be transported by truck, parked or installed on a buyer's lot. Open the following websites for more   information:
https://www.tinyhomebuilders.com/faq   ,
TinyHouseListings.com, Or google search: Tumbleweed

Tiny House Company and Tiny House Company. It is essential that you know the local building regulations and what licenses and variances are needed to build a tiny house in someone's backyard or on your empty lot. In certain jurisdictions, a tiny house is treated as a mobile home and must be mounted on top of a trailer.

14. Sell Advertisements on Restaurant Placemats – This part time business scheme is relatively easy to start and once you have built up a clientele, it is a business that keeps on giving because you will just keep collecting the money even if you do not add new clients. Open the following website and read the article by Lynn Starner. The article provides the basic information on how to start: http://yourbusiness.azcentral.com/advertise-restaurant-placemats-13102.html

Although the article outlines a more sophisticated business plan such as partnering with ad designers, you can start this part time business on a shoestring. Get 2 blank rectangular pieces of paper 12 by 14 inches and 16 by 20 inches. These are the most common placemat sizes. Standard size business cards are 2 by 3 ½ inches. See how many business cards will fit on one placemat. That is the number of spaces you can sell. Essentially, the placemat will serve as a business directory for local businesses. On the middle of the placemat, layout the picture of the restaurant you will give the placemats to. The following sample is a courtesy of "Adsrus the Placemat People":

Create a clean proof of one restaurant placemat to show as a prototype of the finished product. If tastefully done, most restaurants will take you up on your offer to provide them with "free placemats". Why not? You're offering them for free with no strings attached. Your income will come from the advertisers. You will use the advertisers' business cards to imprint on the placemats, so that printing costs should not be very expensive. Build a business plan by creating a spreadsheet with all the costs and projected income. You will need an estimate of the number of placemats a restaurant will need in a period of at least 3 months and the cost for typesetting, designing and printing. A local discount printer will surely be delighted to work with you or you can get a quote from Staples or Office Depot. Do not be too greedy in the beginning. Do not overcharge your clients. $100 to $350 should be reasonable for each advertiser for a period of 3 to 6 months, depending on the number of placements you will print. The more you print the greater the exposure for the advertisers. If you yourself cannot acquire customers, you will need to hire a young sales person, perhaps a high school student to make cold calls or knock on the doors of local businesses to sell this idea to. Most of the placemat advertisers I talked to swear by how effective this type of advertising is. They do not mind paying $300 for three months' advertising. It is cheaper than the cost of the same ad on a local newspaper or magazine. Once you have built a clientele, you can just keep reprinting the placemats, deliver them and watch the money come in.

15. Part Time Messenger, Delivery Service – Make money in your spare time delivering packages, flowers, food, confidential documents, clothes, electronics, gifts, medications, payroll checks, special care items in and around your neighborhood.   Many companies now outsource deliveries to freelance messengers. Contact UberRUSH, 1800 Flowers, EdibleArrangements, uberontime.com, small payroll service companies and other local businesses that might need occasional and reliable delivery service. Tip: When you make a delivery, act in a professional way. Wash your face, dress neatly, put a cap on or comb your hair. Do not give the client the impression that you just got out of bed. Park on the street not on the recipient's driveway. Make the delivery with a smile on your face, have the recipient sign the receipt and make a quick exit. Do not freak out the client by engaging in small talk. Not too many people like talking to quasi messengers. Especially one who is not wearing a UPS or FedEx uniform. Do not linger around waiting for a tip. You will get bad reviews and may not get business anymore from the company...or worse, you may get blacklisted and never receive assignments again. Reliability is an absolute requirement for this part time venture. In general, if you refuse an assignment 2 or 3 times, the company will fire you.

16. Mock Interviewer – This part time job is so much in demand right now.   The nationwide official unemployment rate may be 5% but this low rate is deceptive because it does not take into consideration those who have dropped out of the labor force. Consequently, competition for jobs is really fierce. There are many job seekers who are looking for someone to turn to for mock

interviews. Why not offer them your service? There is no special skill or qualification for this job, although it helps if you actually have experience in interviewing applicants. As long as you can pretend you are a hiring manager, simulate a real interview, be able to ask questions, evaluate how well the interviewee did, then give the client helpful suggestions, you can do the job. Initially, you may offer your service to your state unemployment office. But you may get a lot of clients by advertising in your local newspaper. You can easily make $50 or more per hour with this part time venture that is fun and easy to do. For more information, click on the following website: http://jobsearch.about.com/od/jobinterviewtypes/a/mock-interview.htm

Tips: The gazillions of conflicting information on the internet about the best way of answering various job interview questions can drive you crazy. Even many HR experts disagree on what the correct answers should be on standard, trite job interview questions such as: "What are your strengths and weaknesses?", "Where do you see yourself 5 years from now?", "How would you describe yourself", etc. etc. Many of these common interview questions and various answers are shown on the website below. My advice to you as a **Mock Interviewer** is to put a little bit more emphasis on various exercises designed to give your client (job applicant) more confidence, poise and eloquence. The exercises should include repetition of "questions and answers" on which your client stumbled or otherwise showed weakness. This is what you are getting paid for---to train the client to become more confident and poised not necessarily to supply the correct answers to interview questions which are available on the internet. Click on the website below for additional information on sample interview questions and answers: http://hiring.monster.com/hr/hr-best-practices/recruiting-hiring-advice/interviewing-candidates/sample-interview-questions.aspx

17. Entertainment/Event Promoter – There are three basic components to this business plan. The Act, the venue and the customers. You will love it "when this plan comes together" because you will make a lot of money. The best and easiest way to start this lucrative venture is to put together a business plan and locate a 501(c) (3) or 501(c) (4) tax exempt non-profit charitable organization to partner with. This is called a "Cause Related Marketing Campaign". You should find many of these organizations in your community such as day care and learning centers, adult day care centers, after school centers, veterans' organizations, senior citizens' centers and religious organizations. Once you get them to agree to partner with you, i.e. to let you give them 50% of your profit from the venture, the second step is to find a dependable and reliable entertainer. Since I have actually done this before, I can tell you from my own experience that the best and most reliable acts are celebrity impersonators. I've hired Elvis, Michael Jackson and Tom Jones impersonators but the most successful venture I put together was with the BeatleMania Stage Show. The group was very organized. They themselves checked out the venue to make sure it has the acceptable stage-setup for acoustics, speakers, amplifiers, microphones, mixers, etc. The band's administrator even wrote the online and printed promotional advertising copy. All we had to do was fill in the charitable organization's name on the advertising flyer, e.g. "A Fundraiser for Mother Goose Child Care & Learning Center" then we printed the flyers and the tickets. We charged $30 per ticket advance purchase and $35 at the door. The tickets went on sale 3 months in advance. We completely sold out the 600 + Capacity Theater for the two 90-minute shows that Saturday. The charitable organization took charge of distributing the flyers around the community and even took the orders and charged the customers' credit cards. The organization's volunteers served as door attendants and ushers. My

income statement from the venture looks more or less as shown on the chart:

Gross Sales :	38,000
Less Cost:	
Entertainers	(16,000)
Theater Rental	(2,500)
Management, Promo	
and Other Costs	(6,000)
Net Profit:	13,500
50% Payable to Charitable Organization	(6,750)
NET TAXABLE PROFIT	$ 6,750

Here are a few things to remember with this venture: In most cases the charitable organization you will partner with will not be willing to put up any money up front so be prepared to put up your own capital. You may have to partially or fully fund the cost of the entertainers and the venue rental. Some entertainers demand that the amount for the engagement is fully paid prior to the event. Some theater owners may accept 50% deposit with the balance payable on the day of the event. If you have a good relationship with the charitable organization, they may turn over any sales proceeds to you as long as you can give them an accounting of what it would be used for. If you do not sell enough tickets, you may lose money. It is important to figure out if the area that you will target for ticket sales will patronize the Act that you will hire. For example, if the venue for the event is located in a hip hop town, an Elvis impersonator may not have an audience. A hit can make you a nice profit and earn you future business. A miss can set you back a few thousand dollars and may damage your reputation as a promoter. That is why it is important to know your market.

18. Start a Social Language Club – The objective of a language club is so someone can learn a foreign language quickly. Learning a new language in a social setting is so much better than learning it from books, audio CDs and from teachers in a school setting. If you are bilingual and sociable this undertaking is relatively easy to do and you will enjoy it. Invite some of your friends and relatives who speak your language to act as "shepherds" to start conversations. Advertise on social media that you are starting a language club. Set the admission price or a membership fee of about $25 to $50 per person. Buy a few bags of potato chips and a few family size soft drinks and you're all set. The only rule is for the attendees to enjoy themselves and communicate as much as possible in your language. The venue could be your house, basement, a friend's house, church hall, community center, Public Park, etc. When your club gets bigger, you can start charging more and you can look for a bigger venue. Due to the fact that many travelers want a fast track to learning a foreign language, the attendance might just surprise you. Learning a language through practice is a lot easier and will produce better results than learning from books or tapes.

19. Become a Cross Country Driver - If you enjoy driving long distances and you have an excellent driving record you can start a car delivery and long distance driving service. This can be a fun and enjoyable money making venture. When people relocate from one state to another many of them have more than one vehicle and do not want to drive them to a new location. Typically, you can charge your client $1 to $1.50 per mile plus gas and tolls. In most states insurance is covered by the client's insurance under the "permissive use doctrine". The best way to get started with this venture is to contact businesses in your area that have nationwide branches. Car rental and car leasing companies may also need your services. You may specialize driving exclusively

between two states, for example New York area to Florida, New York area to Texas or New York area to California, etc. Once you develop a network, it is possible to acquire regular business that will allow you to drive back and forth each destination rather than having to fly back home.

20. There are dozens of other ways to increase your income and make money in your spare time such as babysitting, tutoring, waitressing, security guard, gas attendant and many others. The trick is to follow the old adage, "Find something that you love to do. Then find a way to get paid for it."

18. Planning for College

My kids have graduated from good colleges and thank God they are gainfully employed so I don't have to worry about them, financially speaking. But my strategy for funding their college education was not to have any money saved up for that specific purpose because I feared that any amount of savings outside our 401k accounts got counted as a countable asset on our Expected Family Contribution (EFC) on the Free Application for Federal Student Aid (FAFSA) form, causing our eligibility for need-based financial aid to go down. I feared that the additional savings could jeopardize our children's eligibility for financial aid. Instead, we maximized our contributions to our 401k accounts with the intention of borrowing what we may need for college expenses. Fortunately, we only borrowed a negligible amount. We did not spend much because of the following factors:

1. We were able to reduce our "Adjusted Available Income" on the FAFSA form by maximizing our contributions to our retirement accounts. This increased our children's "need based" grants.
2. We only had non-countable assets, i.e. our 401k savings and equity in our principal residence. Very little savings.
3. Both of our children got good SAT scores.
4. They participated in extracurricular activities in high school.
5. They had good GPAs in high school.
6. They had Honors and Advanced Placement courses.
7. They travelled to several foreign countries which looks good on their applications.
8. They completed 4 years of foreign language (Spanish) in high school.
9. They were good at writing essays and made sure their essays did not contain spelling and grammatical errors.

Fortunately, your children will still do well no matter what as long as you plan ahead. Here are a few things you can do:
1. First, realize that college is not for everyone. If you think your child's talents and gifts from God are not geared toward pursuing a 4 year college degree, i.e. they are not college material, there are many other alternatives such as starting a business, going to trade or vocational school, being an artist, getting an associate degree, law enforcement, taking online courses, going to work, joining the military or AmeriCorps. Your children will do just as well and succeed even without a college degree as long as they find something that they can be passionate about. After all, Morley Safer, Richard Branson, Henry Ford, Walt Disney, Rush Limbaugh, Bill Gates and Steve Jobs did not graduate from college. Here are just a few jobs that can generate a lot of income which do not require a 4 year college degree: Electrician, welder, landscaper, nurse's aide, phlebotomist, dental hygienist, personal trainer, model, martial arts instructor, tour guide, carpenter, plumber, painter, Court interpreter, auto mechanic, aircraft maintenance assistant, air traffic controller, flight attendant, inventor, real estate broker, MRI technologist, roofer, truck driver, care giver, casino dealer, butcher, bass

fisherman, mail carrier, journeyman, funeral director, barber or hairdresser, manicurist and pedicurist, skin care specialist, computer repair technician, IT Technician, graphic designer, stage manager, private investigator, home inspector, and many more…obviously too many to mention.

2. If your children are college material, take the following steps as soon as possible:

    a. If your children are not in high school yet, consider moving into a highly rated public high school district in your state. Not only will you get more scholarship offers but it will better prepare your child for college. College is different than high school and many students drop out before the freshman year is over.

    b. Get your children interested in extracurricular activities in school, in sports, academic clubs, debate teams, student body, band, music and drama.

    c. Get your children interested in volunteer work and community service. If you contact your church, temple, synagogue, hospitals and local government you can specify a specific time your child will be available each week and the administrators will work with you. Even if your children accomplish this only in their senior year, it can still make a difference on their resume.

    d. Let your children accept summer jobs as camp counsellor, waiter, dish washer, cook, care giver, office clerk, carpenter, landscaper, driver, etc., etc. This will show the college that your child has some degree of responsibility. This will look good on their applications.

    e. Improve your children's SAT or ACT scores. Most colleges and universities publish the average SAT and ACT scores of their incoming freshmen. The following website shows the averages of hundreds of colleges and universities: https://www.powerscore.com/sat/help/average_test_scores.cfm

Your children can take several steps to improve their scores. There are many books and study guides and practice courses designed to improve SAT and ACT scores. There are practice tests you can buy just by surfing the internet. The Official SAT Study Guide DVD edition or The Official SAT Study Guide 2nd edition are good examples. They can also take the Princeton Review, Kaplan or other college prep study courses. The following are useful websites which should all help the student develop test-taking skills:

http://www.erikthered.com/tutor/practice.html
https://www.graphite.org/website/number2com

https://www.khanacademy.org/test-prep/sat
If you can afford it, it is worth paying whatever these books and courses will cost you. In the long run, the benefit your children will gain from getting higher scores will more than pay for the costs.

f. Check with the high school guidance counsellors which colleges accept graduates from their high school. Some colleges and universities sometimes seek out students from a particular high school. Check with the parents of students who graduated from the high school in previous years about their college search experiences and to see if they would recommend the college their children eventually ended up in. You will get a lot of useful information that can potentially save you thousands of dollars. You will also get an earful from parents who are not satisfied with the colleges their children ended up in. You have to choose carefully because colleges are like dictatorships. For example, if you raised your children in a conservative household, they may constantly butt heads with college professors who have liberal views. They will either get bad grades, drop out or finish college a different person than the person you enrolled. They can be brainwashed from being conservative into being a progressive…and vice versa. To me, this is an important factor in choosing a college. Google: "Most liberal and conservative colleges".

g. The table at the end of this chapter under the topic "College Rankings" came from the Forbes.com website. It should be used for comparison purpose only. The rankings are based on several factors and weights which are listed below:

No. 1: Student Satisfaction (27.5%) Student Evaluations from RateMyProfessor.com (17.5%) Freshman-to-Sophomore Retention Rates (5%) Student Evaluations from MyPlan.com (5%)

No. 2: Postgraduate Success (30%) Salary of Alumni from Payscale.com (15%) Listings of Alumni in Who's Who in America (10%) Alumni in Forbes/CCAP Corporate Officers List (5%)

No. 3: Student Debt (17.5%) Four-year Debt Load for Typical Student Borrower (12.5%) Student Loan Default Rates (5%)

No. 4: Four-year Graduation Rate (17.5%) Actual Four-year Graduation Rate (8.75%) Predicted vs. Actual Four-year Graduation Rate (8.75%)

No. 5: Competitive Awards (7.5%) Student Nationally Competitive Awards (7.5%)

The data is a few years old but my research shows that the numbers have not changed that much. The reason is because cost of living increase (inflation) has been almost non-existent since the "great recession". Many other factors will influence your college choice. If I consider only the rank and cost, Berea College, BYU, Troy, University of Minnesota, Grove City College, ranked at #210, #136, #237, #143 and #279 respectively, would top my list. Unfortunately, there are other considerations such as: incidental expenses and transportation when considering schools that are out of your state, additional tuition fees for out of state students, student population, ethnic and racial composition, male to female ratio and the school's reputation for the degree your children will pursue. The US News and World Report website below provides additional information:

http://www.usnews.com/education

h. Be more analytical when it comes to evaluating your choices. After compiling a list of schools that have a good reputation for the degrees your children want to pursue, create a spreadsheet like the following chart I created:

Rank	College Name	TYP	Tuition & Fees	Tuition & Fees	Fin. Aid Package	Net	Est. Travel & Add. Costs	Approx Annual Tuition & Travel Exp
92	U of Michigan, Ann Arbor, MI	N	41,028	44,761	5,000	39,761	7,000	46,761
62	U of NC, Chapel Hill, NC	N	28,567	33,091	5,000	28,091	7,000	35,091
285	College of NJ, NJ	R	6,949	33,527	22,000	11,527	800	12,327
395	St. Joseph's University, PA	R	7,900	48,360	15,000	33,360	1,000	34,360
7	Swarthmore College, PA	NLA	1,490	50,381	NONE	50,381	1,000	51,381
224	University of Scranton, PA	R	5,651	45,316	32,000	13,316	1,000	14,316
114	Villanova University, PA	R	10,274	49,470	10,000	39,470	1,000	40,470
46	College of William and Mary, VA	N	7,892	39,886	NONE	39,886	7,000	46,886
44	University of Virginia, VA	N	24,541	40,709	5,000	35,709	7,000	42,709

TYP Legend:

N	National University
R	Regional University
NLA	National Liberal Arts
R	Regional University

If your child is accepted by all the schools on the list, and offered the financial aid packages shown, you will realize a huge savings if your child accepts the offer from either the University of Scranton or The College of New Jersey because they offer the most generous financial aid packages. These two colleges are run-away winners. Your first-choice might be Swarthmore College but how much difference will it make to your child's career to graduate from Swarthmore College vs. University of Scranton or The College of New Jersey? If you think it would make a big difference, be prepared to pay $40,000 a year or more in tuition fees and other expenses. This is a big decision. Will your child's second or third choice fail to meet his or her academic and personal goals? Many students are saddled with huge debts, perhaps close to $100,000 by the time they graduate. It takes a very long time to repay such a huge debt. This is not the way your child should start his or her career. Think before you leap. However, if you feel your child would lose interest and motivation to excel in college because the first choice school is out of reach, you, your wife and child should have a serious discussion so as to come up with a sound decision. You will regret making the wrong decision for the rest of your life. If you decide to bite the bullet and enroll your child in the more expensive school, it is worth discussing the financial aid award with the officers of the school. To compare financial aid awards, click on the link below:

https://bigfuture.collegeboard.org/pay-for-college/financial-aid-awards/compare-aid-calculator

    i. Common sense dictates that public institutions in your state are the best bet. In-state tuition for residents is a lot less than for out-of-state applicants. Check out the regional colleges and universities first before national universities and liberal arts colleges. In my experience, regional colleges and universities offer bigger financial aid packages.

    j. Do not disregard community colleges and schools that are "non-rated". My friend Brian, who ended his career as the manager of the Tax Department of a large company graduated from La Guardia Community College in Queens, NY with a Bachelor's

Degree in Business Administration. He made an average of $150,000 per annum over the course of his working life that he was able to retire at 55. Not once did his degree from a community college ever become an issue when he went for interviews. If a community college tuition is all your budget can afford, choose it. Do not take on so much life changing student debt. This will have a profound effect on your life and your children's lives. If your children's friends and high school classmates are all going to top rated schools, and your children are feeling deprived, tell them to get over it and mention my friend Brian as an inspiration. At the tender age of 17, children are very impressionable. They are not mature enough to prevail over what they may consider adversity. It would not take much to make them feel disadvantaged due to your inability to send them to a "better school". Let them read this book. Give them a glimpse of how easily they can follow the steps herein to achieve their goal to financial freedom and to a happy and fulfilling life no matter what college they graduate from. So for your children who have their hearts set on getting a college diploma, their first step to a successful career is to earn the degree. It is less important what college the degree came from.

-College
Rankings
:

Rank	Name	State	Tuition & Fees	Populatio
1	Williams College	MA	49,530	2,072
2	Princeton University	NJ	49,830	7,330
3	Amherst College	MA	50,230	1,697
4	United States Military Academy	NY	0	4,553
5	Massachusetts Institute of Technology	MA	50,100	10,299
6	Stanford University	CA	51,760	17,833
7	Swarthmore College	PA	50,381	1,490
8	Harvard University	MA	50,250	26,496
9	Claremont McKenna College	CA	50,990	1,212
10	Yale University	CT	51,400	10,192
11	United States Air Force Academy	CO	0	4,537
12	Wellesley College	MA	50,026	2,498
13	Columbia University	NY	51,406	23,196
14	Haverford College	PA	51,637	1,169
15	Wesleyan University	CT	51,935	3,149
16	Whitman College	WA	46,212	1,458
17	Pomona College	CA	49,745	1,532
18	Northwestern University	IL	52,120	19,291
19	California Institute of Technology	CA	48,990	2,126
20	University of Chicago	IL	53,310	14,788
21	Carleton College	MN	50,000	1,983
22	Harvey Mudd College	CA	50,073	738
23	Vassar College	NY	51,370	2,389
24	Centre College	KY	39,200	1,197
25	Rice University	TX	43,586	5,357
26	Middlebury College	VT	52,460	2,455
27	Boston College	MA	52,060	14,836
28	Colgate University	NY	51,090	2,844
29	United States Naval Academy	MD	1,000	4,488
30	Dartmouth College	NH	50,547	5,848
31	Colby College	ME	50,120	1,847
32	Kenyon College	OH	49,260	1,644
33	University of Notre Dame	IN	49,030	11,731
34	Tufts University	MA	51,400	10,030
35	Smith College	MA	50,588	3,101
36	University of Pennsylvania	PA	51,299	24,107
37	Washington and Lee University	VA	49,268	2,155
38	Bryn Mawr College	PA	50,060	1,745

39	College of the Holy Cross	MA	49,102	2,898
40	Bowdoin College	ME	50,570	1,723
41	Duke University	NC	50,925	14,060
42	Wabash College	IN	37,750	911
43	Vanderbilt University	TN	52,303	12,093
44	University of Virginia	VA	40,709	24,541
45	Brown University	RI	50,560	8,318
46	College of William and Mary	VA	39,886	7,892
47	Rhodes College	TN	43,680	1,678
48	Davidson College	NC	45,725	1,668
49	Union College	NY	50,060	2,240
50	Lawrence University	WI	42,301	1,496
51	Colorado College	CO	48,000	2,026
52	Georgetown University	DC	54,200	15,318
53	Emory University	GA	49,708	12,755
54	Bates College	ME	51,400	1,776
55	Macalester College	MN	46,730	1,900
56	Bucknell University	PA	50,250	3,759
57	Brandeis University	MA	50,148	5,327
58	Wofford College	SC	40,835	1,429
59	Wheaton College	IL	50,130	2,915
60	Virginia Military Institute	VA	36,573	1,428
61	Lafayette College	PA	49,188	2,382
62	University of North Carolina, Chapel Hill	NC	33,091	28,567
63	Barnard College	NY	51,976	2,359
64	DePauw University	IN	42,175	2,298
65	University of California, Berkeley	CA	47,194	35,396
66	Oberlin College	OH	50,658	2,864
67	Dickinson College	PA	50,334	2,388
68	Principia College	IL	33,075	519
69	Reed College	OR	49,960	1,471
70	Cornell University	NY	50,384	20,273
71	University of California, Los Angeles	CA	45,152	38,220
72	Wake Forest University	NC	49,820	6,862
73	Kalamazoo College	MI	40,416	1,389
74	Hamilton College	NY	50,210	1,872
75	Knox College	IL	38,433	1,379
76	Washington University, St. Louis	MO	52,464	13,339
77	Denison University	OH	45,980	2,200
78	Grinnell College	IA	46,400	1,678
79	Mount Holyoke College	MA	51,516	2,241
80	Skidmore College	NY	51,501	2,777
81	Westmont College	CA	47,786	1,340
82	Juniata College	PA	40,550	1,526

83	Connecticut College	CT	51,685	1,852
84	University of Richmond	VA	49,090	4,249
85	St. Mary's College of California	CA	NA	NA
86	Occidental College	CA	50,409	1,868
87	Sweet Briar College	VA	39,971	828
88	Johns Hopkins University	MD	51,478	19,758
89	St. Mary's College of Maryland	MD	36,494	2,068
90	Furman University	SC	47,040	2,977
91	Drew University	NJ	52,106	2,581
92	University of Michigan, Ann Arbor	MI	44,761	41,028
93	University of Florida	FL	32,093	51,474
94	Cooper Union	NY	51,755	972
95	Wells College	NY	40,280	579
96	Trinity College	CT	50,645	2,504
97	University of Illinois at Urbana-	IL	38,364	43,246
98	Gustavus Adolphus College	MN	39,760	2,503
99	Franklin and Marshall College	PA	50,100	2,164
100	Washington & Jefferson College	PA	41,684	1,519
101	Ursinus College	PA	48,310	1,680
102	Hendrix College	AR	37,758	1,350
103	Randolph-Macon College	VA	39,465	1,201
104	Salem College	NC	35,610	939
105	United States Coast Guard Academy	CT	4,600	975
106	Hillsdale College	MI	NA	NA
107	University of Washington	WA	35,555	39,675
108	Carnegie Mellon University	PA	51,960	10,875
109	Southern Methodist University	TX	47,375	10,965
110	Ithaca College	NY	44,368	6,448
111	St. Olaf College	MN	44,000	3,073
112	University of Southern California	CA	51,881	33,747
113	Westminster College	MO	27,070	1,000
114	Villanova University	PA	49,470	10,274
115	Santa Clara University	CA	50,556	8,758
116	Thomas Aquinas College	CA	31,845	340
117	University of California, Irvine	CA	44,454	26,984
118	Scripps College	CA	51,250	972
119	Nebraska Wesleyan University	NE	30,982	2,086
120	New College of Florida	FL	34,966	785
121	Xavier University	OH	39,130	6,584
122	Luther College	IA	39,550	2,423
123	Gettysburg College	PA	47,830	2,480
124	College of Wooster	OH	43,920	1,884
125	Beloit College	WI	39,736	1,388
126	Southwestern University	TX	38,540	1,270

127	Allegheny College	PA	42,500	2,125
128	Wesleyan College	GA	27,300	739
129	Saint Michael's College	VT	42,000	2,460
130	Loyola University in Maryland	MD	48,410	6,080
131	Rockhurst University	MO	36,278	3,086
132	Muhlenberg College	PA	46,000	2,492
133	University of Rochester	NY	50,550	9,735
134	George Fox University	OR	36,640	3,383
135	Millsaps College	MS	36,054	1,118
136	Brigham Young University	UT	15,330	34,244
137	Agnes Scott College	GA	40,910	832
138	University of Texas at Austin	TX	41,140	49,984
139	University of California, San Diego	CA	44,371	27,520
140	Hobart and William Smith Colleges	NY	50,886	2,078
141	University of Puget Sound	WA	46,035	2,844
142	Pepperdine University	CA	49,750	7,614
143	University of Minnesota, Morris	MN	19,116	1,607
144	Gonzaga University	WA	39,982	7,272
145	Earlham College	IN	42,694	1,336
146	St. Anselm College	NH	42,465	1,900
147	Albion College	MI	38,770	1,860
148	John Carroll University	OH	39,024	3,826
149	Manhattan College	NY	36,810	3,441
150	University of Georgia	GA	33,070	34,180
151	Tulane University	LA	50,030	10,737
152	St. Norbert College	WI	34,707	2,137
153	University of Dallas	TX	37,955	2,977
154	Lake Forest College	IL	43,500	1,400
155	St. John's College	MD	49,818	562
156	Virginia Tech	VA	32,165	30,739
157	William Jewell College	MO	33,630	1,210
158	Marlboro College	VT	42,220	326
159	Doane College	NE	28,600	894
160	Gordon College	MA	36,918	1,717
161	Clark University	MA	42,620	3,330
162	University of California, Davis	CA	45,619	30,568
163	Berry College	GA	33,198	1,795
164	Trinity University	TX	38,521	2,703
165	United States Merchant Marine	NY	9,010	986
166	Hiram College	OH	36,985	1,360
167	Pitzer College	CA	50,800	1,025
168	Colorado School of Mines	CO	35,684	4,704
169	James Madison University	VA	30,196	18,454
170	Sarah Lawrence College	NY	54,854	1,715

171	Pacific University	OR	38,202	3,167
172	University of California, Santa Cruz	CA	46,526	16,615
173	New York University	NY	52,082	42,189
174	Marietta College	OH	35,784	1,606
175	Lehigh University	PA	49,540	6,99
176	Wittenberg University	OH	44,550	1,976
177	California Polytechnic State University	CA	29,295	19,471
178	Capital University	OH	38,120	3,632
179	Covenant College	GA	33,520	1,343
180	Lewis and Clark College	OR	45,576	3,565
181	Sewanee - University of the South	TN	44,020	1,562
182	College of Idaho	ID	27,876	944
183	Hanover College	IN	35,120	926
184	Carroll University	WI	31,954	3,318
185	University of Colorado, Boulder	CO	42,739	32,469
186	University of Redlands	CA	46,932	4,317
187	Willamette University	OR	43,910	2,721
188	The University of Utah	UT	29,749	28,211
189	Illinois Wesleyan University	IL	41,214	2,125
190	College of the Atlantic	ME	41,637	327
191	California Lutheran University	CA	41,765	3,499
192	Pennsylvania State University	PA	37,976	44,406
193	Florida State University	FL	31,896	38,682
194	Texas A&M University, College Station	TX	34,235	48,039
195	Ripon College	WI	33,315	1,057
196	Cornell College	IA	37,260	1,112
197	SUNY, Binghamton	NY	23,906	14,882
198	Austin College	TX	37,187	1,298
199	Providence College	RI	43,910	5,085
200	Brigham Young University, Idaho	ID	12,441	14,276
201	University of Pittsburgh	PA	35,760	27,562
202	Susquehanna University	PA	41,400	2,137
203	Fordham University	NY	51,407	14,666
204	Presbyterian College	SC	39,296	1,177
205	Hampden-Sydney College	VA	40,849	1,120
206	Hampshire College	MA	49,729	1,428
207	University of Denver	CO	47,617	11,328
208	University of Mary Washington	VA	28,768	5,084
209	Whitworth University	WA	38,604	2,704
210	Berea College	KY	9,186	1,549
211	University of California, Santa Barbara	CA	47,061	21,868
212	University of Wisconsin, Madison	WI	33,223	41,620
213	Houghton College	NY	33,020	1,415
214	University of San Francisco	CA	49,030	8,750

215	Whittier College	CA	45,856	2,047
216	Ouachita Baptist University	AR	27,430	1,493
217	St. John's College	NM	50,513	511
218	University of Delaware	DE	31,904	20,500
219	Bard College	NY	51,240	2,158
220	Washington College	MD	44,935	1,394
221	Boston University	MA	51,100	31,766
222	Indiana University, Bloomington	IN	36,343	40,354
223	University of Wyoming	WY	23,030	12,067
224	University of Scranton	PA	45,316	5,651
225	Coe College	IA	37,610	1,326
226	St. Joseph's College	NY	NA	NA
227	University of California, Riverside	CA	44,678	18,079
228	Creighton University	NE	39,458	7,051
229	Hope College	MI	34,832	3,238
230	Loyola Marymount University	CA	49,174	9,011
231	Siena College	NY	35,870	3,305
232	Pacific Lutheran University	WA	38,351	3,652
233	Oklahoma Baptist University	OK	24,378	1,769
234	Utah State University	UT	22,291	15,099
235	College of the Ozarks	MO	24,475	1,334
236	Linfield College	OR	37,234	1,720
237	Troy University	AL	18,308	28,303
238	Wisconsin Lutheran College	WI	30,120	753
239	Case Western Reserve University	OH	48,052	9,814
240	The Master's College	CA	33,812	1,417
241	Mills College	CA	49,760	1,476
242	Georgia Institute of Technology	GA	35,376	19,413
243	Miami University, Oxford	OH	40,618	17,191
244	Wheaton College	MA	35,900	1,655
245	Eckerd College	FL	43,494	2,508
246	Ohio State University	OH	35,793	53,715
247	Emerson College	MA	42,867	4,536
248	Ohio Wesleyan University	OH	44,120	1,959
249	University of Maryland, College Park	MD	36,432	37,000
250	Rollins College	FL	49,587	3,259
251	Bennington College	VT	51,950	759
252	St. Lawrence University	NY	49,010	2,325
253	Wheeling Jesuit University	WV	35,030	1,319
254	Birmingham-Southern College	AL	36,691	1,458
255	Transylvania University	KY	33,610	1,158
256	Seattle University	WA	41,688	7,560
257	Cedar Crest College	PA	38,977	1,872
258	Calvin College	MI	33,910	4,171

259	University of Oregon	OR	31,665	21,452
260	American University	DC	48,001	11,684
261	Saint John's University	MN	37,616	2,063
262	Hamline University	MN	37,786	4,876
263	Stetson University	FL	41,272	3,696
264	Spring Hill College	AL	37,740	1,534
265	The Citadel	SC	33,500	3,328
266	Mount St. Mary's College	CA	42,130	2,363
267	Hollins University	VA	39,505	1,058
268	Goshen College	IN	32,290	957
269	Alfred University	NY	37,374	2,427
270	Converse College	SC	35,600	2,068
271	Bellarmine University	KY	42,496	3,040
272	Randolph College	VA	38,530	568
273	Taylor University	IN	33,498	1,871
274	California Maritime Academy	CA	28,758	875
275	University of Connecticut	CT	37,094	24,273
276	Fisk University	TN	28,715	726
277	SUNY, Environmental Science and	NY	25,639	2,523
278	Emory and Henry College	VA	34,740	1,015
279	Grove City College	PA	20,264	2,499
280	Northwestern College	MN	32,290	3,023
281	Marist College	NY	39,451	5,828
282	Michigan State University	MI	35,388	46,510
283	Augustana College	IL	39,900	2,547
284	University of South Carolina, Columbia	SC	35,097	27,488
285	College of New Jersey	NJ	33,527	6,949
286	Mississippi College	MS	22,865	4,741
287	Union University	TN	29,510	3,655
288	Concordia College-Moorhead	MN	33,090	2,823
289	Huntington University	IN	29,390	1,230

19. Purchase Your Primary Residence

A house will likely be your single biggest investment ever. Statistically, buying a house is cheaper than renting. By the time you are ready to retire the mortgage on the house will probably be paid off leaving you with a nice nest egg of a few hundred thousand dollars. This plus millions of dollars in your retirement fund if you succeed in following the strategies in this book will provide you with a nice retirement income that should last for as long as you live. Buying your principal residence with a low interest mortgage loan is an investment that is hard to beat. The rent you would have paid would go instead towards servicing the loan. Towards interest which is tax deductible and towards the principal. As the principal is reduced, your equity increases. Your property may also go up in value by the time you are ready to sell. You will always be paying property tax but that is deductible too in our current tax system. Finally, the $250,000/$500,000 exclusion of gain from sale of a principal residence for singles/joint taxpayers is one of the best tax shelters that is still in existence as of publication of this book. Check on the IRS website for exceptions and changes to this U.S. code and to make sure the law has not changed, (https://www.irs.gov/publications/p523/ar02.html)

Buying your principal residence that you can afford is different from other investments. This investment may go up or down in value but you still sleep in it. Think of your primary residence as your shelter, the roof over your head, your home and sanctuary, not just an investment. The following formula will give you an idea what price of a house you can afford by calculating the monthly PITI that you can afford to carry:

Principal+Interest+Taxes+Insurance (PITI) $xxxx + All other monthly debt payments $xxxx = Total Monthly Debt Payments $xxxx, multiplied by 12 must not exceed 36% of your annual gross income (debt to income ratio). Example, your gross income is $100,000. PITI plus other monthly debt obligations must not exceed $36,000 a year or $3000 a month. Many banks have been allowing over 40% debt to income ratio provided the debtor pays a mortgage loan insurance which can be as much as 1% of the mortgage balance. This can be dangerous for the debtor. In the event of a financial reversal and loss of income and the homeowner cannot continue making payments, the property may be foreclosed on by the creditor and sold as a distressed property. When this happens the homeowner would most likely lose some or most of his equity in the property. The worst part is that in some states the creditor may be able to go after the homeowner for the deficiency in case the property is sold for less than the balance of the mortgage. Before buying a property it is important for the buyer to accurately assess job security and the prospect of increase or decrease in income in the future. Many homebuyers are confident enough about their job security and their future income that they buy houses they can hardly afford so that initially they become house poor, spending 50% of their income on PITI and other debts. This strategy works for some who are lucky enough to buy at the right time when home values are rising.

The way you can really compare owning to renting is by creating a Pros and Cons comparison table. Plug in real numbers to give you a better idea of where you will be after a period of time.

Pros and Cons of Owning

Pros: No landlord or landlady to deal with. You are at their mercy if you did something they don't like. If you make too much noise, scratch the walls, host too many parties they can increase your rent by 25% in one year or worse, kick you out when your lease is up. A fixed rate mortgage loan is guaranteed for a period of time. You have more freedom to do what you want with your dwelling. You have bigger space and no stomping neighbors going up and down the stairs to deal with. It is great for do-it-yourselfers and for those who enjoy yard work and gardening. In our current tax system, you will receive mortgage tax deduction, property tax deduction, capital gains tax exemption when you sell; have a sense of community, equity build up, appreciation, pride of ownership, availability of an equity loan for emergencies.

Cons: Loss of interest on the down payment and closing costs; depreciation; illiquid asset; it's stressful to buy and sell; broker's fee when you sell; maintenance costs; time you lose in maintenance;

may be farther away from your place of work; higher insurance and utility costs; common fees; it's an albatross around your neck if you get divorced; you cannot instantly move out if a bad neighbor moves in; property taxes; you will lose your equity and your FICO scores will plunge if you can no longer afford the monthly payments and have to move out.

Doing the comparison in an excel spreadsheet and using realistic figures will give you a more accurate result. The following websites are very useful. You can enter your actual numbers to see the result but you must enter accurate variables.

http://www.nytimes.com/interactive/2014/upshot/buy-rent-calculator.html?_r=0

http://michaelbluejay.com/house/rentvsbuy.html

I entered my figures on the said websites, then I created the following excel table to verify my figures. The result is astonishing. I would lose $159,876 if I choose renting to owning on a 15-year projection. This does not even take into consideration the intangibles, some of which were enumerated under the subject "Pros and Cons".

15 Year Projection	OWNING	
4%, 15 Year Fixed		
Price of Dwelling	350,000	
Down Payment	70,000	
Net Loan	280,000	
Annual Percentage Rate (APR)	4%	
Monthly Payment (Principal & Interest)	2,071	
Total Payments	372,803	1
Interest Expense after 15 years = $92,803.40		
Less Income Tax benefit on Interest @ 15%	-13,921	2
Real Estate Taxes, Avg $8400/year	126,000	3
Less Income Tax benefit on R/E Taxes @ 15%	-18,900	4
Maintenance & Repairs, Avg. $3500/year	52,500	5
Homeowner's Insurance, Avg. $1500/year	22,500	6
(a) Total Monthly Expenditure, 15 years (Add 1 to 6)	**540,983**	
Down Payment	70,000	
Closing Costs, 3%	10,500	
Renting a Comparable Dwelling		
15 Year Projection	**RENTING**	
Initial Rent at $1900/mo., 3% Annual Increases	424,055	
Renter's Insurance, Avg $800/year	12,000	
(b) Total Monthly Expenditure after 15 years	**436,055**	
Difference in Total Expenditure (A-B)	104,928	
Renter's Monthly Savings ($104,928/180 mos.)	583	
Monthly Savings + Interest @ 8% APR	198,067	7
Less: Capital Gains Tax 15%	-29,710	8
Downpayment & Closing costs + Interest @ 8% APR	255,360	9
Less: Capital Gains Tax 15%	-38,304	10
Renter's Cash on hand after 15 years (Add 7 to 10)	385,413	11
Property value after 15 years at an average 3% per year increase	545,289	
(Single Individual Capital Gains Exemption on profit=$250,000)		
Owner's Cash on hand after 15 years	545,289	12
Owner's Advantage vs. Renter after 15 years (#12 less # 11)	**$159,876**	

The table only shows a 15-year projection. After 15 years, I practically live rent free. Yes, I will still pay real estate taxes which are tax deductible in our current tax system and I will continue to pay for repair and maintenance and higher insurance and utilities than a renter. But my home "may" continue to appreciate too as years go by.

Brian Lund, freelance writer wrote this article on July 19, 2014, "The Worst Investment You Can Make: Buying a Home". http://www.dailyfinance.com/2014/07/19/the-worst-investment-you-can-make-buying-a-home/ .

In his article, Lund claims that you will end up saving $3 million if you rented a comparable house instead of owning one for $350,000. That is, if you invested the savings you will realize by renting instead of owning a comparable house. Lund adds, *"Of course there are numerous tweaks you can make to this scenario — for example, factoring in your home's price appreciation or the tax benefits — but no matter how you slice it, owning a home doesn't come anywhere close to making financial sense."*

I can cite a few problems with his article:

1. He uses a 30 year fixed rate at 4.5% interest. At the time of writing, you can get a much lower rate for a 15 year fixed.

2. He assumes that the rent for a comparable dwelling is 75% of the monthly principal and interest payment and has no provision for rent increases over a period of 30 years. This is ridiculous.

3. He does not factor in the loss of interest mortgage deduction and real estate tax deduction that will generally put the homeowner into a lower tax bracket. Conversely, he does not consider the fact that there is capital gains tax on the interest the renter's savings earns, so it can put the renter in a higher tax bracket increasing his marginal tax rates, perhaps from 15% to 25% to 28% to 33%.

4. He assumes zero appreciation for your home. There is no way to predict if housing is going up or down but assuming zero appreciation over 30 years is unrealistic. According to

the National Association of Realtors (NAR) existing homes appreciated 5.4% annually from 1968 to 2009 on the average. The nationwide average annual increase of existing homes from 1987 to 2009 according to the Case-Schiller Index was 3.4%. Also, at the time of writing, there is a $250,000 ($500,000 couple) capital gains exclusion on the profit realized on the sale of a principal residence. For additional qualification and updated information, See IRS Publication 523, https://www.irs.gov/taxtopics/tc701.html

On the other hand, long term capital gains are currently taxed at a rate of 15%, see IRS Publication 551, https://www.irs.gov/taxtopics/tc409.html

5. He neglects to consider that after 15 years when your house is paid off, you pretty much live rent free. Yes, you will still pay for real estate taxes, upkeep and higher insurance and utilities than a renter pays but the house is yours. Real estate taxes will continue to reduce your taxable income even after mortgage payments end if you itemize.

6. Finally, he fails to consider that many people will not save the savings they will realize by being a renter. They will find a way to spend it.

In his article "Five Things You NEED to Know before Buying a House", James Altucher declares, *"I hate buying houses. I don't "hate" many things. But I've lost millions of dollars buying houses. The stress is unbearable when you need to sell. And you have no money when you need it. It's a prison. The white picket fence is the prison bars. The bank is the guards looking in. And the need to protect your family keeps you in a solitary confinement of guilt and anxiety and stress."*

Who can lose millions of dollars in real estate? The truth is James is really telling the truth. He really had a string of bad luck that most people will never experience. No one can lose millions of dollars in real estate without really trying. Especially not if the subject real estate is your principal residence. James Altucher indeed lost at least $2 million in real estate. He was unlucky enough to buy at the wrong place at the wrong time. He was a victim of a "perfect storm" of circumstances. Real Estate burnt him that is why he hates real estate and won't go near it anymore. As the story goes, and as various published articles confirm, Mr. Altucher bought a $1.8 million condo in the Tribeca section of Manhattan which is in the downtown area not far from Chinatown. Then he put in at least $1 million in renovations. Shortly thereafter, the 9/11 attacks happened. The location of this condo is not far from ground zero. He ended up selling his condo for $1 million. So I guess he was not exaggerating after all. Contrast his luck with that of a distant relative of mine who is in the advertising industry and claims NOT to know anything about real estate. Let's call her Jane. She bought a pre-construction 2-bedroom condo at the Orion building near the Port Authority bus terminal in NYC. Jane went into contract in 2006 for a pre-construction sale price of $900,000. When the unit was ready for occupancy in late 2007, its value had already increased to $1.2 million. Moreover, the building had a long waiting list of buyers. For some reason not disclosed to me, 3 years later, Jane went into contract to buy another 2 bedroom unit at the just completed Rushmore building on Riverside Blvd in the upper West Side. The pre-construction price of her unit was $1 million. To make a long story short, she sold her Orion unit for $1.7 million and bought the Rushmore unit for $1 million. How is that for buying low and selling high to make a hefty profit? And here's the kicker. She got a 3% 15-year fixed mortgage loan and her 2 bedroom condo is now worth at least $2 million. Call it fortuitous timing or the luck of the Irish, but certainly, NYC real estate treated Jane much better than it did James.

I admit I've lost thousands (not millions) of dollars in rental properties which is why I will NOT recommend them, but rarely can you go wrong in owning your home. Do the math and make sure to consider all the different factors and you will see that typically, owning your home is cheaper than renting a similar dwelling. With regard to Altucher's calling a house a prison, an apartment is also a prison only smaller. The landlord is the warden looking in. You can be thrown out of jail within months if you do something the warden does not like. On the other hand, maybe you can stay for 3 years in your prison of a house even if you stop paying the mortgage. It takes a long time for banks to go through the foreclosure and eviction process. There are many delaying tactics you can employ to delay foreclosure and eviction. Even after foreclosure the bank may have a hard time throwing you out on the street.

Location, location, location

The adage, location, location, location is true, true, true. Two exactly similar homes built on the same date will appreciate differently depending on their location. This is the number one rule in real estate because location is the greatest determining factor in the value of a property. You can fix up a house but you cannot fix up its location.

Look for a house in a nice neighborhood with good schools and a low crime rate and close to your place of work. Check out the following factors: the school district's rating, the crime rate, distance to your place of work, distance to low income housing, commercial and industrial properties, farms, factories, schools, cemetery, railroad tracks, freeways, subway stations, landfills, garbage dumps, recycling, bars, restaurants, main thoroughfares and sports arenas. Determine if the neighborhood is economically stable and observe if the neighborhood is composed of similar types of properties. A house in a fairly homogeneous neighborhood will retain its value better than a similar home in a neighborhood where there are apartments, condominiums and businesses. Check out if the residents take pride in ownership by maintaining their lawns, roofs and exterior of their houses. If the homes have poor landscaping and discarded mattresses, junk car parts and old appliances litter some of the yards, I would not move there. Buy the worst house on the best block. If you live in the Snowbelt choose a house whose driveway faces south east to help the sun melt the ice and snow. If your driveway faces north, you will need a lot of ice-melt, rock salt and de-icer. Houses with south east exposure are better in that part of the country. Make sure you can live with your neighbors. It will be hard to move out after you've moved in. Drive around the neighborhood all hours of the night, on weekdays as well as on weekends to observe if there are undesirable individuals hanging out on street corners. Go to the local police precinct and to the city or municipal building. Ask the police and town clerk questions about the specific street where the house you are considering is located. In most cases, they should be glad to provide information from their own personal knowledge of that neighborhood. The county where the house is located may compile a crime report for different neighborhoods which may be available online.

I prefer a house in the middle of the tract or at the end of a cul-de-sac to one located on the corner. Corners have more traffic and less privacy. Compare property taxes. Real estate taxes can vary a lot. This is an expense you will be paying for a very long time and when the time comes to sell your house the buyer will be looking at the tax expense as well. It would be necessary to put a real dollar figure as well as imaginary dollar value on the pros and cons to determine the amount of money you will really save over a period of time. If you move closer to your place of work, how much money will you save in fuel? How much time will you save in your daily commute? How do they translate in real dollars? You won't be hearing neighbors going up and down the stairs if you own your own house. How much in imaginary dollars is that worth to you?

If you already own a house and plan to stay in your house for at least 7 years, refinance your mortgage if you can get a rate that is at least 2% lower than what you have now and there are no closing costs. Each time you refinance, you will be resetting the mortgage clock to day one. So you will extend the period of your loan unless you are refinancing from a 30 year mortgage to a 20 or 15 year loan. Any extra cash you may receive out of refinancing your home must be used, 1) to pay off credit card debt or other high interest debts, 2) for repair and maintenance of your home, 3) to fund your retirement account.

As part of my financial master plan, as your income increases and you constantly end up with a monthly surplus even after maximizing your 401k contributions, consider moving up to a better house in a better neighborhood with a better school system. See the chapter, "Planning for College" about the importance of a good school system in preparation for college education for your children. It would be better to put that monthly surplus into your own home than wasting it on a BMW or Mercedes, or giving away a big portion of it to the taxman.

20. Good debt, bad debt

Bad debts are those that do not yield a positive return if you invested the amount you borrowed. Pay day loans, department store and credit card charges and other consumer debts are at the top of the list of bad debts. They bear high interests. But if you borrowed money at 4% APR and that money earned a return of 10% APR, that is a "good debt". And if that borrowed money generates another 1% APR on the average for the next 10 years, not only is that a "good debt" but an "excellent debt". This is exactly what happens when you have a mortgage on your principal residence. Mortgage interest payments are generally tax deductible although there are exceptions which you can check on the IRS website: https://www.irs.gov/publications/p936/ar02.html

The benefit of having a mortgage you can afford to pay should be part of your lifetime financial game plan. That is why I just don't understand why Dave Ramsey would recommend paying for your house in cash. Yes, there is a psychological element in knowing that your house is paid off but this is not a good advice in my opinion. I cringe every time I hear debt-free screamers on his radio show proclaiming "I PAID OFF MY $150,000 MORTGAGE. I AM DEBT FREEEEEE!!" I often scream back at the radio, "THAT COST YOU THOUSANDS OF DOLLARS!!!" There is a value to debt. The strategic use of debt is part of wealth building and a lifetime financial game plan. The profit on the spread between the cost of debt and the yield on that debt if invested can be quite substantial. If I have $280,000 in cash to use for purchasing my primary residence but the bank is willing to lend me $280,000 at 4%, 15 year fixed, I will choose to take the loan and invest the $280,000. The tax savings alone will generate a noticeable increase in take home pay. The following table shows the tax deductible interest on a $280,000, 4% 15 year fixed conventional mortgage. The total deductible interest for just the first 6 years is more than $56k.

PMT NO.	PMT DATE	INTEREST @ 4.00%	PRINCIPAL 280,000	RUNNING BALANCE 280,000	INTEREST PER YEAR
PRINCIPAL AND INTEREST PAYMENT, 4% FIXED, 180 Mos. (15 years)					
				280,000	
1	1/10/2015	921	1,151	278,849	
2	2/10/2015	947	1,124	277,726	
3	3/10/2015	852	1,219	276,507	
4	4/10/2015	939	1,132	275,375	
5	5/10/2015	905	1,166	274,209	
6	6/10/2015	932	1,140	273,070	
7	7/10/2015	898	1,173	271,896	
8	8/10/2015	924	1,147	270,749	
9	9/10/2015	920	1,151	269,597	
10	10/10/2015	886	1,185	268,413	
11	11/10/2015	912	1,159	267,253	
12	**12/10/2015**	**879**	1,192	266,061	**10,914**
13	1/10/2016	904	1,167	264,894	
14	2/10/2016	900	1,171	263,722	
15	3/10/2016	838	1,233	262,489	
16	4/10/2016	892	1,179	261,310	
17	5/10/2016	859	1,212	260,098	
18	6/10/2016	884	1,188	258,911	
19	7/10/2016	851	1,220	257,691	
20	8/10/2016	875	1,196	256,495	
21	9/10/2016	871	1,200	255,295	
22	10/10/2016	839	1,232	254,063	
23	11/10/2016	863	1,208	252,855	
24	**12/10/2016**	**831**	1,240	251,616	**10,408**
25	1/10/2017	855	1,216	250,399	
26	2/10/2017	851	1,220	249,179	
27	3/10/2017	765	1,307	247,872	
28	4/10/2017	842	1,229	246,643	
29	5/10/2017	811	1,260	245,383	
30	6/10/2017	834	1,238	244,145	
31	7/10/2017	803	1,268	242,877	
32	8/10/2017	825	1,246	241,631	
33	9/10/2017	821	1,250	240,381	
34	10/10/2017	790	1,281	239,100	
35	11/10/2017	812	1,259	237,841	
36	**12/10/2017**	**782**	1,289	236,552	**9,790**

37	1/10/2018	804	1,268	235,284		
38	2/10/2018	799	1,272	234,013		
39	3/10/2018	718	1,353	232,659		
40	4/10/2018	790	1,281	231,379		
41	5/10/2018	761	1,310	230,068		
42	6/10/2018	782	1,290	228,779		
43	7/10/2018	752	1,319	227,460		
44	8/10/2018	773	1,298	226,161		
45	9/10/2018	768	1,303	224,859		
46	10/10/2018	739	1,332	223,527		
47	11/10/2018	759	1,312	222,215		
48	**12/10/2018**	**731**	1,341	220,874	**9,176**	
49	1/10/2019	750	1,321	219,554		
50	2/10/2019	746	1,325	218,228		
51	3/10/2019	670	1,401	216,827		
52	4/10/2019	737	1,335	215,492		
53	5/10/2019	708	1,363	214,130		
54	6/10/2019	727	1,344	212,786		
55	7/10/2019	700	1,372	211,414		
56	8/10/2019	718	1,353	210,062		
57	9/10/2019	714	1,357	208,704		
58	10/10/2019	686	1,385	207,319		
59	11/10/2019	704	1,367	205,952		
60	**12/10/2019**	**677**	1,394	204,558	**8,537**	
61	1/10/2020	695	1,376	203,182		
62	2/10/2020	690	1,381	201,801		
63	3/10/2020	641	1,430	200,371		
64	4/10/2020	681	1,390	198,981		
65	5/10/2020	654	1,417	197,564		
66	6/10/2020	671	1,400	196,164		
67	7/10/2020	645	1,426	194,738		
68	8/10/2020	662	1,410	193,328		
69	9/10/2020	657	1,414	191,914		
70	10/10/2020	631	1,440	190,474		
71	11/10/2020	647	1,424	189,050		
72	**12/10/2020**	**622**	1,450	187,600	**7,895**	**56,722**
	INTEREST	**$56,722**				

The tax deduction on interest can translate to 10% to 15% of the interest amount depending on your Adjusted Gross Income (AGI) and tax bracket. The higher your marginal rate is, the bigger the deduction.

21. How to earn 8% on your money

If you take a $280,000 mortgage loan on your principal residence, the next question is where can you earn an interest of 8% APR on your $280,000 cash? You can easily make 8% APR in the stock market, see Chapter, **"See, Chapter, "Investment Strategy and Asset Allocation"** in Part III. If you saved this money due to Dave Ramsey's advice, chances are you struggled in the past few years to fully fund your 401k account. You probably contributed only a small amount into your 401k in order to save up the money to pay off your mortgage. Therefore, in the next few years you can comfortably maximize your 401k contributions by using your $280,000. If you and your spouse both work and your companies offer a Roth 401k, this may be a good time to gradually convert your traditional 401k into a Roth 401k over the next few years and pay the taxes from your $280,000. You will be able to afford the maximum contribution of $18,000 a year (plus an additional $5,000 catch up if you are age 50 or over). You and your spouse can contribute $3,000 ($1500 x 2) a month immediately. Check with your company's benefit administrator or double check in the IRS website below to make sure you can contribute the maximum, https://www.irs.gov/uac/Newsroom/IRS-Announces-2016-Pension-Plan-Limitations%3B-401(k)-Contribution-Limit-Remains-Unchanged-at-$18,000-for-2016

The amount that you convert from traditional to Roth if you are under 59 ½ may be subjected to the 10% tax penalty for early withdrawal in addition to ordinary income tax. This will happen if you use any funds that you withdraw from a traditional 401k to pay the taxes on the amount you are converting. The conversion must be done correctly. Your HR benefits administrator should be able to guide you accordingly. You must pay the taxes from your after tax earnings. Also the money that you convert from traditional to Roth are restricted from withdrawal for the lesser of five years or until you reach age 59 ½. If you withdraw the converted funds from the Roth IRA prior to the date the restriction is lifted, your withdrawal will be subject to the 10% penalty.

There are two major factors to an investment strategy, your age and risk tolerance. If you have the same risk tolerance as I do and can tolerate volatility, then follow my "KISS" strategy shown in Chapter, "How I Earned More Than 50% in Just One Year". You will earn at least 8% APR. What is your short-term risk attitude? How much loss can you tolerate? Will 20% to 60% loss drive you crazy or are you willing to stay put and let it ride until your mutual funds recover? If you have a hard time accepting more than a 10% loss of your principal amount, then my investment system may not be right for you and historically speaking your money will earn less if you move your savings into more conservative investments such as bonds and fixed income securities. Check out your risk tolerance on this website: http://calcxml.com/calculators/inv08?skn=#top Also google search: "risk tolerance questionnaire". If your risk tolerance is "conservative", then you are looking for less volatility. Divide 90% of your money into two or three AA+ bond funds and put the rest into a balanced fund. Volatility will be less, and though bond funds are currently earning a low return, 2% to 4% APR, you may still earn an average of 8% APR in the long run if you leave your money alone.

22. Never Buy a Rental Property

Do not make the same mistake I made. Although being an absentee landlord sounds very appealing to many people and seems like a good idea for investing your money, it is not as easy as it seems. I had money I did not know what to do with in the early nineties so I got involved in real estate and bought a total of 8 rental townhouses one at a time in a period of 3 years. Although I never had a problem with 90% of my tenants, the remaining 10% bad apples aged me quite a bit. I am sure no rational individual likes dealing with midnight calls about leaky faucets, smell of gas, broken refrigerators, pest infestations, clogged toilets, etc. etc. etc. But this is what you will be dealing with if you become a landlord. It is more work than you think. You prepare and negotiate leases, prep the property after a tenant moves out, check an applicant's credit record, collect the rent, evict tenant if tenant stops paying, spend money for necessary repairs, etc. etc. etc. The numbers do not lie. If I had only dumped my extra cash into my retirement account instead of supporting the flat and negative cash flows of my rental properties, I would have been ahead by over $500,000.

23. Maximize Contributions to Your Retirement Account

I try to maximize my contribution to my 401k account, which in 2016 is $18,000. I am dollar-cost-averaging into the stock market with my periodic contributions from every paycheck.

I have my money in mutual funds not individual stocks. I have a moderately aggressive risk tolerance which means if I lose 10% to 60% of my money, I will not panic and withdraw the depreciated balance. I will ride the tide and wait it out until the stock market recovers which it inevitably does. I have my money invested as outlined in Part III, Chapter 2, "Investment Strategy – Asset Allocation".

If your employer does not offer a 401k account, you are at a disadvantage but you can still contribute the maximum into an IRA and Roth IRA Accounts. The maximum contribution at the time of writing is $5500 (plus $1000 catch up contribution, age 50 and older). Check in the IRS website about the qualifications and limitation for contributions.

https://www.irs.gov/retirement-plans/roth-comparison-chart

The deferred tax benefit and the compound interest you will earn is incredible. If you and your spouse contributed only $5500 each annually to your 401k accounts, at 8% APR you will have at least a million dollar each in 35 years without counting the company match. See the following chart:

401k Contribution, $5500 a year, average annual yield of 8%				
YEAR NO.	CONTRIB AMOUNT	RUNNING BALANCE		
1	5500	5,940		
2	5500	12,355		
3	5500	19,284		
4	5500	26,766		
5	5500	34,848		
6	5500	43,575		
7	5500	53,001		
8	5500	63,182		
9	5500	74,176		
10	5500	86,050		
11	5500	98,874		
12	5500	112,724		
13	5500	127,682		
14	5500	143,837		
15	5500	161,284		
16	5500	180,126		
17	5500	200,476		
18	5500	222,454		
19	5500	246,191		
20	5500	271,826		
21	5500	299,512		
22	5500	329,413		
23	5500	361,706		
24	5500	396,583		
25	5500	434,249		
26	5500	474,929		
27	5500	518,864		
28	5500	566,313		
29	5500	617,558		
30	5500	672,902		
31	5500	732,674		
32	5500	797,228		
33	5500	866,947		
34	5500	942,242		
35	5500	1,023,562		

24. Minimize Your Tax Bill

Throughout my life, I make it a habit to learn every possible legal tax deduction, tax credit and tax loophole there is in the tax codes to make sure I am not overpaying my taxes. I do not want to pay a penny more than I have to. Much to my surprise, many people especially younger taxpayers have no idea what expenses can be deducted from earnings. A twenty something tax payer recently asked me, "Can I deduct my rent from my wages?" To compound this problem many tax preparers do not ask their clients the questions they are supposed to ask. They bang out as many returns as they can get out during the tax season, collect their fee and have a nonchalant attitude about how much tax their client is paying and how much money they can potentially save them. Hey, it's not their money. Even worse the attitude of many younger workers is not to ask the tax preparer any questions because, "He knows his job". I recently encountered a young couple at a party who casually discussed their tax situation with me. I overheard the discussion when the wife who works as a nurse said, "I'm busting my chops working so many overtime hours and the government is taking so much of it, maybe it is better if I did not work overtime at all". When I joined the conversation and got into their details I found out they have a combined family income of $145,000, two dependent children, and a $285,000 mortgage on their property and they paid over $20,000 in federal tax. I immediately said to myself that there must be something wrong somewhere. So I offered to review their tax return for free. It turned out that the tax preparer took the standard exemption of $16,200 and the standard deduction of $12,600. That's it. Their tax bill would have been cut in half had they taken the itemized deductions. I asked them why the tax preparer did not itemize and deduct the mortgage interest, state tax, charitable contributions, unreimbursed employee expenses, after school child care expense, etc., etc., etc. The husband replied, "Well, he did not ask any questions and we did not think of asking him any questions. After all he is a CPA and he knows what he's doing. We were afraid he might get insulted if we asked…besides he had a long waiting list of clients and he just accommodated us".

"Oh what a waste of $10,000!" I said to myself. I offered to file an amended return for them so they may recover the $10,000 over payment, but the husband said his wife is afraid because they might get audited. "She considers it water under the bridge", he added. Sadly, next year they will again over pay their taxes. They have a misconception that they should not be paying less as a percentage of their gross income, than what they used to pay as single taxpayers. Although they now have many legitimate deductions as a married couple with two children and a mortgage on their house, they are refusing to take the deductions for fear that they are doing something wrong---they think they would be cheating the government and that they will get caught by the IRS.

Because of this experience I compiled the following short check-list below. If you think any of the tax credits apply to you or you may have incurred any of the deductible expenses on the list, discuss them with your tax preparer:

Check list:

- Maximize your deferred retirement contributions
- Ask your employer if an H.S.A. (Health Savings Account) is available through your company. If not, ask him how one may be set up. This is one of the most beneficial and less known tax favored accounts that you can set up to defer taxable income. Learn more in Chapter, "**Enroll in a H.S.A. (Health Savings Accounts**"
- Make sure that you have the correct dependents
- Business losses
- Real Estate Investment losses
- Capital Loss Carryover
- Gambling losses not to exceed your gambling gains
- Excess SS and Medicare taxes (often if you have 2 or more jobs)
- Student loan interest payments
- K-12 classroom and professional development expenses

- Job-related moving expenses
- Alimony payments
- Early withdrawal penalty (Box 2 Form 1099-INT or 1099-OID)
- IRA, SEP-IRA, Simple IRA, and Keogh contributions
- Health insurance premiums if you are self employed
- Attorney's fees related to certain discrimination claims
- Attorney's fees related to certain whistleblower awards from the IRS
- Home mortgage interest (1098 or statement)
- State and local income taxes
- Real estate and personal property taxes
- Sales taxes
- Unreimbursed job-related expenses including subscriptions, organization dues, uniform, home office, utilities & office supplies
- Job-search expenses
- Charitable donations, cash, clothing, books, appliances, furniture, etc.
- Expenses incurred as a volunteer for a charitable organization
- Medical and dental expenses
- Health insurance premiums if not deducted from your gross salary
- Casualty or theft loss
- Depreciation expense on an asset used in an investment activity
- State and local sales taxes in excess of state and local income taxes
- Mortgage insurance premiums

- Points paid on purchase of principal residence
- Real estate taxes paid
- Tax preparation expenses
- Safe deposit fees
- Legal expenses
- Investment expenses
- Hobby expenses
- Fees, subscriptions, tools connected with any income producing activity
- Credit/debit card tax payment convenience fee
- Estate tax paid on income in respect of a decedent
- Unrecovered pension investment
- Bond premiums
- Losses on certain debt instruments
- Child and dependent care expenses
- Retirement savings contribution credit (saver's credit)
- Adoption expenses
- Energy efficient home improvements
- Tuition for college or higher education (Form 1098-T)
- Child and dependent care credit
- Plug-in electric drive motor vehicle credit
- Foreign taxes paid
- Health insurance for displaced worker
- First-time home buyer credit in Washington, DC
- Low income housing credit (Form 8609 & 8586)

This check list was compiled at the time of writing. Some of the items on this list may have been revised, amended or discontinued. Check with your tax preparer and in the IRS website for updates. If you think you have any of the aforementioned deductions, make a list of the amounts and do not hesitate to give it to your tax preparer during your initial meeting. A good tax professional will not be offended that you are pointing out what may turn out as valid deductions and tax credits that he may not know about. In summary, to minimize your tax bill, 1) maximize your contribution to your tax deferred retirement plan, 2) if you constantly receive big refunds after tax filing, reduce the amount of your "federal tax withheld" by increasing your exemptions so that you are not overpaying your taxes throughout the year, 3) take advantage of all legal tax deductions, tax shelters, tax credits and loopholes.

25. Do Not Save for an Emergency Fund

INVESTOPEDIA defines an "Emergency Fund" as: "An account that is used to set aside funds to be used in an emergency, such as the loss of a job, an illness or a major expense. The purpose of the fund is to improve financial security by creating a safety net of funds that can be used to meet emergency expenses as well as reduce the need to use high interest debt, such as credit cards, as a last resort. Most financial planners suggest that an emergency fund contain enough money to cover at least six months of living expenses. Most emergency funds are highly liquid, such as checking or savings accounts. This allows quick access to funds, which is vital in emergency situations."

I myself do not have a 6-month emergency fund. I maintain a checking account with about $2000. That's it. This is the way I look at it: If I follow Dave Ramsey's advice, I will have at least $20,000 in my checking account (6 months' living expenses) earning nothing. Instead, I have the $20,000 stashed away inside my 401k account earning at least 8% a year. Using the rule of 72, savings will double approximately every 9 years (72 / Interest Rate). The chart that follows shows that my $20,000 will have grown to $43,179 in 10 years, to $93,219 in 20 and to $201,253 in 30 years. It does not make financial sense to me to lose this enormous amount of interest. I just don't agree with this strategy. Here is my strategy: Since liquidity is the key, in case of a real emergency, I will use my home equity line of credit on which I will get charged 6% APR. Or I will borrow the money I need from my 401k account at an APR of approximately 4% in today's rates.

| | Emergency Fund |
Year	Amount
	20,000
1	21,600
2	23,328
3	25,194
4	27,210
5	29,387
6	31,737
7	34,276
8	37,019
9	39,980
10	43,178
11	46,633
12	50,363
13	54,392
14	58,744
15	63,443
16	68,519
17	74,000
18	79,920
19	86,314
20	93,219
21	100,677
22	108,731
23	117,429
24	126,824
25	136,970
26	147,927
27	159,761
28	172,542
29	186,345
30	201,253

26. Double Taxation on 401k Loans?

Part of my retirement game plan is to maximize my contributions to my retirement account and borrow from my retirement account in case of real emergencies. So in essence I keep my "emergency fund" inside my 401k account instead of a checking account where it earns no interest. However, **Suze Orman** has been the loudest voice in spreading the misconception that 401k loans are double taxed. In 2006 I sent Suze Orman a private email asking her to stop saying that you will be taxed twice if you borrow money from your 401k account. This is what she wrote in one of her articles and which she often repeated in her seminars: *"Also, never ever borrow against your 401k plan because you will pay double taxation on the money you borrow. Because you don't pay taxes on the money you put into a 401k, when you pay back the loan (which you must do within five years, or 15 years if used to buy a home), you pay it back with money you have paid taxes on. Then, when you retire and take the money out again, you end up paying taxes on it a second time."* I explained that k-loans are not taxed twice. She never replied but I noticed that she stopped repeating this "myth" in her seminars. You did not get taxed on the money you borrowed. After you return the money you borrowed (that never got taxed), why shouldn't you get taxed (only once) when you withdraw the money for retirement? The truth is, you only get double taxed on the interest you pay, as you repay the k-loan. The interest is not a deferral as a contribution would be, so it is true you pay back the interest with after-tax dollars. Do not borrow from your 401k account unless you have to, but rest assured that 401k loans are not taxed twice.

27. Stop Wasting Food, Energy, Natural Resources

You will save a lot of money over your lifetime by conserving food, energy and natural resources. Food is one of the most basic necessities for humans and animals. Animals spend their waking hours hunting for food. Humans do the same although not in the same sense of the word. Many of the wars in history were fought over food. It is a shame that so much food in industrialized nations go to waste. A 2012 study by the Natural Resources Defense Council estimated that America discards up to 40% of its food, or about 20 pounds per person per month. That is the equivalent of $1500 worth of food that a family of 4 throws out each year. Food is about 13% of your budget. Take the necessary steps to minimize the waste. 1) Create a rough plan of your daily meals for a week and write down the ingredients you will need. 2) Do not buy more than a week's supply of food. 3) Avoid buying perishables in bulk. 4) Put smaller portions on your plate. This way you will not overeat or throw out what you cannot finish. 5) Reuse left overs or freeze them if you will not eat them the following day. Most people do not have any problem packing leftovers for lunch to eat at the office cafeteria the following day. 6) Take home your restaurant meal leftovers. 7) If you go to a buffet, all-you-can-eat restaurant, take only what you can finish. Do not be like jerks who pile on food on their plate, take two bites and throw the rest out.

Turn your thermostat down to 65 degrees in the winter and turn it up to 78 in the summer. Turn down your water heater thermostat to about 115 degrees. Replace all your light bulbs with LEDs or CFLs. They are expensive but they will save 90% of the cost of electricity used by regular incandescent light bulbs. Turn off lights, fans and other electrical appliances when they are not needed.

There is so much more to be said about conservation. We should realize that most of our actions impact our earth. The amount of energy we use adds greenhouse gases into the atmosphere. Our televisions, cars, gadgets or the food we eat all produce a carbon footprint. We must strive to do our part. A drop in the ocean will still make a difference.

28. If You Own a Pet, You Must Read This

If you don't have a pet now, don't get one unless you need it for your health and well-being. A pet is another living thing that needs tender loving care and affection. It is not a toy made for your pleasure. Many animal lovers do not realize that animals prefer to be with their own kind not with humans…if they have a choice. What gives us the right to enslave another living thing, neuter or spay it, imprison it in our small apartment 12 hours a day just so we can have something to play with when we get home? A pet, especially a dog, needs companionship. If you cannot adequately provide time for your pet and money for your pet's expenses, please think twice about getting one. A pet, particularly a dog, needs proper nutrition, training, socializing and grooming, boarding and medical care just like other family members. It is a dependent that you cannot claim on your tax return even though you will spend a lot of money taking care of it. Yes, your dog will greet and kiss you when you come home, but believe me it is miserable the rest of its time alone and it has no say about the predicament you put it in. What do you think your dog is doing when it's all alone? It is getting tortured just waiting for you to come home. Just like other family members, you will watch your dog or cat get old, get sick and die. Only it will happen sooner than you think. So why go through this experience? Besides, in retirement don't you want the freedom to travel around without worrying about a pet?

1. How come gloom and doomers never get it right?

The market timing strategy outlined in this book will always outperform the "buy, hold and stay the course" strategy which most financial planners, stock market experts, best-selling personal finance authors and investment gurus espouse. Most financial advisors can competently advice investors on what stocks to buy but most of them do not have an exit strategy to avoid catastrophic losses when the stock market crashes. They say, "Buy, hold and stay the course because stocks eventually recover and always soar to new highs after the crash". But isn't it better to get out of the stock market before the bust and get back in before the boom?

The timing strategy offered in this book is to strive to hit the bullseye twice, i.e. 1) to get out of stocks before the start of the next bear market that follows a recession so as to avoid the typical 30-60% loss of value of stocks and, 2) to get back into stocks close to the bottom of that bear market. **This is a mantra that will be repeated several times in this book to reinforce this technique.** We learn through repetition and repetition may provide a sense of urgency to persuade readers that it is critical to memorize and follow this system so as to avoid a huge devaluation of their portfolio when the crash comes. If you have a tax deferred retirement plan, an IRA, a 401k, 403b or 457b and your money is invested in the stock market, are you prepared to lose as much as 60% of your money when the market crashes? It is not a question of "if" but "when". It is guaranteed the stock market will crash when the next recession arrives, but when will that be?

How come doomsayers never get the timing right? In March 2016, billionaire Carl Icahn raised a red flag on a national broadcast when he declared, *"The public is walking into a trap again as they did in 2007"*. Prophetic economist Andrew Smithers warns, *"U.S. stocks are now 80% overvalued"*.

In his Op-Ed of February 2016, Paul B. Farrell of marketwatch.com forecasts at least a 50% stock market crash and adds, *"But the crash of 2016 really is coming. Dead ahead. Maybe not till we get a bit closer to the presidential election cycle of 2016. But a crash is a sure bet, it's guaranteed certain: Complete with echoes of the 2008 crash, which impacted on the GOP election results, triggering a $10 trillion loss of market cap ... like the 1999 dot-com collapse, it's post-millennium loss of $8 trillion market cap, plus a 30-month recession ... moreover a lot like the 1929 crash and the long depression that followed".* This is a chilling commentary from a respected economist, market expert and columnist of Market Watch, but his prediction did not come true. He finally said, *"So finally I gave up on timing the market---all I know now is that the market truly is random and unpredictable. In fact, only a damn fool would try to outguess it. Flow with it, maybe".* Paul B. Farrell is gracious enough to admit that he does not know anything about market timing.

In his book "The Age of Deception", **James Dale Davidson** predicted a "Black Swan" event with the stock market plunging more than 50% and with the Dow Jones Industrial Averages (DJIA or DOW) dropping 80% in 2016. He promises to tell you what to do to protect your investments and how to "survive and prosper" through the stock market crash that he is certain is coming in 2016. A drop in the Dow of 80% can only mean that he is forecasting a severe recession or worse, a depression in 2016. ***UPDATE***Towards the end of 2016, when it became clear that his prediction of a market crash in 2016 was not going to happen, James Dale Davidson changed his tune and now predicts the economic crash to happen in 2017. He says our economy is like a sandcastle and cracks are forming at the very base. Our entire country rests on an unstable foundation. *"As you can see, all it will take is one grain of sand ... just one ... to send everything crashing. In the end, we will see the stock market tumble by 50% ... real estate will plummet by 40% ... savings accounts will lose 30%, and unemployment will triple",* he continues.

I disagree and here is why: The economy continues to be sluggish and many economists think we are in a secular stagnation. We are following a "lower interest rates longer policy". Fed Chair

Janet Yellen's 25 basis points (.25%) announced benchmark federal funds rate increase scheduled for June 2016 (projected 1.4% total for 2016) should not cause an inverted yield curve (a.k.a. negative yield curved) which is one of the best predictors of an impending recession. The increase may not even happen if leading economic indicators such as GDP and private payroll employment remain stagnant. Copper prices have been holding steady at over $2 per pound. If Copper prices go below $2 per pound and stay there for a couple of months, then I will start worrying. Capacity utilization which is a measure of the output of existing factories for manufacturing, utilities (electric and gas), mining, durable goods and non-durable goods has not been dropping. We are 7 years into this bull market and many financial pundits think that U.S. stocks are overvalued. But I still do not believe there will be a recession in 2017 or 2018. James Dale Davidson is selling his book along with his newsletter subscription for more than $200. Just in case you are sold on his gloom and doom scenario that the Dow will drop 80% in 2017 or 2018, get your money out of equities right now and put your entire portfolio in a money market fund. You will not lose money if the Dow drops 80%. Wait for the crash, then buy back the stocks when their value drop 50%. Why buy his $200 book? In my case I am not convinced that a recession is coming in 2017 or 2018 so I want my money to make a little bit more money before the bust. When will that be? See the timeline under chapter, **"Inverted Yield Curve, a Harbinger of Gloom and Doom"**.

My financial advisor lost 60% of her savings in the stock market crash of 2008 (see the chapter **"How to Lose 60% in the Stock Market"**). I lost nothing by following a reliable stock market timing system. The chart in Chapter, **"Inverted Yield Curve..."** shows a timeline as to when to get out of equities and when to get back in. I got out of equities a year before the crash and avoided a 40% devaluation of my portfolio. Then my portfolio gained more than 50% in 2009. The Federal Reserve Bank of St. Louis reported that household wealth plunged $16 trillion from the beginning of the last recession until it ended in June 2009. As of mid-2013, my financial advisor had not yet recovered all the money she lost. If you succeed in following the strategy in this book, you will never lose money in the stock market. In fact you could make a killing when the next recession hits just by following my stress-free KISS strategy which is explained further under the chapter, **"How I Earned More Than 50% in Just One Year"**. The following two charts are examples of how I was positioned when the yield curve inverted. A more detailed explanation of these charts is in the same chapter:

Mutual Fund 1	PPS		Shares	Total
Jul 17 2006	$ 52	INVERSION		
Jul 17 2007	$ 61	ANNIVERSARY OF INVERSION		
Aug 13 2007	$ 58	GOT OUT OF STOCKS	5,000	290,000.00
Dec 01 2008	$ 30	NBER DECLARED RECESSION STARTED DEC 2007		
Dec 02 2008	$ 31	GOT BACK INTO STOCKS	9,355	290,000.00
Dec 30 2009	$ 50	BALANCE IN THIS FUND AS OF THIS DATE	9,355	467,750.00
		$ INCREASE IN VALUE		$ 177,750.00
		% INCREASE IN VALUE		61.3%

Mutual Fund 2	PPS		Shares	Total
Jul 17 2006	$ 36	INVERSION		
Jul 17 2007	$ 44	ANNIVERSARY OF INVERSION		
Aug 13 2007	$ 40	GOT OUT OF STOCKS	5,000	200,000.00
Dec 01 2008	$ 20	NBER DECLARED RECESSION STARTED DEC 2007		
Dec 02 2008	$ 21	GOT BACK INTO STOCKS	9,524	200,004.00
Dec 30 2009	$ 30	BALANCE IN THIS FUND AS OF THIS DATE	9,524	285,720.00
		$ INCREASE IN VALUE		$ 85,720.00
		% INCREASE IN VALUE		42.9%

2. The Great Recession, No Different From the Rest

It is important to review my published article below to get a clearer picture of my investment philosophy and why I believe the "KISS Principle" of investing and my stress-free "Auto-Pilot" investment strategy are the best and simplest strategies to follow. Investing is not rocket-science. It should be simple and stress-free. Investing should not keep you awake at night worrying about how your investments would do tomorrow.

****

BY ARTHUR V. PROSPER, OCT 18, 2009

Many economists, prognosticators, financial pundits, stock brokers and financial planners have committed a big blunder or a big hoax by proclaiming this recession different from the rest and the worst since the great depression. The fact is I believe this recession is no different from the previous post war recessions. Those who share my belief have made a lot of money in the stock market during this recession. In the first quarter of this year, the majority of financial pundits I watched on TV handed investors a foolish advice, that is "to stay out of the market" unless they have 10 or more years to go before retirement. At that time, some of these investors have already lost 50% of their savings. Who knows how many took their advice and got out of the market thereby missing the strong bull market that started in March and is still going strong as of this minute. In January and February, many financial experts were predicting the Dow Jones Averages to go down to 5,000. In "DIDOSPIN-11,000 DOW, August 7, 2009" when DJIA was 9,370, I predicted the Dow to climb to 10,000 before the end of the year and to 11,000 before the end of next year. It already reached 10,000 last week. Most of the financial experts I watched on the Lou Dobbs and Larry Kudlow Shows collectively stated that "it may take 10 years to recover losses in retirement plans..." Shame on them for being so incompetent or for perpetrating a hoax! Those investors who stayed put have already gained back most of what they have lost and I believe this bull market still has legs before the next significant market correction.

In "DIDOSPIN- Obama's Recession, March 8, 2009", I said "Recessions are part of a normal economic cycle. Soon consumers will come back and resume buying necessities such as refrigerators, TVs, computers, furniture, cars..." How true! A lower than expected contraction in GDP at 1% in the 2nd quarter is believed to have been followed by a small positive increase in GDP in the 3rd quarter, although official stats have not yet been released. I predicted a much bigger increase in GDP the 4th quarter. The increase in GDP is an indication of an increase in consumer spending. **One thing to remember is that GDP stats do not even take into consideration business to business consumption, only the consumption of the ultimate consumer or end-user. This is something that many people are not aware of.**

I secretly scoffed at my boss in January when he told me in a panic that we must dig in our heels in this "worst ever recession". I told him, "We've seen this before, the last one in 2001...." "No, no, no", he adamantly replied, "this is different". How wrong he was! The only difference between this recession and the previous ones is its nickname. This one will probably be known by several nicknames such as "Sub-prime Mortgage Crisis, aka Housing Bubble Burst, aka Auto Industry Crisis Recession, aka as Great Recession". The various nicknames of the 3 previous recessions according to Bloomberg News were: Dot-Com Bubble Burst – 2000 to 2001; S&L Crisis, 1990 to 1991 and the Energy Crisis Recession, 1981 to 1982.

I concede that this will prove to be the longest recession since the Great Depression. But its severity and misery index pales in comparison to the Carter-Reagan recession. According to Bloomberg News, during the 1981-1982 recession, the national unemployment rate was 10.8% at its highest; inflation was 14% and the prime rate went up to 20.5%. In this current recession, inflation is almost non-existent and the prime rate is the lowest it has been in 50 years, source:
http://www.wsjprimerate.us/wall_street_journal_prime_rate_history.htm

Obama's economists projected the unemployment rate will continue to increase and will exceed 10% before the year is over but I will go with my prediction in "DIDOSPIN- Recession Over, June 27, 2009" that it would peak at 9.8%. This means that more than 90% of the working population is employed and is poised to go back into the "buying mode". It is a cycle and consumers eventually buy what they need or want. The stock market rally is a big factor in consumer spending. If a consumer sees his portfolio going up in value, he will have more confidence spending his discretionary income as opposed to saving it for a rainy day. Fortunately, the behavior of the stock market follows a free market pattern that is predictable. The stock market does not like government intervention in the free market economy. It does not like redistribution of wealth; tax increases; government take-over of health care, the banking system and other private industries; cap and trade; interest hikes and increase in deficits. One of the reasons the market is doing so well is that Obamacare and Cap and Trade appear to be in trouble. There are different versions of Obamacare bills that are still under discussion in the congressional committees, and although Cap and Trade bill passed the house, it is not expected to pass the senate.

****end of article****************************

3. What is a stock market crash?

I define stock market crash as a 30-60% (or higher) decline in the stock market major indices, DJIA, S&P 500 and NASDAQ. I do not consider a decline of under 30% a crash but a correction. Corrections will happen periodically in a period of expansion. A decline of 30-60% in these market indices usually signifies that we are in a bear market in the middle of a U.S. recession. The stock market will crash, but when? The answer is when the economy goes into a recession. It is the goal of this book to guide the stock market investor how to look for signs of a recession so that he may exit the market before the start of the bear market that follows and get back in close to the bottom of that bear market thereby avoiding cyclical downturns and catastrophic losses.

4. What will cause the stock market crash?

Ken Little who authored 12 books on investing and personal finance gives the following reasons for stock market crashes: Interest rates, inflation, earnings, oil and energy prices, war and terrorism, crime and fraud and serious domestic political unrest. With all due respect to Mr. Little, what he pointed out are the symptoms of the disease rather than the disease itself. The disease which causes the stock market to crash is recession. The stock market will fall and may turn bearish at the onset of various bad news such as an increase in interest rates and sudden increase or decrease in energy prices, instability of the Euro Banking system and the high jobless rate. But if these factors do not lead to a recession, the stock market should quickly recover from a bear market and continue to rise. Sudden market fluctuation is significant for short-term traders but should not be for long term investors. The market always recovers even after a recession and always soars to new highs during periods of expansions. It would be great if you can predict the highs and lows of the market. You could have made a killing if you had sold in October 2007 when the Dow hit 14,000 and bought your stocks back in March 2009 when it plunged to a low of 6,600. The Eurozone problem, high jobless rate, Syrian war, terrorism, conflict in the South China sea, North Korea and Iran do not worry me as much when it comes to my investments as decrease in retail sales, reduction in hiring, declining commodity prices, industrial production and housing starts. The day-traders may drive down the stock market purely on investor sentiment and the major stock market indices may go down by 20% in just a few days, but it defies logic for a downward trend to continue if all leading economic indicators are pointing upwards to...no recession. This is all intricately connected. If stocks do not recover quickly after a 20% correction and we get into a prolonged bear market, consumer confidence may erode resulting in reduced consumer spending which can then lead to a recession. There should not be a protracted bear market unless we are heading into another recession. If you try to time the market during the boom cycle of the economy you will surely lose. Buying and selling during short term peaks and lows in the stock market in times of expansion is for professional traders who do it for a living. For us ordinary investors, we would be better off to leave our IRA and 401k savings accounts alone, invested in mutual funds until an identifiable recession is in sight. We cannot possibly beat traders and professional analysts who lived and breathed this stuff every day, all day long. We must go back to basics to enable us to assess where we are now in the economic recovery. As of this writing in 2016, we are 7 years into this recovery. The great recession ended in June 2009. The great recession was not followed by a great recovery. The economy is sluggish. GDP has been hovering around 2-3% per annum. Interest rates are low and will remain low for the foreseeable future. There is no sign of a recession at the time of writing.

Stock market crashes are feared by all stock market investors. They result in the sudden reduction of wealth. If you need to get to your money after your portfolio lost 50% of its value, your paper losses will turn into real losses. If you get out of equities after they have lost 50% of their value because you think their value might drop some more, you will lock in your losses. You will not know when to get back in. The timing strategy outlined in this book should serve as a guide. Leave your money alone during boom times, take your money out of stocks ONLY before the beginning of the bear market that follows a recession. Recessions are merely temporary suspension of consumer spending so we can be sure that economic growth will follow recessions. Recessions may become prolonged due to some event that may cause a bank run or collapse of the banking system, another bubble burst or some kind of a natural disaster. Reduction of income; job insecurity; debt increase due to higher interest rates; inflation; diminution of assets, of investments and other tangible property such as real estate will prolong a recession.

5. Pinpointing the official start of a recession

At the time of writing, the total of my 401k account is 100% invested in equities. I can honestly say that I have never lost money in the stock market. The reason is I know the behavior of the stock market---it goes up, it goes down. Historically, in a period of expansion there is a correction of 10% or more every 6 to 12 months. There is a correction of 20% or more every 12 to 18 months. I only check my account when the market is up. I am in for the long term and don't need my money now so why will I stress myself out checking my balance after the Dow goes down 500 points? I know my balance went down. Will it make me feel better to know by how much? Will I turn my paper loss into a real loss? Of course not! What I look out for are signs of a recession. The stock market can turn from boom to bust in just a few weeks during the bear market that follows a recession. Stocks may plunge 60% or more from their recent highs by the time the bear market bottom is reached. For the benefit of the reader who is not sure of the meaning of a recession, a recession is part of a normal business cycle. The economy expands and contracts (shrinks). A recession is a period of contraction. There will be periods of contraction caused by many different factors. But the simplest explanation is, the consumer stops consuming for a brief period of time, as in "recess" in school, i.e. a brief break between the usual activities. The most common financial definition of a recession is "two consecutive quarters of negative growth". The NBER (National Bureau of Economic Research) indicates in its website that this is not the official definition and that only its panel of experts can declare an "official recession" after taking into account a number of monthly factors such as employment, personal income, industrial production as well as quarterly GDP growth. This means that we could be a year into a recession before this panel of experts declares it official. This is exactly what happened during the "great recession" of 2007-2009. By historical accounts, the recession started in December 2007 and the NBER did not call the recession until December 1, 2008. That day the Dow closed at 8,149, 42.5% lower than its most recent peak of 14,164 in October 2007. Then it took the NBER's experts another year before they figured out that the recession ended in June 2009. I like using the DJIA as a barometer of market trend. It is an index of 30 large public companies in diversified industries making it a broader representation of how the U.S. economy and markets are currently trending. In general I use the DJIA, S&P 500 and NASDAQ as the major indices to gauge overall U.S. market performance.

6. Inverted yield curve, a harbinger of gloom and doom

During the great recession my holdings increased by more than 50% in just one year, 2009 by following a system that enabled me to get out of equities before stock prices collapsed and to get back into the same mutual funds close to the bottom of the bear market. **An inverted yield curve (aka Negative Yield Curve) is one of the best and most reliable early indicators of a recession. According to historical data, the yield curve inverted just prior to every U.S. recession in the past 50 years.** The Positive Yield (interest rate earned) Curve is the normal yield for investments. Longer term maturities usually have a higher yield than shorter term. When the yield becomes negative or inverted, market sentiment suggests that the long-term outlook is poor and the yields offered by long-term fixed income will continue to fall. It also spells trouble for the financial sector as what started happening in late 2006. The incentive for depositors to leave their money with the bank for longer periods of time, say 5 to 10 years is to earn a higher interest rate. If the interest rate of return is the same or less for 5 years compared to 1 year, this incentive is gone. This means that profit margins fall for companies that borrow cash at short-term rates and lend at long-term rates, such as hedge funds, banks and mortgage companies. Equity lines of credit and adjustable rate mortgages (ARMs) which are periodically adjusted usually go up since they are based on short-term interest rates. Debtors who got stuck with these loans will need more money to pay for additional interest. They will need to tighten their belts. They will have less money to spend on consumer goods that is why recessions follow an inverted yield curve.

The yield curve is inverted when short-term interest rates on U.S. Treasuries (T-bills) are higher than long term rates (T-notes and T-bonds). Check out the website below:

https://www.treasury.gov/resource-center/data-chart-center/interest-rates/Pages/TextView.aspx?data=yield

As of April 21, 2016, in accordance with the following table from the aforementioned website, the yield curve is not in any danger of flattening:

Date	1 mo	3 mo	6 mo	1 yr	2 yr	3 yr	5 yr	7 yr	10 yr	20 yr	30 yr
4/1/2016	0.2	0.23	0.4	0.6	0.8	0.9	1.2	1.6	1.79	2.2	2.62
4/4/2016	0.18	0.23	0.38	0.6	0.8	0.9	1.2	1.5	1.78	2.19	2.6
4/5/2016	0.19	0.23	0.36	0.6	0.7	0.9	1.2	1.5	1.73	2.13	2.54
4/6/2016	0.19	0.23	0.36	0.6	0.7	0.9	1.2	1.5	1.76	2.17	2.58
4/7/2016	0.2	0.23	0.36	0.5	0.7	0.8	1.1	1.5	1.7	2.1	2.52
4/8/2016	0.2	0.23	0.34	0.5	0.7	0.8	1.2	1.5	1.72	2.13	2.55
4/11/2016	0.19	0.23	0.34	0.5	0.7	0.9	1.2	1.5	1.73	2.14	2.56
4/12/2016	0.21	0.22	0.34	0.5	0.7	0.9	1.2	1.5	1.79	2.18	2.61
4/13/2016	0.21	0.23	0.36	0.6	0.8	0.9	1.2	1.5	1.77	2.16	2.58
4/14/2016	0.21	0.22	0.37	0.6	0.8	0.9	1.3	1.6	1.8	2.18	2.61
4/15/2016	0.19	0.22	0.37	0.5	0.7	0.9	1.2	1.5	1.76	2.14	2.56
4/18/2016	0.16	0.22	0.35	0.5	0.8	0.9	1.2	1.5	1.78	2.17	2.58
4/19/2016	0.18	0.21	0.36	0.5	0.8	0.9	1.3	1.6	1.79	2.19	2.6
4/20/2016	0.18	0.23	0.36	0.5	0.8	1	1.3	1.6	1.85	2.25	2.66
4/21/2016	0.19	0.23	0.37	0.6	0.8	1	1.4	1.7	1.88	2.29	2.69

Thursday Apr 21, 2016

The chart shows 5-year rates are more than double that of the one-year rate, i.e. .6% vs. 1.4% and the 10-year rate is more than triple the one-year rate, i.e. .6% vs. 1.88%. This could mean we are still at least a year away from a negative yield curve. A recession would usually follow within 12 to 18 months of such an event, if history repeats itself. It is prudent to watch the chart diligently. Although the yield curve seems comfortably positive at the moment, the very low long term rates are a reason for concern. This is an indication that the markets think low inflation and low interest rates will continue. Low inflation and low interest rates can mean low growth and slow expansion. We may be experiencing a "new normal" like what Japan has been experiencing since the early nineties, i.e. sluggish growth of 1% to 3% GDP per year with the economy ever teetering on the brink of recession. Low interest rates is always good for stocks because even the most conservative investors have no appetite for treasuries, bonds, money market funds and bank CDs that pay zero to 3% annual yield. Consequently, they have to take a chance on equities.

The yield curve inverted on July 17, 2006 (Inversion) when the 10-year note (T-note) yielded 5.06% and the 3-month bill (T-bill) yielded 5.11%. From a historical perspective, I knew a recession would follow within the next 12 to 18 months so I got out of equities in August 2007 when the Dow was about 13,200 and I put my entire portfolio into a money market fund. (At the risk of being redundant, this statement is repeated several times in this book. Repetition and reinforcement of this message may lead to clarity, especially for readers who are not familiar with the yield curve). That was a defensive capital preservation move. I must admit that I was tempted to go back in when the Dow closed at around 14,100 sometime in October 2007. I thought I got out too soon, but it is a good thing I did not. From that high, the Dow steadily declined until it plunged thousands of points between September and November 2008. I bought back in after the NBER announced the official date of the recession, which according to them started sometime in December 2007. I got back into equities the day after the NBER made the announcement. I was fully invested in the stock market, 100% in equities on December 2, 2008 when the Dow closed at 8,419. With this move, I avoided a 4,781 point value loss in the Dow. Of course I could have taken a chance by waiting a month or two before going back into the market after the declaration. An assumption can be made that the declaration of the official date of the recession by the NBER will initially cause more panic selling. If I waited till February 2009 I would have gotten back in closer to the bottom of the bear market, but I'm happy with my end result. I got out of the market not far from the peak and got back in not far from bottom.

Historically this is what happens: A bear market always lags behind a recession. A bull market always runs ahead of a recovery (end of the recession). How do you know when to get back into the market? A bull market starts a few months before a recession ends. It is difficult for financial advisors and economists to predict that a recession is near its end. They rely on economic data that is outdated when it becomes available. Economists have a terrible track record of forecasting the start and the end of recessions. This is evidenced by the foolish advice of many commentators, financial professionals, economists and other experts, for investors to stay out of equities in 2009. All you have to do is rewind the programs Larry Kudlow Show, Mad Money, Lou Dobbs Show, Squawk Box, Nightline and Bloomberg News. During the first quarter of 2009, I watched daily commentaries from financial expert after financial expert. Their collective advice was for investors to stay out of the stock market "if they cannot afford to lose any of their money". The problem with that advice is that most stock market investors have already lost 50% of their money by that time. And frankly, who can really afford to lose any of their money? These financial experts were caught napping in 2009 and missed the strongest bull market in history when stocks suddenly reversed course and kept going up recovering 60% of their value from the bear market bottom of March 2009. It is important to study the charts carefully so that you can get back into stocks before the start of the bull market that precedes the end of the recession. The timeline on the first chart illustrates DJIA closing prices from July 17, 2006 (Inversion) when the negative yield curve started until the recession ended in June 2009:

DJIA INDEX - HISTORY			
Date	Closing Price		
7/17/2006	10,747		Start of negative yield curve
7/17/2007	13,972		1 year anniversary of negative yield curve
7/18/2007	13,918		
7/19/2007	14,000		
7/20/2007	13,851		
7/23/2007	13,943		
7/24/2007	13,717		
7/25/2007	13,785		
7/26/2007	13,474		
7/27/2007	13,265		
7/30/2007	13,358		
7/31/2007	13,212		
8/1/2007	13,362		
8/2/2007	13,463		
8/3/2007	13,182		
8/6/2007	13,469		
8/7/2007	13,504		
8/8/2007	13,658		
8/9/2007	13,271		
8/10/2007	13,240		
8/13/2007	13,237		
8/14/2007	13,029		
8/15/2007	12,861		

8/16/2007	12,846
8/17/2007	13,079
8/20/2007	13,121
8/21/2007	13,091
8/22/2007	13,236
8/23/2007	13,236
8/24/2007	13,379
8/27/2007	13,322
8/28/2007	13,042
8/29/2007	13,289
8/30/2007	13,239
8/31/2007	13,358
9/4/2007	13,449
9/5/2007	13,305
9/6/2007	13,363
9/7/2007	13,113
9/10/2007	13,128
9/11/2007	13,308
9/12/2007	13,292
9/13/2007	13,425
9/14/2007	13,443
9/17/2007	13,403
9/18/2007	13,739
9/19/2007	13,816
9/20/2007	13,767
9/21/2007	13,820
9/24/2007	13,759

9/25/2007	13,779
9/26/2007	13,878
9/27/2007	13,913
9/28/2007	13,896
10/1/2007	14,088
10/2/2007	14,047
10/3/2007	13,968
10/4/2007	13,974
10/5/2007	14,066
10/8/2007	14,044
10/9/2007	14,165
10/10/2007	14,079
10/11/2007	14,015
10/12/2007	14,093
10/15/2007	13,985
10/16/2007	13,913
10/17/2007	13,893
10/18/2007	13,889
10/19/2007	13,522
10/22/2007	13,567
10/23/2007	13,676
10/24/2007	13,675
10/25/2007	13,672
10/26/2007	13,807
10/29/2007	13,870
10/30/2007	13,792
10/31/2007	13,930

Historically, recession may start on any of these dates

11/1/2007	13,568		
11/2/2007	13,595		
11/5/2007	13,543		
11/6/2007	13,661		
11/7/2007	13,300		
11/8/2007	13,266		
11/9/2007	13,043		
11/12/2007	12,988		
11/13/2007	13,307		
11/14/2007	13,231		
11/15/2007	13,110		
11/16/2007	13,177		
11/19/2007	12,958		
11/20/2007	13,010		
11/21/2007	12,799		
11/23/2007	12,981		
11/26/2007	12,743		
11/27/2007	12,958		
11/28/2007	13,289		
11/29/2007	13,312		
11/30/2007	13,372		
12/3/2007	13,315		Start of recession according to NBER - Dec 2007
12/4/2007	13,249		
12/5/2007	13,445		
12/6/2007	13,620		
12/7/2007	13,626		

12/10/2007	13,727
12/11/2007	13,433
12/12/2007	13,474
12/13/2007	13,518
12/14/2007	13,340
12/17/2007	13,167
12/18/2007	13,232
12/19/2007	13,207
12/20/2007	13,246
12/21/2007	13,451
12/24/2007	13,550
12/26/2007	13,552
12/27/2007	13,360
12/28/2007	13,366
12/31/2007	13,265
1/2/2008	13,044
1/3/2008	13,057
1/4/2008	12,800
1/7/2008	12,827
1/8/2008	12,589
1/9/2008	12,735
1/10/2008	12,853
1/11/2008	12,606
1/14/2008	12,778
1/15/2008	12,501
1/16/2008	12,466
1/17/2008	12,159

CHART 1 SIGNIFICANT DATES RECESSION OF 2007-2008			
	DOW Closing Price		
7/17/2006	10,747	Start of negative yield curve	
7/17/2007	13,972	Anniversary of negative yield curve	SELL
8/9/2007	13,271	End of negative yield curve (almost 13 mos. since inversion)	
10/9/2007	14,165	Peak since inversion	
12/3/2007	13,315	Official start of recession (declared in Dec 2008)	
9/17/2008	10,610	Start of the bear market	
12/1/2008	8,149	On this date NBER declares recession started in Dec 2007	BUY
3/9/2009	6,547	Bear market bottom	
4/9/2009	8,083	Start of bull market	
6/1/2009	8,721	Official end of recession per NBER	
12/31/2009	10,428	Year end, bull market continues	

According to the chart, the markets continued to go up after the yield curve inverted until the Dow peaked at 14,165 on October 9, 2007, about 14 months from inversion date. Then the bear market started on September 17, 2008, 9 months after the recession began. The bear market reached bottom at 6,547 on March 9, 2009. If you had a crystal ball, sold at the peak and bought at the bottom, your assets would have increased by an astounding 75% by the end of 2009. I did not make quite as much but I'm satisfied. If you follow my system you would have sold on July 17, 2007 when the DOW closed at 13,972 and bought back into the same mutual funds on December 1, 2008 when the DOW closed at 8,149 thereby avoiding a 5,823 point loss on the DOW.

Here is the summary of my timing system:

- Allocate your investments as shown under, **"Investment Strategy and Asset Allocation".** Do not touch your investments in times of economic expansions (recoveries). Leave your money alone even if your portfolio loses 30% of its value.

- Monitor the Daily Treasury Yield Curve Rates at least once a month. Click on the website below:

https://www.treasury.gov/resource-center/data-chart-center/interest-rates/Pages/TextView.aspx?data=yieldYear&year=2016

Specifically, compare the 10-year note yield to that of the 3-month bill. Watch carefully if the yields are starting to narrow and flatten.

- When the yield curve inverts, i.e. the 10-year treasury yield falls below the 3-month yield, make note of that date and continue to monitor to see if the inverted yield curve continues. Keep your ears open for news on what action the Feds (Federal Reserve Bank) will take. Most likely, if the Feds increase the benchmark interest rate, the inverted yield curve will continue. If they decrease the benchmark rate, the inverted yield curve will end.

- If the yield curve stays inverted for over a month, make a note of the inversion date. Get out of the stock market when the inverted yield curve ends or when it reaches its one year anniversary whichever is earlier. Sell your stocks and put them in a money market fund or a stable value fund where the principal is guaranteed. This is a defensive move for preservation of your capital so as to avoid the bear market that will follow.

- When the NBER declares that we are in a recession and points to the date when it started, and that date is at least 6 months prior to the announcement date, put your money back into the same mutual funds they were in before you left the market.

Let us examine how your investments would have done in the Recession of 2001 if you followed my system. Review Chart 2:

CHART 2			
SIGNIFICANT DATES RECESSION OF 2001			
	DOW		
	Closing Price		
7/7/2000	10,636	Start of negative yield curve	
9/6/2000	11,311	Peak since inversion	
2/9/2001	10,781	End of negative yield curve (7 mos. since inversion)	
3/1/2001	10,450	Official start of recession	
7/7/2001	10,253	Anniversary of negative yield curve	SELL
11/26/2001	8,567	On this date NBER declares recession started in Mar 2001	BUY
11/30/2001	9,852	End of recession	
10/9/2002	7,286	Bottom of bear market	
3/17/2003	8,142	Start of the bull market	

If you followed my system, you would have sold on or about February 12, 2001 when the DOW closed at 10,947 and bought back into the same mutual funds on or about November 28, 2001 when the DOW closed at 9,712. You would have avoided a 1,235 point decline in the DOW. It is important to remember that 2002 was a particularly difficult year for stock market investors. True to the rule that the bull market starts before the end of a recession, the bull market of 2001 actually started the beginning of October 2001 approximately 2 months before the end of the recession. But there was a major correction that started in the second quarter of 2002 that caused approximately a 30% stock market devaluation. Many economists surmised that the economy was going through a "V" shaped, double dipped recession but the economic indicators did not prove that to be the case. The country's steady recovery from the 9/11 attacks and the proclamation of many economists in November 2001 that the recession was about to end, created a healthy bump in share prices that continued until towards the middle of the second quarter of 2002. In June 2002 stock prices took a sharp downturn with the DOW plunging thousands of points to a low of 7,286 in October, losing 30% of its value from the beginning of the year. Tech stocks were especially devastated with the NASDAQ plunging from its 2000 high of 5,048 to a low of 1,114 in 2002. Most economists view this exceptionally tough year for the stock market as part of a correction after the decade long bull market that led to unusually high stock valuations. But still, you would have been better off than most investors if you followed my system.

7. False negative

If the yield curve inversion occurs then flip-flops from negative to positive during the 12-month period that follows the first inversion from positive to negative, watch the yield curve carefully. If we take the last inversion as an example, the yield curve first inverted on December 22, 2005. Let us call this date a FND (False Negative Date). The rate on a 2 year Treasury bill became higher than a 7 year Treasury note. When this occurs, the corrective action from the Federal Reserve is to lower rates but the opposite happened. The Feds continued to raise interest rates. The yield curve fluctuated back and forth from negative to flat to negative until July 17, 2006 when the yield curve inverted and stayed inverted until towards the end of 2008. By that time the NBER declared that we were a year into a recession and the major market indices showed we were in the middle of a brutal bear market. If you got out of the stock market a year after the FND, i.e. December 22, 2006, the Dow closing price was 12,343. If you followed my strategy you would have bought back into the market on December 2, 2008 when the Dow closed at 8,419. You would have avoided a 3,924 point devaluation of the Dow and gained 3,900 points increase by the end of 2009. Still not too shabby even if you got out of the market on the FND. The danger is that the yield curve may get back to normal (positive) and stave off a recession. So in this respect, it is better to watch for a "true negative", then develop a timeline. A true negative, as defined in this strategy, is when the yield curve inverts and stays inverted for a year. Especially when the 10-year Treasury yield falls below the yield on 3-month treasury bills. When this happens the economy will either be in a recession or close to it. An analytical reader will probably ask, "So, if I get out of the stock market and stayed out for two years, won't I lose 2 years' earnings?" The answer is maybe yes, maybe no. There will be so much volatility in the market the year before a recession hits, there will be wild swings and fluctuations between losses and gains in the major indices. It is likely that you will get out of stocks at the wrong time if you do not follow the timeline. It will be less stressful for you if you sell out earlier rather than later. Take comfort in the knowledge that you will be immune from "the crash" when it happens. Rather than worry, spend your time doing other pleasurable things in life. Play golf, the piano, go to the movies and parties, play with your children, take vacations or find a hobby. Just keep your ears open for the proclamation from the NBER of the official date of the recession. Get back into equities within a month of the official declaration and buy back the stocks you sold at their depreciated price.

8. How to lose 60% of your savings in the stock market

My financial advisor (licensed stock broker) whom we shall call by the name of Rebecca was one of those stock market investors who lost a lot of money during the great recession. In July 2008 Rebecca had her money, close to a million dollars of it, equally divided between a diversified emerging markets fund, a mid-cap growth fund, a large value fund, a specialty natural resources fund and a specialty real estate fund. If you are a stock broker you know which funds I am talking about. Rebecca was very aggressive in her investment choices, bordering almost on reckless and speculative. Well, she paid the price.

We parted ways around the time the interest yield curve started flattening. We had many discussions about the state of the economy and disagreed on how my money should be invested. I told her that I am concerned the interest rate curve inverted from positive to negative and historically…to make a long story short, I fired her. Our paths crossed again around the middle of 2009 at a cocktail party that was hosted by one of the largest banks in the nation who shall remain nameless but whose initials are HSBC. After 3 or 4 Margaritas, she told me her story. She thought her investments along with her clients' investments were doing "OK", with losses of less than 20% for the year at that point, then President Bush delivered his speech on September 24, 2008 announcing the government's bailout of banks with toxic assets. She thought the president's speech caused more of a panic in the market which precipitated an abrupt panic selling. To make her situation worse, she sold all her stocks on or about October 10, 2008 after the Dow plunged approximately 2,500 points between September 25 and October 9, 2008. She thought stocks would continue to go down. But when the Dow gained about 900 points on October 28, 2008, she put her money back into the same 5 funds they were in before. She thought the bear market was close to bottom and stocks would start going up. But stocks kept going down. On or about November 20, 2008, she took what was left of her money out of the market again and put it all in a money market fund, now convinced that the bottom of the bear market has a long way to go. When we met at that cocktail party in mid-2009, all her money was still in a money market fund. None of her money was invested in equities. She did not know that the recession ended (no one knew) and that we were in the middle of the biggest bull market in history. Indeed the NBER did not proclaim, until a year later, that the recession ended in June 2009. That was how she lost 60% of the value of her portfolio. You would think a stock broker knows enough about the stock market to NOT lose 60%. It's a dirty little secret. But the truth is that many stock brokers, financial advisors, investment advisors, economists, speculators, finance gurus, hedge fund managers, market watchers, business forecasters and the so-called stock market geniuses lost money in the last recession just like most people. Warren Buffett lost $25 billion in the 2007-2009 recession cutting his fortune from $62 billion to $37 billion. It is my opinion and belief that the holdings of best-selling Amazon Kindle Books finance advice authors Dave Ramsey, Suze Orman and JC Bogle all lost money from the start of the bear market until it ended…that is if I go by their credo of "Buy right, hold tight and stay the course". Billionaire Carl Icahn, Andrew Smithers, Paul B. Farrell and James Dale Davidson must have lost a lot of money this year if they followed their own advice to get out of stocks before "the crash" that they predicted WILL happen in 2016.

My last contact with Rebecca was towards the end of 2013 when she told me over the phone that she has not yet recovered all the money she lost during the last recession…"good I'm not yet forty five, so I still have plenty of time to recover the money before I retire.." she cheerfully said. I'm glad above it all, she had a cavalier attitude about losing 60% of her money. I LOL, though I never made any disparaging remark. I could have told her, "…and I was paying you 2% for financial advice when I made over 50% return on my money by the time the great recession ended?!!"

I was surprised when I found out that many of Bernie Madoff's clients were banks, financial institutions and asset management firms. He duped banks or firms in Spain, Scotland, Austria, Japan, Switzerland, the Netherlands, France, Italy, Portugal and Singapore (source: http://www.townandcountrymag.com/society/money-and-power/a9656715/bernie-madoff-ponzi-scheme-scandal-story-and-aftermath/).

The founder of Bed, Bath and Beyond, the owner of the NY Mets, the IOC and many schools and universities gave him their money to invest. All he did was give his clients quarterly statements showing their investments made 12 to 20% returns no matter how the markets moved. Had it not been for the financial crisis of 2008 in which many of his clients wanted to withdraw their money, Madoff's Ponzi scheme could have gone on indefinitely. Madoff's case is indeed a study in greed but most of all it's a study in human gullibility, that even the most astute financial professionals can be duped out of millions of dollars. So there, I will manage my own finances, thank you.

9. How I earned more than 50% return on my money in just one year

I face the same challenges as everyone else. But I am a simple man with simple aspirations and ambitions in life. I will be perfectly happy to spend my retirement years fishing, then cooking my catch and finding ways to help my community. My most precious possession is my health. That is why I prefer a stress-free investment strategy. Stress and anxiety can mess up your mind, distort your judgment and cause emotional distress which can lead to depression and a weakened immune system. Suicides increased to 18.9 per 100,000 in 1929 in the year of Wall Street's crash. Some studies correlate economic hardship and increased suicides (source: http://www.huffingtonpost.com/2014/06/13/suicide-recession_n_5491687.html). Fundamentally, there is nothing wrong with the investment strategy of many financial experts to "buy, hold and stay the course", come hell or high water, but I believe that the component I've added to this strategy of getting out of stocks to escape the bear market that follows a recession will not add much stress and anxiety to your life.

I fared well during the last recession based on the very basic knowledge I have about the economy and the stock market combined with my knowledge of history. All you have to watch for is the flattening then inverting of the yield curve. My 401k retirement savings was fully invested in the stock market equally allocated into these five mutual funds: Black Rock Natural Resources, Oppenheimer Developing Markets, AF Euro Pacific Growth, Columbia Acorn Mid-cap and AF Growth Fund. I sold my stocks following my timing strategy and bought them back on December 2, 2008. By the end of 2009, the balance of my portfolio increased by more than 50%. This is after backing out new contributions and their earnings. Exiting the stock market then going back into the same funds you were in before, simply means your money will buy more shares of the same depreciated stock. The following two charts are examples of how the increase in value of your holdings is calculated:

Mutual Fund 1			PPS		Shares	Total
Jul	17	2006	$ 52	INVERSION		
Jul	17	2007	$ 61	ANNIVERSARY OF INVERSION		
Aug	13	2007	$ 58	GOT OUT OF STOCKS	5,000	290,000.00
Dec	01	2008	$ 30	NBER DECLARED RECESSION STARTED DEC 2007		
Dec	02	2008	$ 31	GOT BACK INTO STOCKS	9,355	290,000.00
Dec	30	2009	$ 50	BALANCE IN THIS FUND AS OF THIS DATE	9,355	467,750.00
				$ INCREASE IN VALUE		$ 177,750.00
				% INCREASE IN VALUE		61.3%

Mutual Fund 2	PPS		Shares	Total
Jul 17, 2006	$ 36	INVERSION		
Jul 17, 2007	$ 44	ANNIVERSARY OF INVERSION		
Aug 13, 2007	$ 40	GOT OUT OF STOCKS	5,000	200,000.00
Dec 01, 2008	$ 20	NBER DECLARED RECESSION STARTED DEC 2007		
Dec 02, 2008	$ 21	GOT BACK INTO STOCKS	9,524	200,004.00
Dec 30, 2009	$ 30	BALANCE IN THIS FUND AS OF THIS DATE	9,524	285,720.00
		$ INCREASE IN VALUE		$ 85,720.00
		% INCREASE IN VALUE		42.9%

The preceding tables are only representations of my financial position during the time indicated. They are not my real portfolio.

Recessions are a normal part of a never ending economic cycle. They are inevitable in a free market economy and they are short lived. There will be brief periods when consumers will stop purchasing non-essential goods, then resume their usual buying pattern. Post World War II U.S. recessions have lasted an average of 10 months. The worst thing you can do is to sell your stocks after they have lost 50%. Many certified financial planners (CFPs) are tricky. It was unfortunate that my brother got stuck with one during the great recession of 2007-2009. After my brother's portfolio was cut in half, the advisor directed my brother to get his money out of the stock market and put his entire (depreciated) holdings, 50% into a money market fund and 50% into treasuries. Towards the end of 2009, my brother complained to the financial advisor that he lost a lot of money. The advisor replied, "You really did not lose money. You just did not make much..." My brother almost smacked him in the face. Why tell your clients to get out of the stock market after stocks declined more than 50%? In all seriousness, missing a rally of that magnitude in 2009 was a serious error of commission...and omission on the part of the financial planner. My holdings grew by more than 50% in 2009 while my brother's earned a measly 4% APR. I've done a lot better on my own than when my portfolio was in the hands of my financial advisors. I worked with two CFPs successively and the best result they produced for me was a 9.5% annual yield and that was on a good year when the bulls were running and everyone else was making 17%. I have been doing much better on my own since I fired them. The new fiduciary rules released on April 6, 2016 by the U.S. Department of Labor which does not go into full effect until 2018 requires a financial advisor to place the client's interest first when making recommendations for investing their retirement savings, 401k and/or IRA accounts. The fiduciary's recommendations must not be influenced by the amount or type of compensation he or she receives. I doubt that this would help much. All the fiduciary has to do is make the client sign a disclosure form called "best interest contract exemption" (BICE) which describes how the advisor is paid, e.g. by commission or as a percent of the total investment, and state why the product he sold is in the best interest of the client. An investor usually signs anything that is put in front of him. It would be no different than signing the "suitable investment disclosure" that fiduciaries currently ask clients to sign.

10. Let us review the lesson

1)   An inverted yield curve is a reliable sign of an oncoming recession. 2) The stock market will lose 30% to 60% of its value when a recession hits. 3) Post WWII recessions are short-lived. They last an average of 10 months. 4) When the NBER formally declares a recession, it may already be ending or it has already ended. It happened this way in the recessions of 2007-2009, 2001 and 1990-1991. 5) A bull market is always ahead of the recovery. A bear market always lags an oncoming recession. To simplify this, a bear market starts when a recession is already in full bloom and the

bull market will begin months before the end of that particular recession.

If you can get out of stocks a year before the start of a bear market that follows a recession, like I did, and get back into stocks after the NBER makes an official announcement designating the approximate date of the recession, like I did, you will be very happy. You will avoid the crash. This is sort of like "getting to heaven before the devil finds out you're dead". To help you beat the devil, here are other signs of a recession that you can look out for in no particular order: Reduction in the price of Copper to below $2 per pound; a sustained increase in initial jobless claims and declining job growth; a continuous decline in factory orders, housing starts, existing home sales, industrial production, retail sales and consumer confidence index. A steady decline in consumer spending followed by a sharp drop in commodity prices. If any of these economic indicators persist week after week, a recession is on the horizon. An increase in the Federal Reserve benchmark interest rate in the face of declining indices may be enough to push the economy into a recession. Fed Reserve Chairperson Janet Yellen has been very cautious in raising interest rates. Her conservative monetary policy has been working so as to avoid another recession. She seems to be an independent thinker who is committed in maintaining a goldilocks economy which the market likes. She made it clear in a speech at the Jackson Hole economic symposium in 2014 that she would not arbitrarily follow The Taylor Rule (http://www.businessinsider.com/yellen-on-taylor-rule-jackson-hole-2014-8) which many economists contend stabilizes monetary policy. Indeed if she followed the Taylor rule, she could have raised the Fed rates by an additional 50 basis points every year in 2014, 2015 and in 2016 based on the low inflation and low unemployment rates and the overall economy, in theory, would have been much stronger but there is also a danger that the recovery would be truncated. As it is, with the Fed policy of "lower rates longer", a decade long (or longer) bull market is foreseeable.

Let us suppose you can get out of the stock market before the bear market starts, how do you know when to get back into stocks again? How can you hit the bullseye the second time? Here are signs that the bear market is ending or has ended: The NBER officially declared a recession and pointed to its start; It has been at least 6 months since that date; The Dow has gone down more than 30% from its most recent high; Most of the economic indicators are pointing upwards; Major stock market indices stopped fluctuating wildly and post weekly gains several weeks in a row, pointing to an impending bull market.

11. The KISS Principle and Auto-Pilot Strategy

Investing should be simple. The "KISS Principle" works well as an investment strategy. For the reader who has never heard of this acronym, it can mean a few things: Keep it short and simple, keep it small and simple, keep it simple and straightforward but my favorite variation of it is "keep it simple stupid". The average investor like you and me should not be inundated with jargon such as: leverage, derivatives, future risk, exchange, multiple streams, codility, doji, secular bear market, quadratic vector, marginal cost, hedgehog forecasting, dark pool, contra market, hot asset class, accidental high yielder, standard deviation, shorting, market kinematics, AQR Risk Parity, Sharpe ratio, etc. etc. etc. If you hired a financial professional and he keeps using such jargon, run the other way. Investing should not cause unnecessary stress and anxiety. It should not keep you awake at night. You will make more money using the KISS principle than getting in and out of stocks during dips and rises in stocks in a period of economic boom. Most investors will never manage to get out of stocks before a major correction. If you failed to follow my timing system to get out of the market before the bust, you will be better off to just leave your money alone until the next boom. If the average investors who lost 50% of their holdings in March 2009 kept it simple and left their money where it was, they would have recovered all of their losses within 2 ½ years. Those who listened to bad investment advice and took their money out of equities and got back in only at the end of 2009, did not recover the pre-recession value of their portfolio until after 6 years. For the average investor, it is never a good idea to try to time the market unless you are following the strategy in this book. Buying low and selling high and trading all day long is for stock brokers who do it for a living and are prepared to take that certain amount of stress built into their occupations. For the average investor, if you cannot follow my strategy to get out of stocks before the beginning of the bear market that follows a recession and get back in at the start of the bull market when the recession is about to end, you will be better off with the "auto-pilot strategy"---leave your money alone. Don't touch your money until you have to. You will do just as well as most other investors, making an average of 12% APY in the long run. If you learned from this book and hit the bullseye the first time, i.e. you got out of the market before the bear market started and you put all your money into a money market or stable fund, do not look at the stock market indices again (DJIA, S&P 500, NASDAQ, NYSE, VIX, etc. etc.) while you are out of the stock market. Block all the news from all your senses about how the major indices are doing. If you keep monitoring the market and keep seeing the major indices going up, it can be gut wrenching and the consequences can be disastrous. You might be tempted to go back in and might get caught with all your money back into equities while stocks are taking an even more severe downward spiral. Relax, sit back, watch TV and have a glass of beer or wine. Prepare yourself to be out of the stock market for 2 years. Take comfort in the knowledge that you will not lose 30% or more of your money when the next BIG ONE comes which it inevitably will. When the NBER declares the official start date of the recession and the major indices have plunged 30% to 60% from their most recent high, put your money back into the same mutual funds they were in before you got out of the stock market. You will not be far from the bottom of that bear market if you follow this strategy. See, Chapter, **"Investment Strategy and Asset Allocation".**

12. Managing My Investment Portfolio – 30 minutes

I do not spend much time analyzing and worrying about current events that affect the market. Investing is not rocket science. I know that business, financial, political and economic news are market movers and will cause volatility in the market. So what's the point of worrying? I check the market indices thrice daily, at the opening bell at 9:30 AM, at 12:30 PM then again when the market closes at the end of the day. There is always volatility in the market. If Janet Yellen, Mario Draghi, Angela Merkel or Barack Obama delivers a speech about the economy, the market may go up or down. If there is a new round of quantitative easing (QE), the market will go up. If oil prices go down, the market may go up...or down. So what is the point of watching the market go up and down and stressing over paper losses of 10% to 20%? I am not going to take my money out if my portfolio goes down 20%. I am not going to take my money out if my portfolio goes up 20%. The stock market goes in cycles. Even in "good times" there will be profit taking by the Gnomes of Wall Street which may cause stocks to go down in value. When you sell your depreciated stocks, that is when the Gnomes will snatch them. Even professional stock market traders, wealth managers and hedge fund owners can lose a lot money trying to time the market. Stock market experts themselves have difficulty trying to put together a winning portfolio of stocks, let alone time the market. "A blindfolded monkey throwing darts at a newspaper's financial pages could select a portfolio that would do just as well as one carefully selected by experts", wrote Burton Malkiel in his best seller "A Random Walk down Wall Street". If you choose the wrong stocks like I did (see the next chapter), you can get wiped out. If you get out of equities at the wrong time, you can miss the best 10 days of a bull market. I probably do a lot better than many of the so-called experts with my auto-pilot strategy, to "buy-and-hold" during the boom cycle of the economy and to stay out of the stock market during the "bust cycle" when stocks returned a negative yield.

13. Isn't There a Better Investment Strategy?

I've tried many different investment strategies but I've had no luck. Maybe it's because I want my life to be simple and stress-free. What is better and simpler than leaving your money alone during boom times, letting time and yield work for you then, timing the market with the goal of hitting the bullseye twice when an identifiable recession is on the horizon? If you are able to stay close to the timeline of our timing strategy, it's possible you could make 50% APY on your money during the first year of the recovery. For now until the yield curve inverts, there is nothing wrong with making an average return of 12% APY. I've tried some of the following investment strategies but I do not recommend any of them:

-   Individual Stock Picking – I came into some cash in the year 2000 from the sale of several rental properties. So I bought Yahoo at $90 in 2000 and had to sell it for $8 in 2002. I bought AOL for $109 in 2001 and had to sell it for $26 in 2002. I bought Intel at $65 in 2000 and had to sell it for $18 in 2002. I bought Ford at $26 in 2000 and had to sell it for $10 in 2002. Need I say more? Clearly individual stock picking is not for the ordinary investor like me. I squandered more than $200,000 of cash like it was monopoly money. Now I look at it as the tuition fee for the hard lesson I learned. If I had to do it over again, all I would do is use the cash to maximize my contribution to my 401k which is invested as shown under the chapter, "Investment Strategy - Asset Allocation".

-   Day Trading, Short Selling – I took some courses at an online trading academy, a school that shall remain nameless. It was a total waste of time and money. For most people, day trading and shorting is something that is better left as a complete mystery so as to avoid the unbelievable stress and real losses associated with this activity. Believe me this is not for the faint of heart. If you are one of those people who are avoiding stressful situations in their lives, this is not for you. Bottom line is, you will never make more money in day trading and shorting than you would following my investment strategy.

- Stop Loss Strategy – I took this course after listening to Bill Bresnan's advice on his daily radio talk show. The strategy is to set up a stop-loss for your stocks or mutual funds to trigger a sell order when they have lost a pre-set percentage. It is sort of a red line to trigger a sell order. The stop-loss may be automatically timed but manual monitoring is preferable. Your stocks may drop below the line during the day which will trigger the sell order but then regain their value by the time the market closes. It could become a real mess of frequent selling and buying…requiring a considerable amount of activity in a period of great volatility in the market. Nowadays, it is doubtful that this can even be done with the money inside your retirement account. Most mutual funds have severely limited the number of trades in a month. Some stop-loss setting percentages are 10%, 12%, 15%, 20%, etc. The stop-loss percentages depend on the volume and volatility of the stocks or mutual funds. This is a simple example of how it works: My stop-loss is 10%. The price of the stock is $1 at its most recent high. I sell the stock when it drops to $0.90. The idea behind a stop-loss strategy is that you are convinced that the stock price will continue to drop below the 10% decline you have set, thereby avoiding further losses. That was the reason you set the stop-loss at 10%. If you are not convinced your stock will keep dropping after it declines 10%, then set the stop-loss percent a lot lower to avoid frequent selling and buying activities. If the stock increases in value by 10% from the most recent low, I buy it back. For example, it's most recent low was $0.80, a 20% decline from the original price, then I will buy it back at $0.88. This again means that you are convinced the upward trend in your stock price will continue after it gains 10% from its most recent high. I can only tell you that after trying this for a year, I made less money than my officemates who simply left their money alone.

- Dave Ramsey's Investment Strategy - "The older the better". Pick several mutual funds that have been around for a long long time, the older the better, preferably over 30 years old that have a good average annual return. Just hold them till retirement.

- John Bogle's Investment Strategy - "Buy right, hold tight, stay the course". Allocate your entire portfolio to a broad stock index fund and bond-market fund. Then just watch your money grow.

- J.L. Collins' Investment Strategy – "Buy and hold". Put all your money, 90% into VTSAX and 10% into VBTLX and just hold them. According to him, "the market always goes up" based on his 114 year chart. Never mind if their values drop 50% during a bear market in the middle of a recession. He has no exit strategy. His strategy is "buy and hold". Collins is relying on VTSAX's 40 year annual return of 11.9%. He goes through great length in explaining what an 11.9% 40-year average annual return really means. It is almost painful to read the round-about way he seems to tell investors that he does not believe they will ever make 11.9% annual return on their money in the next many years.

- Joel Greenblatt's Magic Formula Investing Strategy – Buy undervalued stocks by determining the intrinsic value of companies. Use "earnings yield" (EBIT/Enterprise Value) rather than Price-Earnings Ratio (P/E Ratio). Invest only in companies that have a minimum capitalization of greater than $100 million. Exclude utility and financial stocks. Exclude foreign companies. Once you have chosen the companies, keep buying shares and rebalance your portfolio once a year. This appears like this is too much work and too much stress for the average investor like you and me.

- Gambling Man's Buy Low Sell High Timing Strategy – If you are a gambler and do not mind going through some type of stress, this strategy may be for you. We already know that historically, during a period of expansion, the stock market goes through a 10% correction every 12 months or so, and through a 20% correction every 12 to 18 months, you can gamble and time the market by doing this: 1) Start by keeping track of your portfolio balance whenever you want to start. 2) When the Dow goes up 10% from your start date, sell your stocks and put your money into a money market fund (cash equivalents). 3) When the Dow goes down 10% from the date you sold your stocks, put your money back into the same mutual funds they were in before. 4) Repeat the process. The following chart shows a clearer picture of this strategy:

BUY LOW SELL HIGH STRATEGY:				
DATE	DOW	Change	% Change	
Jan 02, 2014	16,441			START DATE
Feb 20, 2015	18,140	1,699	10.33%	SELL
Aug 24, 2015	15,871	-2,269	-12.51%	BUY
Oct 22, 2015	17,489	1,618	10.19%	SELL
Feb 11, 2016	15,660	-1,829	-10.46%	BUY
Mar 14, 2016	17,229	1,569	10.02%	SELL

The chart shows the timeline of the start, buy and sell dates. Theoretically, you will never lose a penny of your principal with this strategy because you will be locking in your gains and the upside profit potential is great. There is a good chance you will out-perform the market. However, there is a downside to every investment strategy, the first one in this case being that this strategy requires nerves of steel. You will have to monitor and keep a chart of DJIA averages daily and prepare to move your money whenever there is a 10% up or down movement. Also, if most of your money is in mutual funds that are "tech heavy", perhaps the NASDAQ averages are what you have to monitor and chart. Finally, you will note that on the previous chart, the fictitious investor following this investment strategy started charting on Jan 2, 2014 and has made a huge profit since then but has been out of the market since March 14, 2016, waiting for a correction of 10% from his own designated high of 17,229. With this strategy, this means the investor will not go back into the stock market until the Dow goes down to 15,506. This can be a nerve-racking experience. The DJIA averages reached an all-time high in August 2016. The Dow averages may not go back down to 15,506 until the next recession.

Another variation of this strategy is the modified buy low sell high strategy as shown on the following chart. In this strategy the investor will buy whenever the Dow loses 10% but will sell only when the Dow gains 15% so as to compensate for new highs.

MODIFIED BUY LOW SELL HIGH STRATEGY:				
DATE	DOW	Change	% Change	
Jan 02, 2014	16,441			START DATE
Feb 20, 2015	18,140	1,699	10.33%	SELL
Aug 24, 2015	15,871	(2,269)	-12.51%	BUY
Jul 12, 2016	18,348	2,477	15.61%	SELL
???	16,513	(1,835)	-10.00%	BUY
???	18,990	2,477	15.00%	SELL
???	17,091	(1,899)	-10.00%	BUY
???	19,655	2,564	15.00%	SELL

You will note that after the starting date, the investor sold after the Dow gained 10%; bought after the Dow lost 10%; sold after the Dow gained 15%; and will buy when the Dow loses 10% and closes at 16,513; and will sell when the Dow gains 15% and closes at 18,990 and so on as illustrated on the chart. In this strategy, the investor must compensate for new highs and new lows. If the market consistently breaches resistance and support levels, the investor must adjust by redefining the new resistance and support levels in his chart. Many stock brokers make a lot of money, 20% APY or more on the spread following some type of "buy low-sell high timing strategy".

Due to my "no stress" game of life strategy, to avoid stress as much as possible, I still prefer my stress-free KISS Principle and Auto-Pilot strategy. I want to sleep like a baby. For those of you who thrive on stress and like gambling a little bit, this strategy may be for you. Feel free to give it a try and let me know how you make out but don't blame me for your losses, if any.

14. Stress-Free Investment Philosophy

When it comes to investing in the market, I prefer the crockpot method to the microwave method. I prefer putting all the ingredients in a slow cooker and come home to a nourishing, delicious meal at the end of the day. I have a long-term gain outlook. If you shove a piece of meat in the microwave in order to get a quick meal, you may end up with a partially cooked or a partially burnt meal. In summary, no prophet can predict when the next man-made or natural disaster will occur. Economists and financial analysts cannot accurately time market slowdowns and recessions. Most of them rely on economic data that is outdated as soon as it becomes available. Watching the yield curve is your best chance of timing the market. If you fail to follow my timing strategy and you suddenly find your portfolio has gone down more than 30%, you will be better off to leave your money alone until it recovers in the next bull market. The downward spiral of a bear market during a recession can be quite rapid. The Dow may lose 20% in just the first 10 days of a bear market then may flip-flop between gains and losses for months until it reaches the bottom. Conversely, stocks may gain 20% in just the first 10 days of a post- recession bull market.

Chance Gardener, the idiot character of Peter Sellers in the movie "Being There" would do just as well in economic forecasting as most economists. Note his simple brand of wisdom: *"In the garden, growth has its seasons. First comes spring and summer, but then we have fall and winter. And then we get spring and summer again. Yes! There will be growth in the spring! As long as the roots are not severed, all is well, and all will be well in the garden."*

1. Your Retirement Plan – Make Yourself Number One

Pay yourself first. Make this your first priority. Do not be like others who only save what is left over after paying all the bills. Contribute 15% to 20% of your gross income to your retirement account. Many people are managing to save more, sometimes up to 50% of their gross income (Sources: http://www.cnbc.com/2017/06/30/how-to-save-30-percent-of-your-monthly-income.html https://www.tiaa.org/public/offer/insights/starting-out/how-much-of-my-income-should-i-save-every-month) If your employer offers a qualified retirement plan such as a 401k, 403b or 457b it is important to contribute the maximum amount allowed by your plan. Check with your plan administrator if you can contribute the IRS maximum amount ($18,000 in 2016 plus $6000 catch up for those 50 years old and older). Check out the IRS website: https://www.irs.gov/uac/Newsroom/IRS-Announces-2016-Pension-Plan-Limitations%3B-401(k)-Contribution-Limit-Remains-Unchanged-at-$18,000-for-2016

Make sure that there are no restrictions that apply to you and your company.   Tax laws change and the contribution limit changes almost every year and it is prudent to always obtain verification before acting on any information obtained from this book. If your company offers both a traditional 401k and a Roth 401k and you qualify for both (there are income limits for a Roth 401k), the advice of many financial planners is to split the contributions 50/50 between the two.   There has been a lot of confusion as to the real winner between a traditional 401k and a Roth 401k. The link below to the IRS website shows a comparison chart between the two:

https://www.irs.gov/retirement-plans/roth-comparison-chart

The main difference between these choices is that with a traditional 401k, you pay your taxes later and with a Roth 401k, you pay your taxes now. With a traditional 401k, you make contributions with pre-tax dollars, so you get a tax break up front, helping to lower your current income tax bill. Your money, both your contributions and earnings grow tax deferred until you withdraw them. At that time, withdrawals are considered to be ordinary income and you have to pay taxes at your current tax rate. (With certain exceptions, you'll also pay a 10 percent penalty if you are under 59½.) With a Roth 401k, it's basically the reverse. You make your contributions with after-tax dollars, meaning there is no upfront tax deduction. However, withdrawals of both contributions and earnings are tax-free at age 59½, as long as you've held the account for five years. So it all comes down to deciding when it's better for you to pay the taxes, now or later. And that depends a lot on what the future may look like for you.

Ed Slott, CPA who calls himself America's IRA Expert, whom many financial experts have referred to as "the number one guy in the IRA field" taped several financial advice programs on PBS. He was named "the best source for IRA advice" by The Wall Street Journal. He is an avid "Roth Lover". Here is an excerpt from one of his taped shows on The Lange Money Hour:
****

Ed Slott: "....like I said, to wake up and do even better planning. So, the government's going to lose all this money, not gain money, because the first thing I would tell older people, who, in the past or now, I'm still encouraging to do Roth conversions, because I believe, like you, that tax-free is always better, especially when you're pulling it out, to pay once and never again. I'm a big believer of that, as you know....... So, if you can start out even with a small amount growing tax-free, that means all of those earnings grow for you, as opposed to a tax-deferred IRA or 401(k). All the earnings are growing for you and Uncle Sam. In other words, you have a partner on every dollar you earn for the rest of your life. The key planning move is to get rid of your partner so you can keep it all. Who wants to share? Start as soon as you start working, the earlier you can, the younger you are, start doing Roth IRAs if your income permits, and Roth 401(k)s at work. This way,

you're starting out great. I'm sixty now, so I didn't have that opportunity until 1998, and still, I didn't even have that opportunity because of income, and 2010 was the first year I was able to convert because they repealed the income eligibility limitations. Now, everybody can convert, and it does mean paying taxes now. But for younger people, they have less. They're probably in a lower bracket. It's nothing. All they're giving up is a tax deduction. And if you get the tax deduction, it sounds good upfront, but then you pay for it for the rest of your life. I'd rather, as your book says, pay it once. You won't even feel it and it's tax-free forever, because, in retirement, to me, there's nothing better than a zero percent tax rate. You can't beat a zero percent tax rate, and that's why I converted everything I could January 4th, the first business day of 2010 when the floodgates opened and the law was repealed….. I like tax-free. Anything you can do now to turn taxable money into tax free is a good move because the minute you do that, all the earnings come back to you, and you don't want to share your earnings with Uncle Sam if you don't have to. You can pay for the privilege. You know, I call it 'there's a mortgage on your IRA.' If you pay it off early, you own it, and everything it earns, you keep, and that's the best way to go into retirement. "
****

Ed Slott claims that if you convert your traditional IRA and 401k into a Roth IRA and Roth 401k, you will be converting your accounts "from accounts that are forever taxed to accounts that are never taxed…You can't beat a zero percent tax", he says. This is not a true statement. The Congressional Budget and Finance Committees employ hundreds of financial analysts and actuaries to create many different statistical charts and actuarial tables before passing any law that affects taxes. The government does not lose money in taxes on Roth IRAs no matter what Ed Slott thinks. Money is taxed at least once. His claim that you will pay "zero percent" tax if you take distributions from your IRA or 401k during years when you have zero earned income may happen once or twice in your lifetime, most likely when you are under the age of 59 ½, when you're in between jobs, in which case you will pay the 10% penalty. Ed Slott is comparing apples to oranges in his calculation. For example, for the sake of a side by side comparison, you cannot say, on the traditional 401k column I will use $10,000 contribution and on the Roth 401k column I will use a $10,000 contribution plus I will add $2000 in taxes making my cash outlay $12,000. Obviously, if you do it this way the Roth 401k will win because you spent $2000 more. Of course the figures will show that you will pay more in taxes 40 years from now since you did not consider the compound interest on the additional $2000 that you did not have to pay when you made the contribution into a traditional 401k. If everything is equal, i.e. contributions, tax rates and annual returns (8% APR used on chart) are all the same, then the Roth IRA and Roth 401k have no advantage over the traditional IRA and 401k as the table shows:

BASIC COMPARISON Traditional 401k vs. Roth 401k	TRADITIONAL Pre-Tax	ROTH After Tax @12% Rate
$8,000 PER YEAR CONTRIBUTION		
FOR 25 YEARS	200,000	176,000
Savings growth after 25 years	631,635	555,839
Less tax rate @ 12%	(75,796)	0
Your retirement savings after 25 years	$555,839	$555,839

Bottom line is that Ed is failing to consider, 1) the deferred tax benefit from a traditional IRA and 401k, 2) the compound earnings of those deferred taxes.

Since it is not as simple as this in real life, I went through the exercise of creating a scenario for the purpose of doing a more realistic comparison. The tables show a 25 year cycle for an individual who earns $60,000 during the 1st year and receives a 3% average increase every year, so that on his 25th year he is making $121,968. His annual contribution to his retirement account is 10%. We make an assumption that the contributions will earn an APR of 8%. And that the tax rate at the time of distribution is 12%.

YR	ANNUAL SALARY	Marginal Tax Rate 10% to 15%	Tax Amount	10% Contribution Pre-tax	Running Bal @ 8% Annual Yield
	TRADITIONAL 401K				
1	$ 60,000	10%	6,000	6,000	6,480
2	$ 61,800	10%	6,180	6,180	13,673
3	$ 63,654	10%	6,365	6,365	21,641
4	$ 65,564	10%	6,556	6,556	30,453
5	$ 67,531	10%	6,753	6,753	40,183
6	$ 69,556	10%	6,956	6,956	50,910
7	$ 71,643	10%	7,164	7,164	62,720
8	$ 73,792	10%	7,379	7,379	75,707
9	$ 76,006	10%	7,601	7,601	89,972
10	$ 78,286	10%	7,829	7,829	105,625
11	$ 80,635	12%	9,676	8,063	122,784
12	$ 83,054	12%	9,966	8,305	141,576
13	$ 85,546	12%	10,265	8,555	162,141
14	$ 88,112	12%	10,573	8,811	184,629
15	$ 90,755	12%	10,891	9,076	209,201
16	$ 93,478	12%	11,217	9,348	236,032
17	$ 96,282	12%	11,554	9,628	265,313
18	$ 99,171	12%	11,901	9,917	297,249
19	$ 102,146	15%	15,322	10,215	332,060
20	$ 105,210	15%	15,782	10,521	369,988
21	$ 108,367	15%	16,255	10,837	411,291
22	$ 111,618	15%	16,743	11,162	456,249
23	$ 114,966	15%	17,245	11,497	505,165
24	$ 118,415	15%	17,762	11,842	558,367
25	$ 121,968	15%	18,295	12,197	616,209
Marginal tax rate at retirement				12%	$ (73,945)
Retirement balance net of taxes					$ 542,264

	ROTH 401K				
YR	ANNUAL SALARY	Marginal Tax Rate 10% to 15%	Tax Amount	10% Contribution Less tax	Running Bal @ 8% Annual Yield
1	$ 60,000	10%	6,000	5,400	5,832
2	$ 61,800	10%	6,180	5,562	12,306
3	$ 63,654	10%	6,365	5,729	19,477
4	$ 65,564	10%	6,556	5,901	27,408
5	$ 67,531	10%	6,753	6,078	36,165
6	$ 69,556	10%	6,956	6,260	45,819
7	$ 71,643	10%	7,164	6,448	56,448
8	$ 73,792	10%	7,379	6,641	68,136
9	$ 76,006	10%	7,601	6,841	80,975
10	$ 78,286	10%	7,829	7,046	95,063
11	$ 80,635	12%	9,676	7,096	110,331
12	$ 83,054	12%	9,966	7,309	127,051
13	$ 85,546	12%	10,265	7,528	145,345
14	$ 88,112	12%	10,573	7,754	165,347
15	$ 90,755	12%	10,891	7,986	187,200
16	$ 93,478	12%	11,217	8,226	211,061
17	$ 96,282	12%	11,554	8,473	237,096
18	$ 99,171	12%	11,901	8,727	265,489
19	$ 102,146	15%	15,322	8,682	296,105
20	$ 105,210	15%	15,782	8,943	329,452
21	$ 108,367	15%	16,255	9,211	365,756
22	$ 111,618	15%	16,743	9,488	405,263
23	$ 114,966	15%	17,245	9,772	448,238
24	$ 118,415	15%	17,762	10,065	494,968
25	$ 121,968	15%	18,295	10,367	545,762
	After tax balance				$ 545,762
	ROTH 401K WINS BY			→	$ 3,498

In this specific scenario, the Roth 401k wins by $3,498 after 25 years. After making other charts of different scenarios, I came to the conclusion that the only projection you have to make is your income in retirement which should show what your future tax rate would be based on the current tax system. If your retirement income will be less than your income now, traditional IRAs are better. If not, ROTH are better and you should take steps now to convert. Some retirees who do not make a correct projection of their retirement income, may be faced with an annual Required Minimum Distribution (RMD) of $100,000 or more. But so what? If you saved over $1 million for retirement, pay the tax on your withdrawals. The taxes will not be as bad as many "financial entertainers" make it out to be. Download my book, **"The Six Million Dollar Retiree" ($6MILretiree")** and open the Chapter, **"Don't Focus on Taxes…"**

https://www.amazon.com/Six-Million-Dollar-Retiree-retirement-ebook/dp/B073XTL47J/ref=sr_1_3?s=digital-text&ie=UTF8&qid=1503082903&sr=1-3&keywords=Arthur V. Prosper

Charts and tables are shown in that chapter that prove taxes are not a big deal for retirees. The income and taxes that you will defer will be making a lot more money while you are still young and working. With a traditional 401k, you will have more money to invest. In your younger years, it is logical to think that you will be putting a bigger portion of your savings into more aggressive investments such as mid-cap, small cap and emerging market funds which have a potential of yielding the biggest returns out of all asset classes of mutual funds during periods of economic expansions. Then as you grow older it follows suit that you would be allocating more of your savings towards more conservative investments.

Other factors such as changes in the tax rates and elimination of certain tax deductions are moot points. They are the big "unknown" at this point. The future of the U.S. income tax system and changes in the law are unknowable. Who knows whether or not charitable contributions, mortgage tax deduction and real estate tax deduction will still be in existence by the time you retire? I like taking what I can get right now than waiting for the future. I prefer not to convert my traditional 401k to a Roth because I want more money to invest right now. No one knows if tax system will be favorable or not. If your company offers both and you qualify for both, you may contribute 50/50 into a traditional and Roth 401k to diversify your lifetime tax expense on your retirement savings but only if your budget shows that you can afford to pay the taxes now.

Certain rules apply to Roth IRA and Roth 401k contributions. Your company's retirement plan administrator should be able to provide you with the necessary information on how to qualify for a Roth 401k and how to convert your traditional 401k into a Roth 401k. The IRS website below has current information. The rules, particularly the income limits and contributions change almost every year so you will need to check the website for updates: https://www.irs.gov/retirement-plans/roth-iras

With regard to your company's matching contributions to your 401k account, it does not matter how much your employer matches. Think of the company match as a bonus---free money. Maximizing contributions to your 401k plan whether your company matches zero or the maximum is an essential part of your financial wealth building game plan. Reducing expenses and increasing your income will help achieve your goal of contributing the maximum each year. The deferred tax benefit and the compounding interest you will earn is incredible.

According to Historical Market Data, the average annualized return of the S&P 500 Index was just about 10% for the past 42 years. The compound interest you will earn on your contributions over your working life cannot be matched by any other investment. If you can contribute close to the maximum, never touch the money and never lose any of the money you contributed, you don't have to bother with any other investment. You can simply sit back and watch your money grow till you retire.

2. Investment Strategy - Asset Allocation

I prefer my portfolio to be self-directed so as to save the 2% to 3% a financial planner typically charges. The expertise these professionals provide is usually, 1) to determine your risk tolerance, 2) pick the appropriate stocks, bonds and mutual funds for your age, 3) periodically review your account for any life changes and objectives. I have had more luck investing my own money than when financial planners were directing my investments.

A 401k account usually has a limited number of funds in a plan but there are many more choices with an IRA at a bank or brokerage firm. If I have an IRA account I will invest my money in a group of highly rated mutual funds through E*Trade, Scottrade or TD Ameritrade following my own strategy defined in the next chapter. At least with these discount brokers you do not have to pay the extra 2% to 3% fee. You will still pay the mutual fund fees which are interwoven within the funds themselves.

Here is the summary of my investment strategy:

- I try to maximize my contribution to my 401k account.
- I have my money in mutual funds not individual stocks. I have a moderately aggressive risk tolerance which means if I lost 10% to 60% of my money, I will not panic and withdraw the depreciated balance. I will ride the tide and wait it out until the stock market recovers which it inevitably does. I am more than 10 years away from retirement so my asset allocation, which I think is a balanced portfolio is 1/8 of my balance into each of these categories of mutual funds: 1) Large-Cap Growth, 2) Large-Cap Value, 3) Mid-Cap Growth, 4) Mid-Cap Value, 5) Small-Cap Growth, 6) Small-Cap Value, 7) Balanced and 8) Bonds (Government or AA and AAA only). I selected each category from the following family of funds: Vanguard, T. Rowe Price, Fidelity, Transamerica, John Hancock, Janus, Oppenheimer, Hartford, Invesco, Dreyfus, BlackRock, Janus, Franklin Templeton, Eaton Vance and American Century. The following website is a good place to

start to find out the best long-term performers in some of the most popular mutual fund categories: http://money.usnews.com/funds.

Example of Allocation

$500,000 Portfolio, $62,500 in each of these funds:

Large Growth

Vanguard PRIMECAP Fund Adm (VPMAX)

Large Value

American Funds Mutual Fund R6 (RMFGX)

Mid-Cap Growth

Janus Enterprise N (JDMNX)

Mid-Cap Value

American Century NT MdCap Val Instl (ACLMX)

Small Cap Growth

Janus Triton Fund D (JANIX)

Small Cap Value

Vanguard Small-Cap Value Index Fd (VISVX)

Balanced Fund

American Funds American Balanced Fund A (ABALX)

Bond Fund

Vanguard LT Govt Bond Index Inst (VLGIX)

The foregoing allocation is only an example. The foregoing funds are not specifically recommended. A current fund's performance may be drastically different from its performance on the date of publication of this book. Do your due diligence before acting on any information obtained from this book.

- I automatically rebalance my portfolio at the end of each quarter.

3. Retiring within 10 years

If I think I will need my money within 10 years, I will reduce volatility by moving the 25% from Small-Cap into high quality short term and long term bond funds, AA or AAA rated only. I will stay away from the so-called high yield bond funds. They probably include lots of junk bonds in their portfolio. My asset allocation will be re-adjusted to 62.5% stocks, 37.5% bonds.

4. Retiring within 5 years

If I am retiring within 5 years and think that I may need some of my principal within that time, I would get out of equities all together. The market may be against me when I need to take out some of the money. So I will divide the balance of my portfolio into several high quality bond funds (government, corporate and municipal) with ratings of AA and AAA only. Although there is less volatility in bond funds than equity funds, the bond fund values will still go down during the bear market that follows a recession. Perhaps not by 30% to 60% like stocks usually do but 20% to 30%. If I do not think I will need to take out any money at all within 5 years, i.e. I can leave my portfolio alone for 5 years, then I will invest the full amount as outlined in the next chapter.

5. Investing in retirement & required minimum distribution (RMD)

I am confident that I will reach my goal in retirement, of having a fully paid house and having enough money to last me well into my 90s if I live that long. When that retirement day comes, I will do a lot of fishing. I do not want to spend much time worrying how my retirement savings is doing today. I want my biggest worry to be figuring out how much money I should donate to charities this week, what kind of fish to catch today, how to cook my catch and what type of wine goes well with my catch. So as soon as I stop working, I will re-allocate my assets this way, 40% in a Large-Cap value fund, 40% in a Mid-Cap value fund, 20% in a short-term government Bond Fund. I will re-balance my portfolio each quarter. I will limit my withdrawals to 4% per annum or the RMD whichever is lower. I will take my withdrawals from the Bond Fund. I will continue to monitor the stock market according to my timing system so I can get out of stocks before the next stock market crash and get back into the same stocks before the start of the bull market that follows the crash.

Note that there is a strict rule on RMDs. Penalty is severe, a whopping 50% on the required undistributed amount. You must take the RMD by April 1 of the year following the year you turned 70 ½. Open these IRS links for more information,

https://www.irs.gov/pub/irs-tege/uniform_rmd_wksht.pdf

https://www.irs.gov/publications/p590b/ch01.html#en_US_2016_publink1000230772

https://www.irs.gov/retirement-plans/plan-participant-employee/required-minimum-distribution-worksheets

The IRS links above will take you to a worksheet to figure out your RMD. If you are still working at age 70 1/2, you don't have to take RMDs from your current employer's 401k plan until you leave your job. This is the "still working exception". To qualify for this exception, you must be considered employed throughout the entire year, own no more than 5% of the company and your 401k plan allows you to delay RMDs. For this reason, it is a good idea to transfer all of your other taxable retirement accounts, traditional 401k and IRAs to your current employer's plan if your plan accepts rollovers so as to avoid the annual RMD if you don't need to take any of the money out. However, if you are already 70 ½, you must first take the RMD from your IRA before rolling the balance over to you company's 401k plan.

RMD rules are complex and the rules often change. The explanations in the IRS website will confuse the average tax payer. A seasoned accountant, retirement planner or tax professional can simplify the rules and customize an RMD plan for you but here is the general idea behind the RMD rules. If your spouse is the sole beneficiary of your IRA or 401k, he or she will inherit your plan and the same rules will apply as if it's his or hers. For unmarried owners of the plan and married owners whose spouses are not more than 10 years younger, and owners whose spouses are not the sole beneficiaries of their plan, the distribution table that follows applies:

Unmarried Owners, Married Owners Whose Spouses Are Not More Than 10 Years Younger, and Married Owners Whose Spouses Are Not the Sole Beneficiaries of Their IRAs)			
Age	Distribution Period	Age	Distribution Period
70	27.4	93	9.6
71	26.5	94	9.1
72	25.6	95	8.6
73	24.7	96	8.1
74	23.8	97	7.6
75	22.9	98	7.1
76	22	99	6.7
77	21.2	100	6.3
78	20.3	101	5.9
79	19.5	102	5.5
80	18.7	103	5.2
81	17.9	104	4.9
82	17.1	105	4.5
83	16.3	106	4.2
84	15.5	107	3.9
85	14.8	108	3.7
86	14.1	109	3.4
87	13.4	110	3.1
88	12.7	111	2.9
89	12	112	2.6
90	11.4	113	2.4
91	10.8	114	2.1
92	10.2	115 and over	1.9

According to the table, if you were 70 ½ years old by the end of the year, and your plan balance is $1,000,000 your RMD is $36,496.35

(balance divided by life expectancy). You must take this distribution by April 1 of the following year but you should take it before year end so you won't get stuck with 2 RMDs the following year which may put you in a higher tax bracket.

The rules are more complicated for plan owners whose spouses are more than 10 years younger and are the sole beneficiaries of their spouse's plan. In the wisdom of our legislators who have hundreds of actuaries, tax experts and economists working for them all day long, they came up with a system for RMD based on "Joint Life and Last Survivor Expectancy". They devised RMD Table II to come up with a "blended" life expectancy for the owner and survivor. The rationale behind this is that the government does not want to wait too long to collect taxes on the older spouse's plan. The website below is an excellent resource for figuring out your RMD. Just enter the required information and click "calculate". A report will show up on the screen and you can print a PDF report of the table.

https://www.calcxml.com/calculators/qua07;jsessionid=F658D4F9462B62CA072EAEC8D35DDDCE?skn=#

If you have retired and are one of the lucky top 10% who have more than a million dollars in your retirement accounts, take at least the annual RMD and pay the taxes. You should not outlive your money if it is invested the way I have outlined in the beginning of this chapter and if you do not lose the typical 30 to 60% drop in assets whenever the market crashes.

If you need more money, take more than the RMD. If your money earns at least 4% APR you will be taking out approximately $40,000 to $65,000 a year until you are over 100 years old. Pay the tax each year. It would not be so bad. Don't be too greedy. You have successfully used the tax system to your advantage, why not pay your due now? Most people have less income in retirement than when they were working. If you're the opposite, be glad, thank God and pay the taxes. If you follow the taxation advice in this book, of maximizing your deferral and taking advantage of all the legal tax deductions, you will have paid much less in taxes by the time you retire than others who will not follow my advice. Some financial advisors recommend buying a QLAC (Qualified Longevity Annuity Contract) at this point to defer RMD and tax payment till age 85, but I would not recommend them. Take the RMD and pay the taxes annually now at this point in your life rather than defer the taxes until you are 85 years old. If you have dependents depending on you for financial support, pay some of their expenses from the after-tax money. Check with your tax accountant if you may be able to claim any of any of them as dependents (qualifying relatives) on your tax return so as to reduce your taxes. Better still, if you have too much money, give a big portion of it to charity to reduce your taxes or just invest the after tax money as I have outlined in the beginning of this chapter.

If you are adamant about minimizing taxes in retirement, another option that many finance gurus (aka "Financial Entertainers") advocate is to form a charitable foundation to reduce taxes. Click on the link below to learn more:

http://www.thebusinessofgood.org/get-engaged/starting-a-foundation.aspx

According to these finance gurus you may be able to deduct many business expenses (*wink wink*) from your tax returns if you have a foundation. Examples of these "business expenses" are: vacations, cruises, casino trips, cars, yachts, gardening, janitorial services and many other expenses. In a recent guest appearance on WOR radio, a NYC based station, **Bill Bresnan**, who was a popular radio talk show host in the 1990s, said you can use your yacht or go on a cruise and deduct the expenses from your taxes if your trips were related to your charitable work. He gave examples such as, attending a party in Paris, investigating wildlife in the Galapagos or touring Costa Rica to observe birds in the wilderness so you can decide if it is worth it to donate money to the Audubon Society. He concluded by saying, "The IRS does not like it but there is nothing they can do until Congress changes the tax system. You are not breaking the law". As for me, do I really want to get involved in any of this in my old age? If I have 2 million dollars at the age of 70, I will never spend it all in my lifetime. And how much money to leave my children is really not that important to me nor to them. So all I want to plan for today, tomorrow and the following day is, "where am I going fishing?" I also want to plan a trip every couple of months to every exotic location in the world I can think of. Right now I am thinking of Bora Bora, Bhutan, Myanmar, Galapagos, Maldives, Alice Springs, Victoria Falls, Machu Picchu, Cape Town and hundreds of other tourist spots on my bucket list. Geeeeeez, I can't wait!

6. Other investments before and during retirement

100% in Bonds - If your risk tolerance is a lot lower than mine, i.e. if a 10% to 50% drop in the stock market will drive you crazy, then put your entire portfolio into 4 different bond funds that are rated AA+. Avoid a fund that has junk bonds in it. Select funds that have a "below average risk" rating. You will not receive a return of 13% to 20% APR during bull markets as you would in Small Caps or Emerging market equity funds, but in the long run, say 15 years, you will average just slightly lower. Best of all, you can put your money in and forget it.

For those of you who are about to retire, saved a substantial amount of money, say $2 million or more of cash and are hoping to live off the passive income from dividends and leave the principal to your heirs, check out high quality dividend paying stocks from solid companies with a record of profitability which are not likely to go out of business in this lifetime. Click on the website below for more information:

http://www.dividend.com/

For example, you can divide your $2 million equally into several quality dividend stocks such as Astra-Zeneca, Glaxo-Smith-Kline, Hanes Brands, Nike, Walt Disney, Apple, Microsoft, Intel Corp, Pepsi-Cola, Coca-Cola, Johnson & Johnson, 3M Company, Procter & Gamble, McDonald's, AT&T, General Electric, Anheuser-Busch, Nestle', Exxon-Mobile, Chevron, Phillips, Stanley Black & Decker, Deere and IBM.

The aforementioned companies are used as examples only and are not specifically recommended. Do your due diligence as to the financial strength and viability of each company.

7. Annuities, what are they?

Car leases and annuities are the most mysterious deals most people will ever encounter. In my experience with both products, the salesperson employs diversionary tactics and mumbo jumbo to convince you that you are getting a good deal. He will avoid telling you the equivalent effective annual interest rate you will be paying in case of an auto lease or that you will be receiving in case of an annuity. Instead, the salesperson will divert your attention towards the monthly payments you will be paying or receiving and other benefits and advantages these product may have over others. Annuity salesmen will neatly hide the deficiencies of these products within the very fine print of the contract that you will need a lawyer to review it and to tell you that what you are getting is a bad deal. That is the reason I have included this chapter in this book.

Think of annuities as "reverse-insurance". With an insurance policy, the sooner you die, the better it is financially speaking to your beneficiaries. You will pay less in premiums and your beneficiaries will immediately receive the tax-free death benefit. With an annuity, you either give the insurance company a lump sum or fund the annuity account with regular payments for a promise of a guaranteed income for a definite period of time or for as long as you live. The longer you live, the more money the insurance company will pay out. Some annuity contracts have long term care clauses and some of them have death benefit options.

I have concluded that annuities are not for me. I am looking for growth of my investments and I am willing to take the risk following my own system of saving and investing for a high return. But for people who are looking for preservation of capital, not growth, guaranteed return and do not mind turning over a big portion of their lifetime savings in one lump sum to an insurance company or fund an annuity contract (accumulation phase) for a period of time in return for a promise of principal protection, guaranteed income and perhaps to take care of the cost of long term care, annuities may be for you. The following information came from the U.S. Securities and Exchange Commission:

An annuity is a contract between you and an insurance company that requires the insurer to make payments to you, either immediately or in the future. You buy an annuity by making either a single payment or a series of payments. Similarly, your payout may come either as one lump-sum payment or as a series of payments over time.

People typically buy annuities to help manage their income in retirement. Annuities provide three things:

- Periodic payments for a specific amount of time. This may be for the rest of your life, or the life of your spouse or another person.

- Death benefits. If you die before receiving payments, the person you name as your beneficiary receives a specific payment.

- Tax-deferred growth. You pay no taxes on the income and investment gains from your annuity until you withdraw the money.

There are three basic types of annuities, fixed, variable and indexed. Here is how they work:

- Fixed annuity. The insurance company promises you a minimum rate of interest and a fixed amount of periodic payments. Fixed annuities are regulated by state insurance commissioners. Please check with your state insurance commission about the risks and benefits of fixed annuities and to confirm that your insurance broker is registered to sell insurance in your state.

- Variable annuity. The insurance company allows you to direct your annuity payments to different investment options, usually mutual funds. Your payout will vary depending on how much you put in, the rate of return on your investments, and expenses. The SEC regulates variable annuities.

- Indexed annuity. This annuity combines features of securities and insurance products. The insurance company credits you with a return that is based on a stock market index, such as the Standard & Poor's 500 Index. Indexed annuities are regulated by the state insurance commissioners.

Some people look to annuities to "insure" their retirement and to receive periodic payments once they no longer receive a salary. There are two phases to annuities, the accumulation phase and the payout phase.

- During the accumulation phase, you make payments that may be split among various investment options. In addition, variable annuities often allow you to put some of your money in an account that pays a fixed rate of interest.

- During the payout phase, you get your payments back, along with any investment income and gains. You may take the payout in one lump-sum payment, or you may choose to receive a regular stream of payments, generally monthly.

All investments carry a level of risk. Make sure you consider the financial strength of the insurance company issuing the annuity. You want to be sure the company will still be around, and financially sound, during your payout phase.

Variable annuities have a number of features that you need to understand before you invest. Understand that variable annuities are designed as an investment for long-term goals, such as retirement. They are not suitable for short-term goals because you typically will pay substantial taxes and charges or other penalties if you withdraw your money early. Variable annuities also involve investment risks, just as mutual funds do.

Insurance companies sell annuities, as do some banks, brokerage firms, and mutual fund companies. Make sure you read and understand your annuity contract. All fees should be clearly stated in the contract. Your most important source of information about investment options within a variable annuity is the mutual fund prospectus. Request prospectuses for all the mutual fund options you might want to select. Read the prospectuses carefully before you decide how to allocate your purchase payments among the investment options.

Realize that if you are investing in a variable annuity through a tax-advantaged retirement plan, such as a 401(k) plan or an Individual Retirement Account, you will get no additional tax advantages from a variable annuity. In such cases, consider buying a variable annuity only if it makes sense because of the annuity's other features.

Note that if you sell or withdraw money from a variable annuity too soon after your purchase, the insurance company will impose a "surrender charge." This is a type of sales charge that applies in the "surrender period," typically six to eight years after you buy the annuity. Surrender charges will reduce the value of -- and the return on -- your investment.

You will pay several charges when you invest in a variable annuity. Be sure you understand all charges before you invest. Besides surrender charges, there are a number of other charges, including:

- Mortality and expense risk charge. This charge is equal to a certain percentage of your account value, typically about 1.25% per year. This charge pays the issuer for the insurance risk it assumes under the annuity contract. The profit from this charge sometimes is used to pay a commission to the person who sold you the annuity.

- Administrative fees. The issuer may charge you for record keeping and other administrative expenses. This may be a flat annual fee, or a percentage of your account value.

- Underlying fund expenses. In addition to fees charged by the issuer, you will pay the fees and expenses for underlying mutual fund investments.

- Fees and charges for other features. Additional fees typically apply for special features, such as a guaranteed minimum income benefit or long-term care insurance. Initial sales loads, fees for transferring part of your account from one investment option to another, and other fees also may apply.

- Penalties. If you withdraw money from an annuity before you are age 59 ½, you may have to pay a 10% tax penalty to the Internal Revenue Service on top of any taxes you owe on the income.

Variable annuities are considered to be securities. All broker-dealers and investment advisers that sell variable annuities must be registered. Before buying an annuity from a broker or adviser, confirm that they are registered using BrokerCheck and click on this website, FINRA's BrokerCheck website.

In most cases, the investments offered within a variable annuity are mutual funds. By law, each mutual fund is required to file a prospectus and regular shareholder reports with the SEC. Before you invest, be sure to read these materials.

If the preceding article from the SEC does not yet discourage you on buying annuities, read on. Fixed and Indexed annuities are in essence insurance contracts. Most of them are sold by insurance companies such as Allstate, Fidelity Insurance, John Hancock, Met Life, AXA, Prudential and others. Variable annuities are in essence insured investments in mutual funds and are generally sold by brokerage firms. Annuities are not guaranteed by the government. Your money will disappear if the annuity provider disappears. The most common slogan of annuity salesmen is: "You make money when the stock market goes up, but you won't lose money when the stock market goes down". They insure the "annual percentage yield" on fixed and indexed annuities and you pay a premium for that guaranteed return. The annual expenses can be as much as 3% a year. Example, if an annuity is indexed to the S&P 500 which averaged 10% in one year, your annuity will earn a return of 7% that year. On the other hand, you are protected on the down side and your annuity will still earn a minimum return even in a year when the S&P 500 had a negative yield. I prefer my own investment and allocation of asset strategy.

Before signing a contract, make sure to read the fine print. Better still, in your first meeting with the broker, request a prospectus that you can take home with you. It is important to ask about principal protection (insurance), annual fees on fixed and variable, long term care rider, investment options, death benefits and annuity payout options.

If you still think that an annuity may be right for you, the website below is an excellent source for additional information for fixed annuities.

https://www.immediateannuities.com/information/annuity-rates-step-1.html

Enter the lump sum amount you want to annuitize today. Enter your age and other pertinent information. Various offers of monthly payouts will pop up for the amount you want to annuitize. If you click on the (?) the terms are explained in plain non-legalese language. The payout amounts shown represent interest and return of principal. After the page with your information pops up, you will notice that there are different pay outs and types of coverages such as "Joint Life", "Single Life" and "Period Certain" options, e.g. for life, 25, 20, 15, 10 and 5 years. After I entered information for a person who just reached full retirement age (FRA) which at the time of writing is age 66, has $300,000 to invest and wants a monthly payout for a 10-year period certain, with no cost of living increase, I received a best offer of $2,780 monthly payment. This annuity payout represents a 2.18% annual percent return on the money. You may confirm the rate of return by clicking on the website below. Enter the initial principal amount = $300,000 and monthly withdrawal = $2780.00 annuitized over 10 years, then click calculate to see the annual growth rate.

http://www.bankrate.com/calculators/investing/annuity-calculator.aspx

My opinion is that I can do a lot better than a 2.18% APR by investing on my own.

The payouts include principal and interest, so the interest portion of the annuity is taxable as ordinary income. Click on this IRS website for information on how the interest is calculated, https://www.irs.gov/taxtopics/tc411.html

8. When Should You Collect Social Security?

At present, you may begin collecting SS benefits at 62 but your benefits will be reduced by 1 to 25% of the benefits you would have received at FRA. The percent of reduction will depend on the number of months you are shy of your FRA. The SSA website, https://www.ssa.gov/ has a lot of resources that can help you calculate your benefits, estimate the best age to start receiving retirement benefits and other things to consider to help you make a decision. The rules have not changed for individuals born before January 2, 1954. Since the various SS benefit claiming strategies are complex especially for couples, widows and widowers and divorced people, I created the following table to show my own personal claiming preference for people born on or after January 2, 1954:

SOCIAL SECURITY ROAD MAP	CLAIMING STRATEGY
SINGLE NEVER MARRIED	Wait at least until full
	retirement age.
MARRIED	Wait at least until full
	retirement age, for the
	following reasons: "File and
	suspend" strategy was
	eliminated as of May 1, 2016. A
	married person who reaches
	FRA must actually collect
	benefits in order for the spouse
	to collect spousal benefits.
	"Restricted applications"
	strategy which allows a spouse
	to file an application to claim
	spousal benefit but defer
	collecting their own until age
	70, was also eliminated. If you
	were born before January 2,
	1954, check with the SSA for
	the exceptions and what
	options may be available to you.
	https://www.ssa.gov/
MARRIED AT LEAST 10	Wait at least until FRA. Then file
YEARS, DIVORCED AT	for either your own benefits or for
LEAST 2 AND CURRENTLY	spousal benefits. SSA will pay the
SINGLE	higher of the two.

DIVORCED, HAS REMARRIED	Wait at least until FRA. You
& CURRENTLY MARRIED	cannot claim under your
	ex-spouse's benefits since you
	are currently married.
WIDOW/WIDOWER	Wait till FRA if you can. You may
	receive reduced survivor's benefits
	as early as age 60. If you are
	disabled, benefits can begin as early
	as age 50. If you wait till FRA, you
	will collect the same amount your
	deceased spouse was collecting at
	the time of death. If your spouse did
	not start collecting benefits yet at the
	time of death, you will receive the
	higher of 100% of your spouse's
	maximum benefits at FRA or 100% of
	your own. If you start collecting prior
	to FRA your benefits will be further
	reduced if you earn more than
	$16,920 a year.
	Click on the link below for more
	detailed information:
	https://www.ssa.gov/planners/survivors/ifyou5.html
SURVIVING DIVORCED	You can get benefits just the same
SPOUSE, MARRIED AT LEAST	as a widow or widower, but check
10 YEARS, CURRENTLY SINGLE	on the website above for updates on
OR REMARRIED AFTER THE	qualifications and various options.
AGE OF 60	Rules and limits often change.

The SSA states "...the rules are complicated and laws change..." They advise that individuals should call their number, 1-800-772-1213 for up to date information before making any decisions.

There are many different ways to collect your benefits and there are many factors that can influence your decision and timing as to when you should apply for benefits. There are personal considerations that are unique to your situation such as your health, financial needs, income and tax rate. The SSA cannot give you advice. They can only provide the facts. Once the facts are known pertaining to your own unique situation, you can compare your options by putting the numbers on a spreadsheet.

There is no doubt that pressure is on Congress to keep looking at ways to keep the social security system solvent for the foreseeable future. The ideas that were thrown around during the 2016 Presidential Primaries included increasing retirement age and increasing the wage limit, which in 2016 is $118,500. The legislators closed what they considered loopholes in the system, i.e. "file and suspend" and "restricted applications".

File-and-Suspend
The "file-and-suspend" strategy worked best for married couples that had a significant difference in their social security earnings records. Under the law in effect until May 1, 2016:
1. A higher-earning spouse claims social security benefits based on his or her earnings record. Once that claim is made, the lower-earning spouse applies for a spousal benefit based on the higher-earning spouse's earnings record.
2. The higher-earning spouse files for benefits then voluntarily chooses to suspend until age 70 to maximize his or her own benefits. The lower-earning spouse continues to receive the higher spousal benefit during the suspension period, and the higher-earning spouse accumulates more retirement credits equivalent to an 8% annual increase.
3. When the higher-earning spouse dies, the lower-earning spouse is eligible for survivor's benefits based on the deceased spouses' increased benefit.
4. The higher-earning spouse may suspend the benefit until age 70. At that time, or anytime between the initial application and age 70 the suspended benefits are claimed retroactively. The receipt of the suspended benefits are only delayed not lost. As of May 1, 2016, the higher earning spouse can no longer file and suspend. He or she must actually file and collect to allow the lower earning spouse to collect spousal benefits. There is no longer an advantage for the higher earner to defer benefits to age 70.

Restricted Application
The "restricted application" strategy worked best for married couples

that have similar social security earnings records and are about the same age.

Using this strategy allows the lower-earning spouse, at full retirement age, to claim a spousal benefit based on the other spouse's earnings record. At the same time, the lower-earning spouse will postpone receiving their own benefit based upon their earnings record. As with the "file-and-suspend" strategy, the lower-earning spouse's delayed benefits will increase by approximately 8% a year until turning age 70 or before if that couple decides it is no longer an advantage to defer the benefits to age 70.

If you were born before January 2, 1954, check with the SSA how the new rules affect you. Click on the website below to find out the approximate value of your social security benefits:
https://www.forbes.com/sites/baldwin/2016/03/15/whats-your-social-security-benefit-worth/#7a24d6c464d8

9. Retirement Ideas

- **Moving to retirement friendly states**

You have greater flexibility on how to spend your retirement years if you are in good health, with good mobility and very little restriction on your diet. If you have no health issues that compel you to favor one state over another, you can move to states that are friendly for retirees, or even to other countries that are viable. When I retire I will consider moving to states that have great year round weather, easy access to good health care, a low crime rate, low income tax, sales tax and property tax rates, low insurance rates and low cost of living. Salt water fishing is what I hope to be doing every day of my retired life. That is why I want to be close to the gulf, ocean or sea. Others may want to live close to golf courses, biking trails and hiking trails.

According to CNN and the U.S. News and World Report, the states chosen in 2016 with a combination of favorable factors were Florida, Texas, Nevada, Colorado, Washington State, South Carolina, South Dakota, Utah, Idaho, Wyoming, New Mexico, Montana, Delaware, Arizona and New Mexico. Bankrate.com has a different rating system which combines only a variety of statistics, i.e. cost of living, crime rate, health care quality, weather and well-being. The rankings for the year 2015 are shown on the following chart:

Rank	State	Cost of living	Crime rate	Community well-being	Health care	Tax rate	Weather
1	Wyoming	18	5	5	32	3	8
2	South Dakota	26	11	6	9	2	29
3	Colorado	32	25	4	13	16	3
4	Utah	15	22	8	11	30	6
5	Virginia	20	4	17	14	24	10
6	Montana	33	19	3	27 (tied)	13	9
7	Idaho	2	2	36	38	22	7
8	Iowa	13	12	14	6	20	39
9	Arizona	27	41	9	21	15	5
10	Nebraska	14	20	20	15	21	21
11	Maine	38	3	22	3	37	27
12	North Dakota	29	10	15	12	18	43
13	Wisconsin	25	13	13	2	47	46
14	Minnesota	30	15	7	5	42	48
15	New Hampshire	39	7	21	1	7	49
16	North Carolina	21	33	23	16	31	19
17	Kansas	8	32	25	36	28	17

18	South Carolina	24	48	19	23	9	16
19	Tennessee	6	47	37	33	4	24
20	Pennsylvania	31	16	33	24	38	22
21	Texas	17	38	11	48	6	23
22	Rhode Island	41	18	26	7	43	12
23	Vermont	42	1	29	10	41	35
24	Mississippi	1	23	43	43	10	42
25	Delaware	34	42	27	8	35	18
26	Massachusetts	45	21	30	4	39	11
27	Nevada	37	44	38	46	8	4
28	Florida	28	39	12	29	17	28
29	Michigan	9	29	39	20	26	45
30	New Mexico	22	50	16	47	14	1
31	Alabama	7	43	28	27 (tied)	12	41
32	Kentucky	5	9	49	42	29	33
33	Georgia	10	35	41	40	19	20
34	Illinois	23	24	35	26	46	36

35	Washington	36	36	24	17	25	40
36	Ohio	16	27	47	30	32	37
37	Indiana	3	30	46	39	27	34
38	Missouri	12	37	45	35	23	38
39	California	49	31	10	41	45	2
40	New Jersey	43	8	32	18	48	15
41	Maryland	40	34	34	19	44	13
42	Connecticut	46	6	18	25	49	14
43	Alaska	47	46	2	37	1	50
44	Oklahoma	4	40	48	50	11	26
45	Hawaii	50	26	1	22	36	32
46	Louisiana	19	49	42	49	5	44
47	Arkansas	11	45	44	45	34	30
48	Oregon	44	28	31	34	40	31
49	West Virginia	35	14	50	44	33	47
50	New York	48	17	40	31	50	25

The previous chart ranks each state using six categories chosen when weighted equally. But the statistics for various locations within each state may vary widely. Many states allow various jurisdictions (counties) within their state to add local sales taxes. In addition cost of living, health care, crime rate and weather can vary from city to city. To cut to the chase, here are my personal favorite retirement cities. My desire to be close to salt water has been taken into consideration. If you have other interests such as golfing, tennis, theatre, museums, cultural events, biking, hiking and mountain climbing my choices may not agree with yours:

- **Top Retirement Cities:**
   Punta Gorda, Cape Coral and Port Charlotte, Florida; Dauphin Island and Gulf Shores, Alabama; Long Beach, Gulport, Ocean Springs and Biloxi, Mississippi; Port Arthur and Rockport, Texas; Myrtle Beach and Charleston, South Carolina; Dewey and Bethany Beach, Delaware; Portland, Eugene and Medford, Oregon; Ocean City and Belmar, NJ.

   After family and friends, I consider good climate, availability of good health care and low crime rate as the primary reasons for choosing a retirement location. State income tax on retirement income and social security benefits, sales taxes, property taxes, various fees, tolls, insurance rates and cost of living pretty much balance themselves out. So to me, these are secondary factors. If one tax is lower in a certain jurisdiction, another type of tax is higher to offset it. The cost of insurance and the cost of living are also balancing factors in most locations. Take Florida as an example. It has no state income tax but sales taxes, property taxes and home insurance premiums are high.

   After considering the primary factors, I would continue to figure out which state to move into through the process of elimination. I would first eliminate the states that tax social security benefits and retirement income. Then, for many retirees who have accumulated millions of dollars in assets, it is a good idea to cross out the states that levy estate and inheritance tax. As of the time of writing, here is the list of the jurisdictions that do not impose a state estate tax or a state inheritance tax:

1. Alabama
2. Alaska
3. Arizona
4. Arkansas
5. California
6. Colorado
7. Florida
8. Georgia
9. Idaho
10. Indiana
11. Kansas
12. Louisiana
13. Michigan
14. Mississippi
15. Missouri
16. Montana
17. Nevada
18. New Hampshire
19. New Mexico
20. North Carolina
21. North Dakota
22. Ohio
23. Oklahoma
24. South Carolina
25. South Dakota
26. Texas
27. Utah
28. Virginia
29. West Virginia
30. Wisconsin
31. Wyoming

Here is the list of jurisdictions that collect a state estate tax or a state inheritance tax at the time of writing:

Connecticut - estate tax and gift tax
Delaware - estate tax

District of Columbia - estate tax
Hawaii - estate tax
Illinois - estate tax
Iowa - inheritance tax
Kentucky - inheritance tax
Maine - estate tax
Maryland - estate tax and inheritance tax
Massachusetts - estate tax
Minnesota - estate tax
Nebraska - inheritance tax
New Jersey - estate tax and inheritance tax
New York - estate tax
Oregon - estate tax
Pennsylvania - inheritance tax
Rhode Island - estate tax
Tennessee - estate tax
Vermont - estate tax
Washington - estate tax

Tax laws change and the preceding information may no longer be current. Reform and repeal of estate and inheritance taxes have been frequent in various states in the last few years. Check on the website below for updated information: http://wills.about.com/od/stateestatetaxes/fl/States-Without-an-Estate-Tax-or-an-Inheritance-Tax-in-2015.htm

Another website that is full of important resources is,

https://smartasset.com/retirement/retirement-taxes
This website has an interactive retirement calculator, 401k calculator, SS calculator, retirement state tax friendliness calculator, home buying calculator and many more. Here are the "tax friendliness" ranking of each state from this website:
Very Tax Friendly
States that either have no state income tax, no tax on retirement income, or a significant tax deduction on retirement income. In addition, states in this category have friendly sales, property, estate and inheritance tax rates.
Alaska

Florida
Georgia
Mississippi
Nevada
South Dakota
Wyoming

Tax Friendly

States that do not tax Social Security income and offer an additional deduction on some or all other forms of retirement income. Generally, states in this category also have relatively friendly sales, property, estate, inheritance and income tax rates.

Alabama
Arkansas
Colorado
Delaware
Idaho
Illinois
Kentucky
Louisiana
Michigan
New Hampshire
Oklahoma
Pennsylvania
South Carolina
Tennessee
Texas
Virginia
Washington
West Virginia

Moderately Tax Friendly

States that offer smaller deductions on some or all forms of retirement income. The sales, property, estate, inheritance and income tax rates in this category range in friendliness based on the degree of retirement deductions available.

Arizona
District of Columbia
Hawaii

Indiana
Iowa
Kansas
Maryland
Massachusetts
Missouri
Montana
New Jersey
New Mexico
New York
North Carolina
North Dakota
Ohio
Oregon
Utah
Wisconsin

Not Tax Friendly

States that offer minimal to no retirement income tax benefits. These states also do not have particularly friendly sales, property, estate and inheritance tax rates.

California
Connecticut
Maine
Minnesota
Nebraska
Rhode Island
Vermont

- **Moving to retirement friendly foreign locations**

If you can get past moving away from relatives, friends and acquaintances, many retirees become perfectly content living in foreign countries where the climate is great, good quality health care is cheap and the cost of living is half of that in America. U.S. News and World Report and International Living Magazine consistently rank these foreign locations at the top of their list: Santa Fe and Panama City, Panama; Belize; Medellin, Colombia; Vilcabamba and Cuenca, Ecuador; Granada and San Juan del Sur, Nicaragua; Cuepos and San Jose, Costa Rica; La Cieba and Trujillo, Honduras; Buenos Aires, Argentina; La Serena and Viña del Mar, Chile; San Miguel de Allende, Campeche, Puerto Vallarta and Guadalajara, Mexico; Costa del Sol and Estepona, Spain; Algarve and Lisbon, Portugal; Phuket and Pattaya, Thailand; Penang and Kuala Lumpur, Malaysia. The chart was compiled by Forbes and The Huffington Post. They used 10 different variables and weighted them equally which resulted in the rankings shown on the chart:

Country	Buy or Rent	Benefits & Discounts	Visas & Residence	Cost of Living	Fitting In	Entert'mt & Amenities	Health Care	Healthy Lifestyle	Infrastructure	Climate	FINAL SCORES
Panama	86	100	100	89	97	100	89	95	90	89	93.5
Ecuador	100	99	83	90	92	95	85	95	85	100	92.4
Mexico	89	88	90	88	91	96	87	86	90	88	89.3
Costa Rica	88	79	87	86	95	88	92	98	88	83	88.4
Malaysia	94	67	87	90	95	100	94	90	87	74	87.8
Colombia	88	65	80	92	89	94	94	95	90	90	87.7
Thailand	90	72	70	90	90	96	88	80	89	83	84.8
Nicaragua	96	72	77	98	88	84	80	97	70	80	84.2
Spain	82	69	77	82	81	90	86	88	93	88	83.6
Portugal	82	75	77	85	81	81	81	88	93	86	82.9
Malta	80	75	78	83	94	82	83	75	93	85	82.8
Honduras	77	72	87	78	100	76	79	75	87	82	81.3
France	63	75	77	57	88	96	88	80	93	83	80.0
Belize	74	83	80	78	98	70	83	85	67	78	79.6
Peru	87	57	75	95	85	74	84	72	80	85	79.4
Italy	62	70	70	74	82	90	80	85	92	83	78.8
Philippines	63	75	67	85	92	90	88	67	89	69	78.5
Uruguay	67	63	67	65	90	98	88	73	90	83	78.4
Dom. Rep.	92	72	63	85	88	78	80	77	80	67	78.2
Ireland	80	75	77	65	98	84	72	72	93	65	78.1
Cambodia	76	57	80	100	83	89	75	83	63	74	78.0
Guatemala	82	63	77	91	75	78	75	70	76	85	77.2
Vietnam	70	63	60	90	65	58	74	72	57	76	68.5

It is my opinion that this ranking system is slightly flawed since some of the factors such as health care, climate and cost of living should be weighted more than other factors. Other relevant data that must be considered which were not included in the ranking system are the crime rate, safety and security, political stability of the countries and strength of their currencies. Climate, health care and taxes are certainly important for retirees, but any sudden policy and political changes by the host nation will affect the retiree. It is hard enough trying to figure out the judicial system of the U.S., but you will be completely helpless in the Courts of Mexico, Nicaragua and Colombia if any legal issues come up for any reason. You will be at the mercy of local lawyers whose language you may not even understand. You practically will no longer be under the protection of the United States. Another point for consideration, most of these nations will require you to directly deposit your social security and retirement income into a local bank. If the account is not a U.S. Dollar account, the exchange rates may fluctuate wildly and you may lose money due to policy and political changes and currency devaluations. For the preceding reasons, I will never retire in a foreign country. To me, the risks far outweigh the benefits.

- **Moving into a resort hotel**

The elderly joke about moving into a Holiday Inn when you retire is not a joke after all. The anonymous writer of the joke says, *"With the average cost for a nursing home reaching $188 per day, there is a better way when we get old and feeble. I have already checked on reservations at the Holiday Inn. For a combined long-term stay discount and senior discount, it's $49.23 per night. That leaves $138.77 a day for breakfast, lunch, dinner in any restaurant I want, or room service. It also will leave enough for laundry, gratuities, and special TV movies. Plus, I'll get a swimming pool, a workout room, a lounge, and washer and dryer. I'll also get free toothpaste, razors, shampoo and soap. And I'll be treated like a customer, not a patient."*

But take note of this comment from a certain retiree by the name of Janet Beaudet, *"Our room included TV, electricity, telephone, towels, bedding, desk, WIFI, furniture etc. The hotel was located in a parking lot with 7 restaurants, Pharmacy, medical facilities on the bus stop. A brook with picnic tables was across the street and we spent time feeding the ducks, etc. We had a kitchenette and made simple meals when we did not eat out. The grocery store was in walking distance but they delivered the* *groceries to our room and helped put them away. It was like living in paradise. If we did not have 4 children and 11 grandchildren at home we would have sold our house and stayed there indefinitely. I pay $6464.00 a month for 2 room suite including meals, some help getting dressed, occasional bed checks. I have to provide all my own furniture, linens, telephone, TV. My opinion is that if you can find a great location with a negotiated long term rate in a facility that is approved for long term tenants (zoning laws do not allow it in all hotels) and do not require extensive help and are willing to tip generously a hotel can be much better than Assisted Living and Cheaper."*

Many popular hotel chains are now offering extended stay. It would not take much effort to shop around for the best deal for a year-long stay in the most ideal location you can find. These are some of the hotel chains that offer extended stay plans: Marriott, Mainstay Suites, Hilton, Hampton Inn, TownPlace Suites, Homewood Suites, Candlewood Suites and many others. Many of them advertise full kitchen and free Wi-Fi, free hot breakfast and evening social hours, health club, pool, lobby and outdoor space designed for socializing and free grocery delivery. When your year is up, you may want to move to a different exotic location or negotiate a renewal.

- **Cruise Ship Retirement**

This is yet again another rumor that has been making the rounds for years, i.e. a cruise ship retirement is cheaper than the cost of a nursing home. It turns out this happens more than you think but here is what my research reveals: The cost of an independent living facility is less than the cost of a cruise. The cost of an assisted living facility is more than the cost of a cruise. And the cost of a nursing home where you need level 3 care, i.e. assistance for activities of daily living (ADLs) and 24 hour on demand nursing care will cost a lot more than the cruise. However, a cruise ship will not be able to provide assistance for ADL and level 3 care. Due to our aging population, many of the popular cruise lines are now seriously discussing how to provide long term care on cruise ships. Obviously, the ships will have to be retrofitted to make them suitable for long term assisted living. For more information on one of the cruise lines contact, www.HealthcareAtSea.com.

10. Paying for Long-Term Care

Before we can discuss various ideas and strategies on how to deal with the expenses for long-term care (LTC), particularly expenses for a nursing home, assisted living facilities and in-home care, first you have to understand that no matter how prudent and austere you have lived your life, which hopefully resulted in a substantial wealth accumulation, the cost of long-term care can wipe out your lifetime savings. You may think that you have saved enough for retirement, and if you succeed in following the strategies outlined in this book for wealth accumulation, you may very well accumulate more than a million dollars in liquid cash and real estate by the time you reach full retirement age. But the cost of long term care assistance, (particularly if you and/or your spouse have to spend the rest of your life in a nursing home) can wipe out all your assets. According to the U.S. Department of Health and Human Services (HHS), about 70% of people turning 65 will need long term care services at some point in their lives. Long-term care is not necessarily medical care but rather "custodial care" which provides individuals with assistance for the Activities of Daily Living (ADLs). Custodial care is not covered by Medicare. There are 3 ways of paying for custodial care. By cash, Medicaid, or private insurance.

The following information came from Medicare.gov. Various ideas and strategies are explored towards the end of this chapter:

11. How can I pay for nursing home care?

There are many ways you can pay for nursing home care. Most people who enter nursing homes begin by paying for their care out-of-pocket. As you use your resources (like bank accounts and stocks) over a period of time, you may eventually become eligible for Medicaid.

Medicare generally doesn't cover long-term care stays (room and board) in a nursing home. Also, nursing home care isn't covered by many types of health insurance. Don't drop your health care coverage (including Medicare) if you're in a nursing home. Even if it doesn't cover nursing home care, you'll need health coverage for hospital care, doctor services, and medical supplies while you're in the nursing home.

There are several other ways you can pay for nursing home care:

Personal resources

You can use your personal money and savings to pay for nursing home care. Some insurance companies let you use your life insurance policy to pay for long-term care. Ask your insurance agent how this works. When your personal resources are depleted, you will be eligible for Medicaid.

Help from your state (Medicaid)

Medicaid is a state-run program. The state laws vary with regard to income eligibility and asset requirements. Once you qualify for Medicaid, nursing home care costs, LTC and in-home care giver costs will be paid by Medicaid. Most people who want to apply for Medicaid have to reduce their assets first. There are rules about what's counted as an asset and what isn't when determining Medicaid eligibility. There are also rules that require states to allow married couples to protect a certain amount of assets and income when one of them is in an institution (like a nursing home) and one isn't. A spouse who isn't in an institution (community spouse) may keep half of the couple's joint assets, up to a maximum of $119,220 in 2015, as well as a monthly income allowance. However, some states are more generous and may allow the community spouse to keep a maximum of $100,000 in countable assets regardless of whether or not this represents half of the couple's assets. For more information, call your Medicaid office. You can also call your local Area Agency on Aging to find out if your state has any legal services where you could get more information.

Transferring assets and reducing income in order to qualify for Medicaid is not illegal. It is not unethical or immoral. It is the right thing to do if you want to preserve your lifetime savings for the benefit of your heirs....as long as you accomplish this in accordance with the law. Medicaid/Nursing Home Planning is no different from tax planning to avoid paying unnecessary taxes. Transfers of assets for less than fair market value may subject you to a penalty that Medicaid won't pay for your nursing home care for a period of time. How long the period is depends on the value of the assets you gave away. There are limited exceptions to this, especially if you have a spouse, or a blind or disabled child. Generally, giving away your assets can result in no payment for your nursing home care, sometimes for months or even years.

Federal law protects spouses of nursing home residents from losing all of their income and assets to pay for nursing home care for their spouse. When one member of a couple enters a nursing home and applies for Medicaid, his or her eligibility is determined under "spousal impoverishment" rules. Spousal impoverishment helps make sure that the spouse still at home will have the money needed to pay for living expenses by protecting a certain amount of the couple's resources, as well as at least a portion of the nursing home resident's income, for the use of the spouse who is still at home. For more information, call your Medicaid office. To apply for Medicaid, call your Medicaid office. They can tell you if you qualify for the Medicaid nursing home benefit or other programs, such as the Programs of All-Inclusive Care for the Elderly (PACE), or home and community-based waiver programs.

Not all nursing homes accept Medicaid payments. Check with the nursing home to see if they accept people with Medicaid, and if they have Medicaid beds available. You may be eligible for Medicaid coverage in a nursing home even if you haven't qualified for other Medicaid services in the past. Sometimes you won't be eligible for Medicaid until you've spent some of your personal resources on medical care. You may be moved to another room in the Medicaid-certified section of the nursing home when your care is paid by Medicaid. To get more information on Medicaid eligibility requirements in your state, call your Medicaid office.

You may have to pay out-of-pocket for nursing home care each month. The nursing home will bill Medicaid for the rest of the amount. How much you owe depends on your income and deductions.

Long-term care and residential care have categories of different care levels. Generally, Medicaid will pay the bill for eligible seniors.

The following table shows a comparison of different care facilities and their approximate costs as of this writing:

HOUSING OPTION	PURPOSE	APPROX. COST
Assisted Living	For people who need help with both simple and complex ADLs	$7000/MO. Medicaid for eligible seniors and low income individuals
Board and Care Homes	People who need help with complex ADLs	$4500/MO. Medicaid for eligible seniors and low income individuals
Skilled Care Facilities	For people with significant short-term care needs	$7500/MO. Medicaid for eligible seniors and low income individuals Medicare usually covers for 20 days if medically necessary
Long-Term Care Facility	For people who will not return to independent living	$90000/PER YEAR covered by Medicaid and long-term care insurance

The state cannot put a lien on your home if there is a reasonable chance you will return home after getting nursing home care or if you have a spouse or dependents living there. This means they cannot take, sell or hold your property to recover benefits that are correctly paid for nursing home care while you are living in a nursing home in this circumstance. In most cases, after a person who gets Medicaid nursing home benefits passes away, the state must try to get whatever benefits it paid for that person back from their estate.

They cannot recover on a lien against the person's home if it is the residence of the person's spouse, brother or sister (who has an equity interest and was residing in the home at least one year prior to the nursing home admission), or a blind or disabled child or a child under the age of 21 in the family.

Long-term care (LTC) insurance

This type of private insurance policy can help pay for many types of long-term care, including both skilled and non-skilled care. LTC insurance can vary widely. Some policies may cover only nursing home care. Others may include coverage for a whole range of services like adult day care, assisted living, medical equipment, and informal home care. If you have LTC insurance, check your policy or call the insurance company to find out if the care you need is covered. If you are shopping for long-term care insurance, find out which types of long-term care services and facilities the different policies cover. Also, check to see if your coverage could be limited because of a pre-existing condition. Make sure you buy from a reliable company that's licensed in your state. Federal employees, members of the uniformed services, retirees, their spouses, and other qualified relatives may be able to buy LTC insurance at discounted group rates. Get more information about LTC insurance for federal employees from this website:

 https://www.opm.gov/healthcare-insurance/long-term-care/

Summary

- Medicare does not cover medical services for cognitive ailments like dementia, or simply because you are unable to handle some of the basic activities of daily living like eating, drinking, walking, dressing, bathing and grooming. A full time caregiver for in-home assistance will cost approximately $230 a day in 2016 dollars.

- Long term care in a nursing home will cost approximately $90,000 a year in 2016 dollars. The average nursing home stay is about 3 years.

- Medicare covers 100% of nursing care in a nursing home, board and care convalescent centers, or in-home care but only for 20 days and only if medically necessary following a hospital stay of more than three days. It will also pay for physical therapy, wheelchairs, walkers, hospital beds and even hospice care for those with less than six months to live.

12. Exploring different strategies in dealing with LTC expenses

It would be great if we can choose how to die and when to die. Since we cannot, we have to explore the few options available to us. According to statistics shown below, only 31% of us will die never needing long term care. Private LTC insurance is very expensive. You cannot buy insurance only when you need it. Even if you are in good health, the older you get the more the premiums would cost. Estimated Years of needing Long-Term Care after turning Age 65:
More than 5 years 20%
2 to 5 years 20%
1 to 2 years 12%
1 year or less 17%
None 31%

If you are in good health, take care of yourself and are feeling lucky that you will be among the 31% who will never need LTC, then you can take a chance and not do anything. But the worst case scenario if you go by the above averages is you will spend $230 a day (in 2016 dollars) for 5 years for a total of $419,750 in today's dollars. This is only for one person. After spending down your cash, the state government will take care of you through the Medicaid program.

At age 50, long-term care may not be something that you are thinking about. But premiums are obviously a lot cheaper at 50 than at 65 or at 70. At age 70, the premiums will be so much more expensive and you will be subjected to a rigorous underwriting process which may include urine and blood tests and cognitive testing such as memory recall, reasoning and basic math. 45% of applicants 70 years and older are declined. If you are healthy and never smoked, at 50 you can buy a fixed rate lifetime policy for about $1500 per annum. You will spend $60,000 in premiums over 40 years. That is $120,000 for a couple. If you factor in the interest that money could have earned over 40 years, using the rule of 72 where your money doubles every 10 years or so, that is a cash outlay of over $400,000 per person by the time you reach 90. You may die without ever needing LTC. At 65, the premiums for a fixed lifetime policy could be about $2500 per annum. You will spend $62,500 in premiums if you live to be 90. That is $125,000 for a couple without factoring in the interest the premium payments could have earned. Again, you may never need long-term care. A typical policy is shown as follows:

State	NJ
Birthdate	1/2/1966
Age	50
Facility Daily Benefit	$300
Facility Benefit Period	3 Years
Home Care Daily Benefit	100%
Monthly Home Care	Monthly
Elimination Period	0 Days
Marital Discount	Both Insured
Payment Option	Annual
Gender	Male
Monthly Benefit	$9,000
Maximum	$324,000
Assisted Living	100%
Cash Benefit	30%
Cash Benefit Amount	$2,400
Premium	$1,500

State	NJ
Birthdate	1/2/1951
Age	65
Facility Daily Benefit	$300
Facility Benefit Period	3 Years
Home Care Daily Benefit	100%
Monthly Home Care	Monthly
Elimination Period	0 Days
Marital Discount	Both Insured
Payment Option	Annual
Gender	Male
Monthly Benefit	$9,000
Maximum	$324,000
Assisted Living	100%
Cash Benefit	30%
Cash Benefit Amount	$2,400
Premium	$2,500

My LTC Strategy

Since my health and longevity are big unknowns, I prefer the flexibility of not losing a penny on insurance premiums if I never need long-term care. So my preference is to deposit the money I would have paid for LTC insurance into my Roth 401k, sort of self-insurance. If it earns an APR of 8%, I will have $454,865 if I started at 50 until I reach 90 years of age and $215,877 if I started at 65. See the following charts:

Age	Savings	Addition	Earned Interest	Total Savings
50	$0.00	$1,500.00	$120.00	$1,620.00
51	$1,620.00	$1,500.00	$249.60	$3,369.60
52	$3,369.60	$1,500.00	$389.57	$5,259.17
53	$5,259.17	$1,500.00	$540.73	$7,299.90
54	$7,299.90	$1,500.00	$703.99	$9,503.89
55	$9,503.89	$1,500.00	$880.31	$11,884.21
56	$11,884.21	$1,500.00	$1,070.74	$14,454.94
57	$14,454.94	$1,500.00	$1,276.40	$17,231.34
58	$17,231.34	$1,500.00	$1,498.51	$20,229.84
59	$20,229.84	$1,500.00	$1,738.39	$23,468.23
60	$23,468.23	$1,500.00	$1,997.46	$26,965.69
61	$26,965.69	$1,500.00	$2,277.26	$30,742.94
62	$30,742.94	$1,500.00	$2,579.44	$34,822.38
63	$34,822.38	$1,500.00	$2,905.79	$39,228.17
64	$39,228.17	$1,500.00	$3,258.25	$43,986.42
65	$43,986.42	$1,500.00	$3,638.91	$49,125.34
66	$49,125.34	$1,500.00	$4,050.03	$54,675.37
67	$54,675.37	$1,500.00	$4,494.03	$60,669.39
68	$60,669.39	$1,500.00	$4,973.55	$67,142.95
69	$67,142.95	$1,500.00	$5,491.44	$74,134.38
70	$74,134.38	$1,500.00	$6,050.75	$81,685.13

71	$81,685.13	$1,500.00	$6,654.81	$89,839.94
72	$89,839.94	$1,500.00	$7,307.20	$98,647.14
73	$98,647.14	$1,500.00	$8,011.77	$108,158.91
74	$108,158.91	$1,500.00	$8,772.71	$118,431.62
75	$118,431.62	$1,500.00	$9,594.53	$129,526.15
76	$129,526.15	$1,500.00	$10,482.09	$141,508.24
77	$141,508.24	$1,500.00	$11,440.66	$154,448.90
78	$154,448.90	$1,500.00	$12,475.91	$168,424.82
79	$168,424.82	$1,500.00	$13,593.99	$183,518.80
80	$183,518.80	$1,500.00	$14,801.50	$199,820.31
81	$199,820.31	$1,500.00	$16,105.62	$217,425.93
82	$217,425.93	$1,500.00	$17,514.07	$236,440.01
83	$236,440.01	$1,500.00	$19,035.20	$256,975.21
84	$256,975.21	$1,500.00	$20,678.02	$279,153.22
85	$279,153.22	$1,500.00	$22,452.26	$303,105.48
86	$303,105.48	$1,500.00	$24,368.44	$328,973.92
87	$328,973.92	$1,500.00	$26,437.91	$356,911.83
88	$356,911.83	$1,500.00	$28,672.95	$387,084.78
89	$387,084.78	$1,500.00	$31,086.78	$419,671.56
90	$419,671.56	$1,500.00	$33,693.72	$454,865.29

****

Age	Savings	Addition	Earned Interest	Total Savings
65	$0.00	$2,500.00	$200.00	$2,700.00
66	$2,700.00	$2,500.00	$416.00	$5,616.00
67	$5,616.00	$2,500.00	$649.28	$8,765.28
68	$8,765.28	$2,500.00	$901.22	$12,166.50
69	$12,166.50	$2,500.00	$1,173.32	$15,839.82
70	$15,839.82	$2,500.00	$1,467.19	$19,807.01
71	$19,807.01	$2,500.00	$1,784.56	$24,091.57
72	$24,091.57	$2,500.00	$2,127.33	$28,718.89
73	$28,718.89	$2,500.00	$2,497.51	$33,716.41
74	$33,716.41	$2,500.00	$2,897.31	$39,113.72
75	$39,113.72	$2,500.00	$3,329.10	$44,942.82
76	$44,942.82	$2,500.00	$3,795.43	$51,238.24
77	$51,238.24	$2,500.00	$4,299.06	$58,037.30
78	$58,037.30	$2,500.00	$4,842.98	$65,380.28
79	$65,380.28	$2,500.00	$5,430.42	$73,310.71
80	$73,310.71	$2,500.00	$6,064.86	$81,875.56
81	$81,875.56	$2,500.00	$6,750.05	$91,125.61
82	$91,125.61	$2,500.00	$7,490.05	$101,115.66
83	$101,115.66	$2,500.00	$8,289.25	$111,904.91
84	$111,904.91	$2,500.00	$9,152.39	$123,557.30
85	$123,557.30	$2,500.00	$10,084.58	$136,141.89
86	$136,141.89	$2,500.00	$11,091.35	$149,733.24
87	$149,733.24	$2,500.00	$12,178.66	$164,411.90
88	$164,411.90	$2,500.00	$13,352.95	$180,264.85
89	$180,264.85	$2,500.00	$14,621.19	$197,386.04
90	$197,386.04	$2,500.00	$15,990.88	$215,876.92

The money is mine if I never need LTC. I will invest the money inside my 401k account. This is sort of self-insurance, a strategy which I really like.

How to qualify for Medicaid benefits for LTC

Monthly income and countable assets are two determining factors for Medicaid benefit eligibility. As of the time of writing, an applicant cannot earn more than $2199 per month and must not have more than $2000 in countable assets. When your countable assets are down to $2000, Medicaid will take over. Some assets are exempt from valuation such as the value of your home if it is $500,000 or less (some states have a higher exemption limit), your car with a value of $4500 or less, funeral burial funds of $1500, personal property that is essential to self-support and life insurance. Not all nursing homes and home health care providers accept Medicaid. In some cases, you may be moved to another room in a Medicaid-certified section of the same facility. Medicare.gov states, "The state cannot put a lien on your home if there is a reasonable chance you will return home after getting nursing home care or if you have a spouse or dependents living there. This means they cannot take, sell, or hold your property to recover benefits that are correctly paid for nursing home care while you are living in a nursing home in this circumstance. In most cases, after a person who gets Medicaid nursing home benefits passes away, the state must try to get whatever benefits it paid for that person back from their estate. They cannot recover on a lien against the person's home if it's the residence of the person's spouse, brother or sister (who has an equity interest and was residing in the home at least one year prior to the nursing home admission), or a blind or disabled child or a child under the age of 21 in the family."

Transferring assets to qualify for Medicaid

There is a 60-month "look back" period for transfers made after February 8, 2006. It is logical to think that you will not transfer any of your assets to your children or other heirs until you are faced with the sad reality that you must go to a nursing home. It is human nature that given the choice you would rather give the money to your children (let the government take care of you) than give it to the nursing home. The government knows this that is why "the penalty period" was established when the Deficit Reduction Act of 2005 (DRA) was enacted. The penalty applies for transfers made within

60 months from the date that transferor moved to a nursing home and had applied and been approved for Medicaid if not for the transfer. You will be eligible for Medicaid if your total cash in the bank is less than $2000. However, Medicaid will not pay during the length of the penalty period which is calculated by dividing the amount of transfer by the average cost of nursing home care in your state. The penalty period starts after Medicaid approves your application. If the amount of transfer was $75,000 and average cost of monthly nursing home care in your state is $7500, the penalty period is 10 months, i.e. $75,000/$7500. The chart illustrates the timetable for a person who has enough money to pay the nursing home for 8 months:

AMOUNT OF TRANSFER	$75,000
MONTHLY NURSING HOME RATE	$7,500
PENALTY PERIOD ($75000/$7500)	10 Months
Admitted to nursing home	1/2/2016
	2/2/2016
	3/2/2016
	4/2/2016
	5/2/2016
Applied for Medicaid	6/2/2016
	7/2/2016
	8/2/2016
Spent savings down to less than $2000	9/2/2016
	10/2/2016
Approved by Medicaid	11/2/2016
10-Month Penalty starts	12/2/2016
	1/2/2017
	2/2/2017
	3/2/2017
	4/2/2017
	5/2/2017
	6/2/2017
	7/2/2017
	8/2/2017
	9/2/2017
10-Month Penalty ends, Medicaid pays from this date	10/2/2017

The reader who is paying attention will surely ask, "Well, who will pay the nursing home bills from January 2, 2016 through October 2, 2017?" The answer is you are responsible for the bills not the person you transferred the money to unless that person signed the admission agreement as a "responsible party" or "guarantor". The nursing home's collection agency will go after you not the transferee. Most people want to do the right thing so the practical solution is for the transferee to voluntarily return the $75,000 as payment towards the nursing home bills. Another timetable is shown below. This is whereby the Medicaid applicant has no more than $2000 in countable assets. The applicant applies immediately upon admission to the nursing home:

AMOUNT OF TRANSFER	$75,000
MONTHLY NURSING HOME RATE	$7,500
PENALTY PERIOD ($75000/$7500)	10 Months

Admitted to nursing home, countable assets not more than $2000 & immediately applied for Medicaid	1/2/2016
	2/2/2016
Approved by Medicaid	3/2/2016
10-Month Penalty starts	4/2/2016
	5/2/2016
	6/2/2016
	7/2/2016
	8/2/2016
	9/2/2016
	10/2/2016
	11/2/2016
	12/2/2016
	1/2/2017
10-Month Penalty ends, Medicaid pays from this date	2/2/2017

- **Permitted transfers.** The following information was published and is available on the website, Medicaid.gov:

While most transfers are penalized with a period of Medicaid ineligibility of up to five years, certain transfers are exempt from this penalty. Even after entering a nursing home, you may transfer any asset to the following individuals without having to wait out a period of Medicaid ineligibility:

• Your spouse (but this may not help you become eligible since the same limit on both spouse's assets will apply).

• Your child who is blind or permanently disabled.

• Into trust for the sole benefit of anyone under age 65 and permanently disabled.

• In addition, you may transfer your home to the following individuals (as well as to those listed above):

• Your spouse.

• Your child who is under age 21.

• Your child who has lived in your home for at least two years prior to your moving to a nursing home and who provided you with care that allowed you to stay at home during that time.

• A sibling who already has an equity interest in the house and who lived there for at least a year before you moved to a nursing home.

13. How to reduce income to qualify for Medicaid

If your income exceeds the eligibility threshold, which at the time of writing is $2199 a month, the best thing to do is to consult a Medicaid Planning professional or an Elder Care attorney to set up a Qualified Income Trust (QIT) such as an Income Cap Trust, Miller Trust or a Pooled Income Trust that you can contribute into thereby reducing your income. As an example, if you receive $1500 from SSA and $1500 from other sources, $801 will be deposited into the QIT to exclude it from your monthly income, thereby qualifying you for Medicaid benefits. Every month your trustee will have to use the money in the QIT to pay for your care including turning the available amount to the nursing home or assisted living facility. Medicaid pays the rest of your expenses. Upon your death, the state is entitled to reimbursement from the money left in the QIT. Medicaid laws are complex and they vary from state to state. This is not a do-it-yourself project. You need a lawyer to set up a QIT. Maybe you will spend $2000 to $7,000 on legal fees to set up a QIT for the less complicated ones, but you will qualify for Medicaid if the trust is done correctly.

14. Creative Ways of Hiding Assets to Qualify for Medicaid

The following are other strategies that I do not endorse. They are included in this book for entertainment only. In fact, some of these egregious activities may land you in jail. But it is a fact some people have been employing these tactics to qualify for Medicaid. I learned about these activities when I interviewed some retirees who have gone through the experience. One retiree who shall remain nameless said, "There is a fine line between right and wrong, between legal and illegal." Another retiree said, "It's only illegal if you get caught". Yet another retiree said, "as long as in my mind I am telling the truth, I have no guilt and I have not perjured myself. The government has nothing on me". I discovered these are some of the ways some retirees hide cash from Medicaid:

- **In a bank's safe deposit box** – This will sound like a strange story to some people, but this happens more often than you think. A retiree by the name of Perry D (not his real name) lives in California. He and his wife are counting on Medicaid for their LTC. Between the two of them, they receive about $3500 a month in SS benefits which they will have to turn over to the nursing home in return for long term care if the need arises. Medicaid covers anything Medicare does not cover such as long term nursing care, assisted living facility and custodial care (home health care). He and his wife are both 70 years old and they keep $185,000 cash in 2 safe deposit boxes in two different banks. Perry is a law school drop-out so he knows a little about the law. He tells me that keeping money in a safe deposit box is perfectly legal as long as the money is not ill-gotten. Perry and his wife are in marginal health. Both are diabetics and are worried that they might need LTC in a nursing home or may have to move into an assisted living facility in a few years. Their house with a market value of $380,000 is all paid for. Their two children are included in the deed as joint tenants with their parents with right of survivorship and they use the house as their principal residence. Perry and his wife lease their 2 cars and have no other countable assets except for the $185,000 cash hidden in the safe deposit boxes. Multiple persons can be named as lessees so he has his name, his wife and two children on the rental agreements although they did not give their children keys to the boxes. Yes Perry admits he could be earning at least 1% interest on this money but he is more worried about having to turn over the money to the health provider when the time comes if it's not hidden. As a precaution, he drafted the following sworn affidavit which he keeps with the money:

Affidavit and Certification

This is to certify that we gifted the following amounts to our children:

Date	Amount	Name	SS#
1/2/2003	$11,000	John D	SS# ***-**-4156
	$11,000	Susan D	SS# ***-**-4157
1/2/2004	$11,000	John D	SS# ***-**-4156
	$11,000	Susan D	SS# ***-**-4157
1/2/2005	$11,000	John D	SS# ***-**-4156
	$11,000	Susan D	SS# ***-**-4157
1/2/2006	$12,000	John D	SS# ***-**-4156
	$12,000	Susan D	SS# ***-**-4157
1/2/2007	$12,000	John D	SS# ***-**-4156
	$12,000	Susan D	SS# ***-**-4157
1/2/2008	$12,000	John D	SS# ***-**-4156
	$12,000	Susan D	SS# ***-**-4157
1/2/2009	$13,000	John D	SS# ***-**-4156
	$13,000	Susan D	SS# ***-**-4157
1/2/2010	$13,000	John D	SS# ***-**-4156
	$13,000	Susan D	SS# ***-**-4157
	$190,000		

Affiants' Signatures: Perry D _____,
Mrs. Perry D,   _____

Subscribed and sworn to before me this _____
day of _____,20xx , City, County, State.

Notary Public

Perry told me that he has never encountered a problem. Except for the loss of 1% to 2% annual interest, he is happy with what he is doing. He thinks that if he and his wife ever need LTC, which can be any day now, Medicaid will take care of them. They will tell the absolute truth that they have no cash in the bank and that they did not make any transfers of cash within the 60-month look back period. Of course they have to watch that the balances of their individual checking accounts under their separate names do not go over $2000 each. They withdraw their social security benefit payments (about $1750 each) immediately upon receipt, spend the money to maintain their daily needs and lifestyle, then put the remaining cash, if any, into the safe deposit boxes. Perry gave me more details. The Affidavit does not have to be backdated since the affiant is merely attesting to what happened in the past. Perry and his wife did not withdraw large amounts of cash from their savings. Over 5 years ago, they withdrew $5000 a month or less over the course of three years which they systematically transferred into the safe deposit boxes. Perry tells me that the money keeps growing. They do not spend that much money on their daily needs so they always have something extra to put into the safety deposit boxes at the end of the month. They will need to update the affidavit as needed.

- **In a foreign bank account** – A retiree by the name of Jesse H is 68 years old. He and his wife live in Illinois. They receive $2000 each monthly from the SSA. They crossed the Canadian border 5 years ago and opened an account at a TD bank in Windsor, Ontario. The account is a "joint account" with their 3 daughters. He tells me they only had to show two IDs, their passports and credit cards. They opened the interest bearing savings account, no other questions asked. They systematically transferred their liquid assets totaling the equivalent of CAN$390,000 into the account. They told the bank they are planning to buy a house in Ontario and needed a place to park their money. At the end of the year, the bank sends them a T5NR slip for the 10% withholding tax on the interest the money earned. This is the counterpart of IRS form 1099INT but the T5NR slip makes no reference to any

U.S. taxpayer's SS number because this form is for non-residents. Since ¾ of the money in the account legally belongs to their daughters, in the beginning of the year Jesse asks his three daughters this question, "Will you gift your mother and me $10,000 each?" Their daughters always say yes, so they are allowed to withdraw up to CAN$60,000 ($10,000x3x2) if they need it and not have to worry about their daughters having to file a gift tax return. Last year they took some money out and went on a 130-day world cruise. With regard to the requirement to file IRS Form 8938, Statement of Specified Foreign Financial Assets, Jesse tells me they are not required to file since together with their daughters and their spouses they do not satisfy the reporting threshold of more than US$100,000 per married couple in foreign assets. I've interviewed other retirees who have hidden bank accounts in foreign countries such as India, Malaysia, Indonesia, Italy, Germany, The Bahamas, and many other Caribbean and South American Countries. Most of the people I've interviewed who hold foreign bank accounts claim that they comply with IRS regulations shown on the link below.

https://www.irs.gov/businesses/small-businesses-self-employed/report-of-foreign-bank-and-financial-accounts-fbar

- **In a fire proof safe** – This is the story of Hazel J, a 72 year old widow retiree. She does not think she has enough money to be concerned about as other retirees. She lives in Washington State. She has 3 adult children but they live far away from her. Her 2 bedroom condo is fully paid for and has a market value of $280,000. She added her children as co-owners of the condo more than 5 years ago. As a precaution she signed an affidavit stating "It is my intention to return home after my discharge from the hospital or any nursing home and/or health care facility…" Her cash on hand is less than $100,000 and her SS benefit is around $1800 a month. She has been in and out of nursing homes in the past two years, the expenses all paid by Medicare and Medicaid. First she had a hip replacement. After 20 weeks at a rehab center she was transferred to an assisted living facility. When she applied for Medicaid assistance, she told the authorities that she has no countable assets. She tells me that the $100,000 cash hidden in her vault does not belong to her but to her children and grandchildren. She withdraws money from that vault only with the permission of her children and grandchildren when they want to give her some money. After she got well and was able to take care of ADLs, she returned home. She still needed custodial care 3 times a week at home which Medicaid paid for. After a year or so, she needed knee surgery and the process started all over again. Right now she is looking to get into an assisted living facility. All through her retired life, she keeps her cash in a fire proof safe deposit box dropped into a secret vault underneath the concrete floor of her garage. Her cash is in denominations of $20s, $50s and $100s. She tells me that she takes extra precaution by wrapping the money in zip lock bags to protect it from moisture. She has been doing this since her husband died a few months after she retired at 66.

- **In a domestic S. Corporation, Limited Liability Corporation (LLC) or Partnership** – Adam H and his wife are both 70 years old. In their early 60s, they asked their lawyer to set up an LLC. The membership units of the LLC are owned by an irrevocable trust that the lawyer set up simultaneously. They transferred most of their liquid assets to this LLC. If they ever need LTC, they can apply for Medicaid and will likely get approved since Medicaid will not find assets under their names and social security numbers. Adam tells me this is perfectly legal as part of estate planning. Adam adds, this is not a do it yourself undertaking. You will need a lawyer to create an estate plan since the provisions of the plan can be complex. One of the most important provisions of the plan is to define the conditions under which the funds may be withdrawn. The funds in the Trust are no longer yours once you turn them over to the Trust. But you and your spouse will qualify for Medicaid. The cost of creating a plan is approximately $2,000 to $10,000 depending on how simple or complex the plan is.

- **In a Life Estate** – Rachel, a 69 year old widow told me this story. She has no immediate family members. Her only income is her social security pension of $1900 a month. She owns a fully paid for house that is valued at $300,000. She has no immediate family members but she has friends who live close by and she loves the neighborhood. She would never dream of moving anywhere else. She can no longer afford the real estate taxes and maintenance on the property. So she donated her house to a 501(c) nonprofit corporation. The corporation's lawyer set up a life estate whereby Rachel can live in the house for as long as she lives. In return, the corporation which now owns the house provides necessary maintenance and the property is now exempt from real estate taxes. Rachel qualifies for Medicaid. She tells me that you need a lawyer to set up a Life Estate. You cannot do this on your own.

15. Estate Planning, asset protection – Setting up a trust to avoid probate, exposure to creditors and predators

Estate planning goes hand in hand with asset preservation, planning for retirement and long term care. Here is a check list of things to consider as part of your estate planning package:

- **Create or update your will and living will**
  1. Take an inventory of your assets and define who will receive them and how much.
  2. Include a Living Will clause, health care declaration and a power of attorney which gives someone you choose the power to make decisions if you are mentally incapacitated. Here is an example of a living will clause, "if my physician determines that I am brain dead, any medical life support and life sustaining treatment must be terminated".
  3. Make a declaration how you want your funeral handled, e.g. "I want my body to be cremated and my ashes scattered in the Atlantic Ocean".
  4. Name a personal guardian for your minor children.
  5. Name an executor and trustee of your estate.

- **Draw up a power of attorney (POA)**

The purpose of this important document is to give another person the authority to make important decisions on your behalf. A specific POA grants authority over a single or specific matter, whereas a general POA grants blanket authority in all matters as permitted by law. If the grantor of a POA dies or becomes incapacitated, the POA becomes invalidated. A "Durable POA" will survive the death or incapacitation of the grantor. There are do it yourself forms but it is better to consult an attorney to create a will, living will and durable power of attorney than doing it yourself. The attorney will ask you the right questions in order to find out what you want to accomplish out of these legal documents.

- **Set up a Revocable Living Trust ("RLT") to skip probate.** If you only have a will, your estate will not escape probate which is an expensive and time consuming court procedure to validate your will. If you have minor children, that is one of the best reasons you should consider setting up a Revocable Living Trust and naming the Trust as the primary or contingent beneficiary of your retirement accounts and life insurance policies. Your lawyer can set up the Trust with you and your spouse as Co-Trustees and another person as a secondary Trustee. If you and your spouse should pass away at the same time, this will enable The Secondary Trustee that you selected to accept the funds into the trust to be used in accordance with your directions, i.e. for your minor children's living expenses, schooling, etc. In the absence of a Trust, your estate will have to pass through probate and the court will have to appoint a guardian for the benefit of your minor children until they reach the age of 18. You can set up the Trust so you yourself can appoint a guardian and you can direct The Guardian what to do after your death and at what age your minor children will receive their inheritance. Even if you do not have minor children, The Trust will still serve you well by letting your estate skip probate. While you're living, you can still access and use the assets because you are the Trustee. There are many things to consider when setting up a Revocable Living Trust and an estate planning attorney should be able to readily hand you a questionnaire that will help in drafting the various provisions of the Trust. Among the many different considerations are: 1) the assets that will go into the Trust (the more assets you put into the Trust the better), 2) location of the assets (each state has different rules), 3) beneficiaries, 4) your marital status, e.g. if divorced, relationship with ex-spouses and how that may affect the Trust and beneficiaries. You can pretty much transfer into the Trust most of your assets, real estate, life insurance, patents and copyrights, jewelry, valuable works of art, stamp and coin collections, stocks and bonds, cars and even cash in the bank. The more assets there are in the Trust the better it will be for your beneficiaries when you die. The assets in the trust will pass on to your beneficiaries without probate. You can add assets to your Trust anytime and can always sell, give away or take back the assets since you are the trustee. However, a Revocable Trust will not shield your assets from frivolous lawsuits, creditors and predators. For asset protection, you will need an Irrevocable Trust.

- **Set up an Irrevocable Trust ("IT").** The purpose of setting up this type of trust is to transfer wealth, protect assets from creditor claims and frivolous lawsuits, to delay or reduce taxes, to avoid the Medicaid "spend down" provision for nursing home care. There are many different trusts for different purposes. Any mistakes in the wording of the trust will prove to be costly. A skilled and experienced trust attorney can set up an "IT" correctly once you define your objectives. Bottomline: The assets you will transfer into an "IT" are no longer yours. The assets will be protected from frivolous lawsuits, creditors and predators if you get sued but you will no longer have access to the assets. If you file for bankruptcy, the assets you transferred into the "IT" will not be counted. The assets in the trust will pass on to your beneficiaries without probate upon your death.

- **Fill out beneficiary forms to avoid probate.** Naming a beneficiary for bank accounts, 401k and brokerage accounts allows the funds to skip the probate process which can be quite lengthy. The balance of the accounts are automatically payable to the beneficiary upon your death in most states. In some states, banks require a specific beneficiary form called "payable on death (POD) beneficiary designation form". In some states, stock brokers where your investments in stocks and bonds are held, will need a specific form called Transfer on Death (TOD) form to transfer the investments to your beneficiary upon death without probate court proceedings which can be expensive.

- **Organize and store your documents and inform your executor of their location.** A simple storage system is to keep documents in a binder and put the binder inside a fireproof safe. Some of the documents you should keep in the binder are the following: Will, trusts, deeds, stock certificates, bonds, annuities, insurance policies, bank accounts, mutual funds, safe deposit box contracts, IRA and 401k account documents, credit card statements, mortgage loans, promissory notes, utilities, social security card, passport.

    You need a lawyer to set up a trust and create a will. Mistakes in these documents can be costly and may result in unintended consequences for your heirs, so the legal fee a good attorney will charge is worth the price. Do you want any of your in-laws to inherit some of your assets? An estate planning attorney will give you a questionnaire that covers all bases which should answer various questions such as this one.

- **Life insurance for estate planning.** See the next chapter for a comparison between buying a life insurance policy and leaving your IRA account alone as inheritance for your heirs when you pass. Check with your tax accountant, insurance agent, financial advisor or estate tax attorney to find out if it makes sense to set up an Irrevocable Life Insurance Trust (ILIT) for your current situation. Your age, health and the size of your estate will be factors whether or not permanent life insurance makes sense for you. See Chapter, **"Insurance**

Policy vs. IRA" in the book, *"The Six Million Dollar Retiree"*,
https://www.amazon.com/Six-Million-Dollar-Retiree-retirement-ebook/dp/B073XTL47J/ref=sr_1_6?s=digital-text&ie=UTF8&qid=1507830248&sr=1-6&keywords=Arthur V. Prosper

The chapter in the aforementioned book has several charts showing "what if" scenarios to help you decide whether or not your beneficiaries will receive more money upon your demise if you buy a life insurance policy or just let them inherit your retirement savings.

- For 90% of retirees, inheritance and estate taxes will not be an issue since $5.49 million of your estate is exempt from federal estate tax at the time of writing and many states exempt a big portion of the estate or do not have an inheritance and estate tax at all. The idea of buying life insurance at retirement is so your beneficiaries can receive the tax free life insurance proceeds upon your death and will have immediate access to cash to pay estate tax on your estate. If there is no estate tax to pay, life insurance earmarked for estate tax is not necessary. But read my book, *"The Six Million Dollar Retiree"*, for additional considerations.

You must take RMDs when you reach the age of 70 ½. If you don't need the RMDs, the advice of some retirement planners is to use your RMDs to buy a universal life insurance policy to generate more wealth for your heirs. This can be accomplished by buying a standard permanent life insurance policy yourself or by setting up an irrevocable life insurance trust (ILIT) which will be the entity that will buy and own the policy. Between these two choices, setting up an ILIT to own the policy is preferred. There are many IRS rules and requirements with regard to a standard policy outside of a trust. For example, while you're still alive ownership of the policy must be completely transferred to the beneficiaries; you must relinquish control over the policy; you will have no authority to add or delete any beneficiary; policy must have been in effect three years prior to your death to be valid. The ILIT is simpler, more straight-forward and relatively inexpensive to set up. You must see a reputable retirement planner or a competent estate attorney to assess whether or not this is for you.

16. Enrich Your Life by Exploring the World

Travel used to be unaffordable. Many Americans waited till retirement when they felt they had enough money to explore the world. Unfortunately, by retirement age most people are not fit enough to climb up and down tour buses, let alone walk to tourist attractions to take pictures. Whenever I join sightseeing tours, I always feel sorry for senior citizens who beg the tour guides to let them remain on the bus on stop-overs requiring a short walk to a certain tourist spot.

Why wait until retirement to explore the world? Why not do it now and enrich your life and the lives of your children? After all, if you follow the wealth building advice in this book you are destined to have enough money to last your lifetime. Take two meaningful trips every year. Explore the national parks for at least two weeks in summer and go overseas for at least a week between November and New Year's Day. Most companies offer a 2-week paid vacation each year, and many companies offer 3 weeks after a certain period of employment. Most companies in Western Europe offer at least one month vacation every year. Travel is easier than you think. Nowadays, you do not need a travel agent. You yourself, on your own, can book your flights, car rentals and hotels online through travel websites like Travelocity, Orbitz, PriceLine, Kayak, Expedia, TravelAdvisor.com, Hotel.com and Bookings.com. For local sightseeing tours, I like Grayline and Viator. You can snag some "real bargains" from any of the aforementioned websites such as: $125 a night at Elbow Beach Hotel in Bermuda in the month of May and accommodations at four star hotels for about $100 per night during the low season in Rome, Paris, London, Munich, Amsterdam and Geneva. Because I have been following my own advice, I have visited most of America's 58 National Parks. My favorites are Arches, Canyonlands, Bryce Canyon, Glacier Bay, Zion, Grand Canyons, Yellowstone, Sequoia and Volcanoes National Park. I love driving so I do not mind driving thousands of miles while enjoying the scenery on the way to a certain destination. Some of the most scenic routes I've driven on America's highways are from Hilo to Kona in the big island of Hawaii; Highway 1 from Half Moon Bay to Santa Cruz; Highway 5 Sacramento to

Vancouver, Canada; Highway 70 Denver to Provo, UT; Highway 191 Crescent Junction to Bluff, UT; Highway 89A from Lake Powell to Kanab; Lolo Pass Road from Mt. Hood Highway 26 to Lost Lake, Oregon; Highway 75 from Sault St. Marie to Mackinaw City; Skyline Drive, Shenandoah National Park; NYC to Montreal via Taconic Parkway; Highway 81 from Scranton to Syracuse. Whenever time permits, I find a way to rent a car to take in the scenery and explore the countryside even in foreign countries. The most memorable road trips I've taken were from Puerto Vallarta to Guadalajara; London to Bristol; Chamonix to Pisa; Salzburg to Venice; Torino to Rome and Berlin to Luxembourg. I estimate that I have spent over $200,000 in travel expenses in the past 20 years. For me, this is money well spent. Travel has been good for my family and me, for our health and well-being. My children had travelled to several foreign destinations before entering high school. The priceless experiences opened their eyes on how other people outside America live, on what side of the road they drive, the languages they speak and the food they eat. Most importantly, I've opened my children's eyes on how lucky and privileged they are to be living in America. I was born with wanderlust. As soon as I complete one journey, I am planning and looking forward to the next one. That is why I just don't understand people who have not yet caught this "disease". I have a friend who can well afford to travel but who says he does not want to go to Hawaii because "it's too far". There are those who fly to exotic places then sit by the pool reading a book and sipping margaritas all day long. I have a friend who goes to Cape Cod in the summer and flies to Las Vegas in November, year after year.

Whenever I travel to a new place, I like exploring the food, talking to the locals even in sign language and going to the market places where they go. I can only hope that you readers will catch wanderlust and find yourselves booking trips to wonderful destinations such as Bhutan; Seychelles; Maldives; Goa, India; Machu Picchu, Peru; Kathmandu, Nepal; Durban, South Africa; Alice Springs, Australia; Petra, Jordan; Masada National Park, Israel; Chamonix, France; Interlaken, Switzerland; Naples, Italy. Before you leave this world, don't you want to see the land of the midnight sun, the Alps, Pompeii, Stonehenge, the Eiffel Tower, the

Great Wall of China, Taj Mahal and a phenomenon called Aurora Borealis? For just once in your life don't you want to experience an overnight stay at one of those ice hotels in Finland? Think of the money you will spend as a small investment for your mind and spirit. Many years from now if you end up in a nursing home and cannot walk anymore, you might still remember those amazing trips that you took in your youth and tell stories of your wonderful experiences to anyone who would be kind enough to listen.

17. Staying Healthy and Fit as You Age

I must preface this chapter by warning the reader that this is not an attempt to give medical advice. I included this chapter to relate my own personal story for entertainment purpose only or for whatever benefit it may give the reader. Do not act on any information in this book without consulting your doctor.

If a doctor goes by my family health history it would be easy for him to conclude that I only have a short life to live. My paternal grandfather and ALL my paternal granduncles died of either heart disease, heart attacks or strokes. Many died in their forties and fifties. My paternal grandmother and most of my paternal grand aunts died of diabetes also at a relatively young age, in their fifties and early sixties. My father's side of the family was always plagued with elevated triglyceride, high cholesterol levels and high blood pressure. My mother's side of the family was plagued with asthma, emphysema and chronic pulmonary diseases. None of my grandparents, grand uncles and grand aunts died of old age.

Due to my family history and my own ignorance, in my first 30 years of life my diet consisted of low fat, low protein and high carbohydrates. For breakfast I ate bread, pancakes, donuts, muffins, cereals, waffles, bagels and cakes. I avoided eggs (because they have high cholesterol content), bacon, sausages, butter, cheese, ham and steaks. For lunch I loaded up on pasta, bread, rice, French fries and all types of starches you can imagine. My dinner consisted mostly of different types of starches and vegetables with very little meat (because they are high on cholesterol). My annual check-up just a few days shy of my 30th birthday revealed that I had hypoglycemia and my doctor recommended that I change my diet. I must have misunderstood him because the way I changed my diet was to add on more meat to my diet without easing off on my sugar and starch intake. The result was disastrous. I gradually gained weight and the result of my blood test a year later confirmed that whatever I was doing was not working. I had elevated cholesterol and triglyceride levels, my glucose was high and my blood pressure was consistently 160/90. It was only then that it became clear to me that my doctor's advice was for me to reduce carbohydrate intake---not necessarily to increase protein. It was extremely difficult to heed my doctor's advice. I am the type of person who can consume a 1.5 quart container of Breyers vanilla ice cream in one sitting. Oftentimes I even added vodka or brandy to it. But just the same, chances are if I opened a 1.5 quart container, it did not make it back to the freezer.

My day of reckoning came in the mid-90s when I went to San Francisco for a 2 day conference. My flight was scheduled to depart at 3pm from Newark airport. I worked for a tour operator so I often travelled first class for free. I planned to forgo lunch to take full advantage of the perks, the in-flight first class meal and free adult beverages. I had a big corn muffin at my desk about 8 that morning and around 10am, someone brought out a big cake on the occasion of an office mate's birthday so I took a big piece of it. I was hungry when I got to the airport at 2pm but I said to myself "I can bear it" for another half hour until boarding time. I don't know how it is now since I have not been in first class for quite some time but back then, the airline crew pampered first class passengers and served them alcoholic drinks as soon as they were seated. We had priority boarding and by the time the last passenger boarded, I had already consumed 2 glasses of champagne. Before the plane moved I finished three more drinks, 3 shots of Chivas and gobbled up an assortment of appetizers. Then the flight attendants cleaned up and folded back our tray tables. As the plane was taking off, I felt a little nauseous and could not wait until the "fasten your seat belt sign" was turned off. I had a window seat and the seat next to mine was vacant so I was able to quickly get up and run towards the lavatory. The next thing I remember I am lying on the aisle and I am hearing a woman's voice on the PA announcing "if there is a doctor on the plane please come over..." I soon realized I passed out on my way to the lavatory. A stewardess has loosened my belt, unbuttoned my pants and held me down when I tried to get up, saying "stay on your back sir, the doctor is coming". Soon the doctor was examining me while I was lying on the floor and asking me questions. "Do you have any medical conditions? Why do you think you passed out?" By then I've regained my senses so I calmly replied, "I have hypoglycemia and I think I had too much to drink with too little to eat". "You should take a return flight as soon as this plane lands. You need a full examination", he suggested. The stewardess helped me get up and got me back to me seat. "Do you have pain in your chest?" she asked, pointing to her own chest. "No, why? And where are my glasses?" I inquired with a puzzled look on my face. "They're in your shirt pocket, you took a really hard fall". I took my eye glasses out of my pocket. They were bent out of shape and I had to twist them back into shape so I could wear them. I felt better two hours into the flight after eating the first class meal the airline served. I refrained from any alcoholic drinks and only ordered diet coke, tea and coffee. I felt soreness in my chest area so I went to the lavatory to check it out. When I unbuttoned my shirt I noticed a 2 inch by 2 inch welt in the middle of my chest. I also noticed a bruise on my forehead just above my right eye. The locations of the injuries led me to believe that when I lost consciousness, I must have fallen forward, face first then bumped my forehead on the back of an empty seat then my chest hit the armrest. I learned two important lessons from this eye opening experience. First, when you become unconscious you will feel no pain. There must be something in our brain that disconnects the pain receptors. A protective mechanism that protects us from pain. Second, I was not healthy.

So when I got back home, I immediately called my PCP and related my experience on the plane. He ordered different types of tests for me which were done over the course of 2 months. These included blood work, electrocardiogram, nuclear stress test and glucose tolerance test. His diagnosis is that I was pre-diabetic, I had hypertension and elevated cholesterol. So, at the age of 32, my doctor put me on Lipitor to lower my cholesterol and a beta blocker for hypertension. And he threatened to put me on diabetes medication if I fail to shape up. To make a long story short, I struggled for 7 years, gradually gaining weight, experiencing palpitations, extreme fatigue, drowsiness at around 3pm, insomnia and sleep apnea. I am only 5'8" and weighed almost 200 Lbs. If I walked only a few blocks or climbed the stairs I had trouble catching my breath. My life changed when my son who was then in high school asked me, "Dad, why don't you walk around the yard instead of spending the entire day in front of the television?" The rhetorical question hit me like a lightning bolt. The next day, I walked around the yard for 15 minutes just to show my son that his dad is not a lazy bum. Then each day, though I struggled, I picked myself up and walked a few more steps until I started jogging, then running a mile, then 2 miles a day. I got my old bike repaired and biked for long periods on weekends, sometimes for 4 hours almost non-stop. Although I lost 10 pounds quickly due to the physical activity, I was not able to take control of my diet until I accidentally came across a book entitled "Protein Power" by Drs. Michael and Mary Eades. Two statements in the book became etched in my mind, "The body does not need carbohydrates..." and, "...fats in the absence of carbohydrates are good..." (Paraphrased). Since I secretly love fats anyway, I resolved to give the diet a try. I followed the high protein diet by eating 2 eggs and bacon for breakfast, broccoli and fried chicken or a burger with no bun for lunch and chicken, fish, pork chop or steak and leafy green vegetables for dinner. It was terrible at first! I badly craved for some bread, pasta, potatoes, rice and sweets. But after only 15 days on this "protein power diet", what a surprise! I lost 15 pounds! The best part is that my blood work taken 1 month after I began this diet showed my cholesterol, triglycerides and glucose all went down to normal levels. My blood pressure was consistently much lower than normal for 3 months so my doctor took me off the hypertension medication. I continued taking only the Lipitor.

That was 15 years ago. I have an occasional craving for sweets and starches and on those occasions, I make an exception and still consume a 1.5 quart container of Breyers vanilla ice cream in one sitting just to get it out of my system. But generally, I remained faithful to the diet and I try to limit my carbohydrate intake to 35 grams a day. I feel much stronger today, physically and mentally than 20 years ago. My weight is down to 165. I kept up with walking, jogging and running at least half an hour every day. In fact, I stopped taking Lipitor 2 years ago but did not tell my doctor. Thank God my blood test readings are still all normal even without taking any regular medications. My doctor keeps telling me, "Continue doing whatever you're doing....", so I continue eating eggs, bacon and steaks. I have so much energy that I now go to the gym thrice a week for strengthening and conditioning.

In summary, I eat a low carb diet, exercise at least half an hour each day, I almost always drink 2 glasses of wine with dinner, I drink at least 8 glasses of water every day, I usually get 7 to 8 hours of sleep and I go out of my way to avoid any type of stress. Stress can cause anxiety and depression and can weaken the immune system. When I'm feeling stressed out and I feel that my mind is in turmoil, I do the following:

- While sitting in front of my desk, I put my elbows on my desk, my hands on my face, empty my mind so I am thinking of nothing, which is similar to what others may refer to as meditation, hold my breath, try to tense all the muscles in my body from head to toe, then exhale. I repeat the process 3 or 4 times.

- Then I push my chair back, grasp the front of my desk and do 15 squats, as shown on the picture below. I do at least 3 sets of this exercise every day. Squat exercises offer many types of benefits. Click on this link to find out more: http://www.beautyandtips.com/sports-and-fitness/10-benefits-of-squats-and-why-every-girl-should-try-doing-squat-exercises/

- If I am home, I do plank exercises or push-ups and sit-ups, doing as many repetitions as I can.

Life is good. Why not make it even better in retirement!

PART IV: OTHER IDEAS FOR CREATING HARMONY & BALANCE IN YOUR LIFE

1. Document Storage and Retrieval System

Getting organized is an integral part of a rich, happy and well balanced life. If you are like most people in the United States and most developed countries, you probably have more stuff than you know what to do with. Although you may think that most of "that stuff" is important, something you cannot part with, a lot of it is really junk. You have to take steps now to make your dwelling more habitable. The biggest category of junk that takes up a lot of space is "important documents". Fortunately, with the advancement of technology we have more options now than years ago for storing and retrieving important documents. Years ago, I used to create folders for each category of "important documents" and filed them in Transfiles (storage boxes) by year. Needless to say, the last time I moved, I spent a lot of money in moving expenses just to bring boxes after boxes of Transfiles with me to my new house. Nowadays this is how I deal with important documents:

- Tax Returns – Automatically saved in my Tax Preparation Software. No hard copies.
- Tax Returns Supporting Documents – W2s, 1099s, 1095s, 1098s, etc. I scan them and keep them as PDF files under a subdirectory entitled "Taxes-2016". I shred the originals.
- Bank Statements and Cancelled Checks – I went paperless many years ago and enrolled in online banking. So I view my banking activities online. I also use the "bill pay" service of my bank so I pay online and save the postage.
- Credit Card Statements - I went paperless and view my credit card transactions every other day. I also enrolled in the credit card company's automatic minimum monthly payment option.

I pay the statement balance of my credit cards in full as soon as the month closes, but this is a safety net approach. In case I get temporary amnesia and forget to pay the balances in full before the due date, the automatic minimum payments will kick in and I will never be delinquent.

- Non-Business Receipts – I used to have boxes and boxes of these receipts before I wised up. Then I started shredding them. Since receipts no longer have personal identifiers and credit card numbers are redacted on the receipts, now I simply throw them out.
- Tax Deductible Receipts and Bills – I scan them and save them as PDF documents under the "Taxes-2016" subdirectory. I throw out the originals.
- Household Bills - I scan them and save them with the name of the vendor then I move them to a subdirectory entitled "Invoices-2016". I throw out the originals.
- 401k Statements, IRA Accounts, Brokerage Accounts – I went paperless so I view all these accounts online.
- Contracts, Health Insurance Records, Important Correspondence, Personal Notes and Letters, Photos, Souvenirs, Mementos. If they can be scanned, I scan them and file them as JPEG or PDF files under the appropriate name, then move them to a subdirectory entitled "Misc-2016". I throw out the originals.
- Insurance Policies, Deeds and Mortgages, Automobile Titles, Wills, Birth Certificates, Passports, Marriage Certificates, Divorce Records, Individual Stocks and Bonds, and Other Legal Documents, I keep them in a fireproof box that I bought from Staples for about $135.

Purge your computer files around the month of May every year. Delete documents from 4 years ago to make room in your computer for current documents. My suggestion to keep documents for 4 years is to play it safe because according to the IRS Section 6501, there is a three year statute of limitations on tax audits. But the three year limitation is from the time you mailed your return. If today's date is April 1, 2016, they may audit your tax return for the year 2012 if you did not mail it before April 1, 2013. There is no statute of limitation if the IRS suspects the taxpayer filed a false or fraudulent return.

2. Don't be a Hoarder

Now that you have a blueprint on how to keep documents that you should keep, let us deal with the stuff that you don't have to keep. This chapter does not address "compulsive hoarding". If you are a compulsive hoarder and you hoard more than the things shown below, you will need more than this book to unclutter your life. The following shows the things that I used to hoard and the steps I have taken to unclutter my precious and limited living space:

- Clothes, socks, shoes, gloves, hats, costumes – I hated throwing clothes away even the very old ones and the ones that don't fit anymore. I only threw out the ones that were soiled and worn out. My clothes continued to accumulate since I kept buying more. Solution: I threw out or gave away clothes that I have not worn in a year. Now if I buy a piece of clothing, say a pair of pants, I get rid of an older pair of pants. It is sort of a like-kind exchange.
- Books, magazines, old newspapers, encyclopedias, dictionaries, maps, bibles, catalogs, posters – I kept them all to use as reference for the future. Solution: I threw most of them out, now that all the information is available on the internet. I sometimes still receive magazines in the mail and books as gifts from friends, but I throw them out or donate them to the library as soon as I finish reading them. I get

maps from AAA before a trip, then throw them out after the trip.

- Old calendars, notebooks, pens, old bond paper, rulers, lined pads, rubber bands, various office supplies – some of this stuff is 20 years old. Solution: I threw some of the stuff out and gave away the rest. I am careful not to bring home any of this stuff anymore.
- Old invitations, greeting cards, thank you cards, travel post cards, entrance stubs to concerts, sporting events and amusement parks – I kept them all for their sentimental value. Solution: Now I throw them out as soon as the event is over.
- Old phones, broken computer parts, electrical cords – I used to keep them thinking that they would be useful someday or that I will get around to repairing them...one day, but the truth is I will just buy whatever I need instead of going through several old storage boxes. Solution: I immediately throw out anything broken or something that does not work the way it's supposed to work.
- Cassette tapes, CDs, VHS Tapes, and DVDs – I find discarding any of these items the hardest job of all because there is a sentimental value attached to most of them especially the old VHS tapes and the cassette tapes. I suppose my solution for the cassettes and VHS tapes is to convert them into DVDs but this would take time and cost money. So for now they are occupying an entire cabinet in my basement. I would appreciate suggestions from readers on how to deal with these.
- Rusty and broken tools, half empty can of paint, insecticide, weed killer, cleaning solutions, solvents, old car battery, broken fishing pole, plastic forks and knives, empty wine bottles, broken vacuum cleaner, plastic Chinese take-out containers, shoe boxes, wooden tennis racket, old tennis balls, broken flower pots ---- are just some of the "stuff" I found in my garage this morning. Solution: As soon as I come home this afternoon, I guarantee the reader, this "stuff" is all going into the trash can or recycling bin. And from now on, I will immediately get rid of any partially used cans of anything.

For some people, having a garage/yard sale several times a year is part of the solution. I can only say it's not for me. My entire household, a family of 5 only made $300 for an entire weekend of haggling with stingy buyers the first and last time we held a yard sale. If I add the money we spent advertising in the local paper and the time we spent creating and putting up road signs, setting up portable tables, laying out the items, making up price stickers and sticking them to the items then closing up shop, one can easily conclude that I am a loser when it comes to garage sales.

3. Stress-Free Personal Time Management

This chapter deals with how to manage your time outside the office. Your professional goals are different from your personal goals. How you manage your time at work is dictated by the goals you have to accomplish for your employer. If you are having trouble meeting deadlines, you will not last long in that job.

According to the U.S. Bureau of Labor Statistics (USBLS) employed people ages 25 to 54 with children under 18 spend their 24 hours a day this way: 8.9 hours working and related activities, 7.7 hours sleeping and the rest of the time, more than 7 hours a day is at your discretion to spend as you wish. Personal time outside the office is your own time but if you cannot manage your personal time, you will pay the price. No one will fire you if you miss the tax deadline but you will pay a late filing fee. It will cost you unnecessarily if you constantly miss deadlines for paying bills, filing certain applications, renewing licenses and permits, answering invitations, etc. If you keep deferring certain repairs and maintenance on your house and cars, fail to return important calls and emails and miss medical and dental appointments, you will not get fired but you will pay a price. This is the way I spend my discretionary 7 hours in a day:

Managing My Investment Portfolio – 30 minutes

See Part II, chapter 11, "Managing My Investment Portfolio – 30 minutes". By following my investment strategy which I describe as "wealth preservation on auto-pilot", I do not spend much time analyzing and worrying about current events that affect the market. So I only spend 30 minutes a day managing my investment portfolio.

Paying Household Bills, Meeting Deadlines – 1 hour

With technology as advanced as it is today, there is no reason why you should still wake up late, miss an appointment, forget to return a call, miss making payments and forget important dates and filing deadlines. Like many people, I too used to procrastinate. Now I pay each bill through the bank's "bill pay service" the day after I receive them. If the bill is a hardcopy, I scan the bill and store it electronically as I have described in the previous chapter. I throw out the original. When I get a greeting card, I look at it, smile then throw it out in the garbage can. When I get an invitation that requires a response (RSVP), I answer it the following day. This goes the same for license and registration renewal notices and various applications with deadlines. I take care of them the following day after receipt. I open my mail every day. Any unsolicited mail goes straight into the waste basket.

Household Chores, Leisure and Sports

Because I do not spend much time monitoring my investments and paying household bills, I am left with plenty of time to spend on more meaningful activities such as watching TV, reading, eating, drinking, going to the gym, mentoring youngsters and engaging in sports activities with them, doing household chores, yard work and thinking of money making projects to earn extra income. If I remember something that I need to do while doing other things, I use my phone to type a reminder or record a message.

4. How to Store and Safeguard Passwords

Simple, weak and easy to remember passwords can make you more vulnerable to hackers. On the other hand, trying to remember difficult passwords can really be a time waster. Since I designed my own password system, I have not had any problems in remembering my passwords nor have I been a victim of hacking. This is the system I designed: In Outlook, I create a "new mail" addressed to myself. I copy and paste the website under subject (e.g., Wells

Fargo Bank), then I type "login & password". The login can be your nickname, just add 3 numbers. For example, Bob543. For the password use a state or food as "the constant" with a combo of caps, symbols and numbers. Capitalize any letter except the first letter so as to make the password stronger. For example: caliF@1972 or steaK@1972. The website will confirm that these are strong passwords. Now the trick is to disguise these passwords so only you know what they mean. Since I store them in outlook under my incoming emails directory, the subject matter on the email will appear this way:

https://www.wellsfargo.com/ - login: Bob543 - password: state@19**. Or password: food@19**. The combination of capitalizing the last letter and the "@" sign after it, makes the password very strong. The two numbers after the "@" sign will remind you what the remaining two numbers (disguised by asterisks) are. The last four numbers should not be your birth year. They should be random numbers that cannot be easily associated with you but that you will easily remember. This scheme can get confusing if you use many different states or types of food. Use only one constant in each category. Additional example, boxeR@1972 will be disguised as dog@19**. I am sure you get the idea. You do not have to use outlook to store passwords but I like it since I can search the subject matter for the website and simply click on the link. You may store them on a Word document, on an Excel spreadsheet or on your mobile phone.

5. Do Not Take Unnecessary Risks, Don't Do Anything Stupid so you may Reach Retirement

To make you a winner in the game of life, it is absolutely necessary to avoid doing something stupid. It also includes staying clear of dangerous situations. In the blink of an eye, doing any of the things listed on the following "stupid list" may change your life forever or worse, end it. Life in this world is so fragile. We face danger daily. There is no need to tempt fate by going out of your way looking for danger. If we just follow our animal instinct of self-preservation, we can avoid a lot of dangerous situations. Even a mighty pride of lions will not attack a herd of water buffalos if the buffalos outnumber them by a lot. It is our human intelligence, emotions and thrill-seeking behavior that keep us constantly in peril. Our intelligence is what prods us to take stupid chances and live dangerously because we think we are smart enough to overcome any peril. Sometimes we think we are smarter than we really are. We will avoid lots of dangerous situations if we just listen to our animal instinct and let it prevail over our perceived superior human mental ability. Take these as examples. If there is a war somewhere, don't take a vacation there. If there is a hurricane forecast for Florida, don't go there. If you cannot swim, don't go into deep waters. Some true to life examples of stupidity that I have read in the news: Alex Honnold climbs mountains without ropes; Michael Kennedy died playing football on skis; JFK, Jr. flew his Piper Saratoga plane at night even though he did not know how to read the plane's navigation instruments. Experts believe he experienced spatial disorientation causing his plane to crash; "Grizzly Man", Timothy Treadwell thought he could talk to bears and that they understood him. He was discovered dead and partially eaten by one of his beloved grizzlies. How about this for stupidity and thrill seeking irrational behavior: After Christopher McCandless graduated from Emory University with a double degree in History and Anthropology, he hitchhiked from South Dakota to Alaska. A hunter found his decomposing body inside a junk bus a month after he died of starvation as many authorities speculate.

An Alaskan Park Ranger Peter Christian wrote:

"When you consider McCandless from my perspective, you quickly see that what he did wasn't even particularly daring, just stupid, tragic, and inconsiderate. First off, he spent very little time learning how to actually live in the wild. He arrived at the Stampede Trail without even a map of the area. If he [had] had a good map he could have walked out of his predicament [...] Essentially, Chris McCandless committed suicide."

I read somewhere on the internet that, "Being stupid is like being dead. Only others know it." No offense to any reader. The following is a "stupid list" I compiled as I am writing this book, and my apologies ahead of time to those who do not think that any of the following is stupid:

- Drinking and driving, texting and driving.
- Smoking
- Stretching out your credit card debt by making minimum monthly installments.
- Buying life insurance on your minor children.
- Ignoring a lawsuit.
- Antagonizing someone in your office who has the power to get you fired.
- Spending your entire week's salary on the lottery because the jackpot has reached $300 million.
- Claiming zero exemptions so you will receive a huge refund at the end of the year.
- Lying to the IRS, Police, FBI and CIA.
- Driving 50 miles an hour on the passing lane of a freeway.
- Stopping on a driving lane of a highway to check your tires.
- Letting your cell phone ring while on a job interview.
- Visiting North Korea, Iran, Iraq and Syria.
- Jamming on your brakes to stop for a squirrel that is crossing the road.
- Shoplifting.
- Stopping 3 car lengths from the intersection while waiting for a red light to turn green.
- Sneaking into a movie house without a ticket.
- Backing up your car without looking behind you.
- Sneaking out of a restaurant without paying your bill.
- Passing a school bus with flashing red lights.
- Selling your stocks after they have gone down 50%.
- Stopping your car in the middle of a railroad track to look and listen.
- Taking 2 parking spaces in a parking lot of a busy pub.
- Having unprotected sex with a stranger.
- Stopping your car and clicking your blinkers to let deer know you are giving them the right of way.
- Gambling with money that you cannot afford to lose.
- Backing up on the highway to get back to the exit you've missed.

- Taking a dip in a lake that has a sign that says, "Danger-ALLIGATORS".
- Joining a class action lawsuit to collect a $5 settlement.
- Doing drugs.
- Getting involved in a road rage argument or fight; arguing or fighting with a stranger.
- Giving your social security number, license number, bank account number to someone you don't know.
- Buying liability insurance on your rental car when it's covered by your automobile liability insurance; and buying collision damage waiver (CDW) insurance when it's covered under your credit card agreement.
- Sitting for 4 hours through a timeshare presentation to get 2 discounted Disney tickets.
- Buying a timeshare.
- Cosigning or guaranteeing someone else's loan.
- Partnering, borrowing or lending money to a relative or a friend.
- Walking in the middle of the road because car drivers will see you and avoid running over you.
- Admitting to something you did not do.
- Posting something on social media that you will be ashamed of.
- Ignoring a traffic ticket.
- Leaving just your name and phone number on an answering machine of someone who does not know you, e.g. "This is Jason. My number is 646-555-3482."
- Feeding a bear.
- Petting a bison.
- Swimming with sharks.
- Leaving a child alone with a pit bull, Doberman, Rottweiler or German shepherd.
- Running in Central Park in the dark.
- Riding a bike without a helmet.
- Disobeying the instructions of a police officer; and a pilot or airline stewardess while you're on board their plane.
- Leaving your baby inside your car "for just a moment".
- Not using seat belts.

- Inserting your fingers into an animal's mouth to see if it will bite.
- Spending more than you make.
- Going to North Korea and stealing a banner from a North Korean hotel.
- Trying to disarm a person with a weapon.
- Parking your car and leaving your car engine running for more than 5 minutes.
- Filling up your plate with food at a buffet restaurant, taking a few bites, throwing out the rest.
- Buying real estate without an attorney.
- Hiking in Iran.
- Investing your retirement money on a get-rich-quick scheme or exotic venture you don't understand.

PART V: <u>Live a Rich, Happy, Healthy, Simple and Balanced Life</u>

Life does not have to be complicated. If you succeed in following the life strategies in this book, your children will end up well, your investments will provide you with a nice retirement nest egg that will last for as long as you live, you will minimize stress in your life and you will have more time for leisure and for activities that help keep your mind and body healthy. This book is not the magic bullet for success but a playbook to improve your odds for achieving success. There will be unexpected twists and turns in your life but the principles and strategies in this book will help lead you to the correct path to success and keep you on track to achieve all you want in life. If you have goals, dreams and aspirations in life, you have a sense of direction but you still need a road map to take you from here to there. I hope this book will serve as that road map for you.

Having a balanced life for me does not only mean having equal portions of work, play and family life. For me, it does not only mean having a sound mind, body and spirit. What I believe is that it is within us to muster the forces of nature to be on our side by reforming our own behavior in order to achieve a well-balanced life. If you do "the right thing", the right thing will come back to you. This is not necessarily karma but the realization that there is positive and negative energy in the universe that is out of our control and beyond our comprehension. Besides time, light, darkness, gravity and centrifugal force, there are forces in the universe we will never comprehend---laws of science, frequencies, vibrations, fields of energy, quantum mechanics, and our life force energy that affects people around us. I believe that doing the right thing will harness and call on all these forces to rally behind us. If it won't take too much effort on our part, why not choose to do the right thing? In doing so, I believe we will achieve the unity of mind, body, emotion and spirit which will awaken the genius in us. It is combining the fundamental rules of life with common sense, with the sum of our knowledge and with the unexplainable power of the universe.

Why is it that there is a certain order in this world? Who

invented numbers, math, the alphabet, musical notes, minutes in an hour, hours in a day, days in a month and months in a year? Who invented daylight savings time? And why do we blindly follow this world order from birth? Who invented vocabulary so that every word we utter means something? And who makes us agree with the meaning of each word? Who invented tall buildings and why do many people agree to live in them? Why do we agree to spend 90% of our short life on earth going to work every day instead of eating, drinking and mating like other animals? This is because, I believe we are different and the mind of The Creator dwells in us. We have a purpose in life. That is the only explanation that makes sense to me.

I am not religious. But I believe there is a greater power that put us here on earth. I believe that there are physical laws of nature and there are some unknown forces that contribute to our success and failure. Whether IT is called The Force, The Creator, God, Mother Earth, The Almighty, Allah, Jehovah, Zeus, Brahma, Vishnu and Shiva, however IT, HE or SHE is called in different cultures, a greater power created the universe. I believe "the big bang" is the explanation of nothing. How can something exist where nothing existed before? How can something come from nothing? A smart aleck would ask, "oh yeah, then who created God?" My answer is simply this, "No one created God. That is why He is God". In his book, "*The Age of Reason*," Thomas Paine wrote that: "...everything we behold carries in itself the internal evidence that it did not make itself." And Antony Flew (1923-2010), a son of a Methodist minister who was once a leading Atheist but accepted the existence of God later in his life, wrote: "How can a universe of mindless matter produce beings with intrinsic ends, self-replication capabilities and coded chemistry?" I cannot be convinced that out of the billions of solar systems in the universes, man just happened to evolve from micro-organisms 6 million years ago into a god-like creature with a complex body with trillions of living cells and a highly developed brain that created flying objects, the nuclear bomb, self-driving cars, robots and computers. A god-like intelligence that can cure illnesses, wipe out infectious diseases, prolong life, build tall buildings, put man on the moon, create wonders such as the IPhone, Internet, Facebook, Google, Amazon and Uber. Certainly, there is an intelligent design to our genetic composition. The human brain is powerful. Napoleon Hill said, "Whatever the mind of man can conceive and believe, it can achieve". And Norman Vincent Peale said, "Change your thoughts and you change your world".

I believe that the mind of God dwells within each and every one of us, and the power of God is within us helping us see the unlimited possibilities in our lives. A Supreme Intelligence rewarded us with a super mind aligned with the universe. There is no question of the infinite power of the human mind. I believe that there is a certain order in the universe that controls us and that there is a natural code of ethics and moral conduct most people observe...even without the 10 Commandments and laws of men. That there is a balancing force that will compensate for any deviation that happens in our lives. I believe there is an energy that balances everything we do in life, unknown forces that are beyond our comprehension that affect our lives. If we are grateful for all our blessings, we will continue to be blessed and doors will open. How we live our lives matters. Doing the right thing, being considerate to others, considering other people's feelings, to me, are effortless ways of balancing one's life. The following are some of the things I believe contribute to a rich, healthy, happy and balanced life:

- Teach your children good manners, good citizenship and respect for others, especially their elders. Good behavior will help build your children into law abiding citizens with good moral character. From my own observation, it seems that many parents no longer teach their children good manners and respect for others. Most recently I've observed 6 to 12 year old children cutting in front of the buffet line at a five star hotel and their parents just don't do or say anything to discipline them.
- Be honest, polite, trustworthy, fair and ethical in your business and personal life. Always consider other peoples' feelings. You can succeed in life without throwing anyone under the bus.
- Don't blame and criticize friends, relatives, loved ones and yourself for past mistakes. We make decisions on the available information we have at the time. It is inevitable that in hindsight, we made some bad decisions. Let it go. Learn through failure. Do not compare your current life to happier

days gone by. Past is past, now is now. Focus on making a better future for yourself and your loved ones.

- Give to others as much as you can afford. This includes random acts of kindness not just monetary donations. Examples: offering rides to senior citizens and the disabled; buying burgers for children in an after school center; helping a blind or an old person cross the street; opening doors for old people or people in a wheelchair; offering your seat in a bus or train to anyone who needs it; helping someone trying to get a stroller down the steps; paying for groceries or making up the amount if a person in front of you in a supermarket does not have enough cash. Every day of your life you will always find opportunities to perform random acts of kindness. When you take those opportunities, you'll feel great.

- Be analytical in all phases of your life. Always assess risk vs. reward and determine the worst case scenario, then formulate plan B and C. Follow the same principle in managing your money. Always assess cost vs. benefit. I'll give a few examples. I bought my wife a Ronco Rotisserie BBQ cooker for $79 a few years ago. She used it only once. A few months later, I bought her a NuWave Oven for $119 which she uses almost every day. Which was the better buy? Which had a better value? You can apply this principle to every product and service you buy throughout your life. A Murray lawn mower cost me only $175 but it only lasted 3 seasons. After that I bought a Honda lawn mower for $600. It's still almost as good as new after 5 years. Never buy a whole pack of anything if you only need one even if the price for that pack is just slightly higher than one unit. Examples, batteries, light bulbs, washers, screws, nuts and bolts.

- Always take the path of least resistance in all phases of your life. This will pay off in the long run. Do not add any unnecessary stress and dissonance in your life. This does not mean to shy away from every challenge and opportunity that knocks at your door. It just means you must be more analytical in balancing the cost vs. the benefit of every challenge and opportunity. A good example is dispute resolution in an office environment. It is very common to have disagreements with superiors and subordinates. Accept the fact that you will not always get your way. And in taking the path of least resistance, you may lose a few battles but you may end up winning the war. In the process you are sure to experience less emotional distress than if you have an inflexible unwavering attitude. Do not fight too many battles at the same time. Take up arms only after dispensing with the current battle at hand.

- Don't be a whiner. Count your blessings and always have a positive attitude. Always look at the brighter side of life. Always see the glass half full instead of half empty. If you keep complaining about every little problem you encounter, you will continue to encounter them and they would most likely snowball into bigger problems. Conversely, being a perpetual optimist is a force multiplier. If you feel and act like a winner, you will continue to win. Believe in your vision. Believe in yourself even when no one else does.

- Reverse Murphy's Law. This could be a continuation of the preceding paragraph. Reverse "If anything can go wrong, it will". Lately, I have just been hearing people around me complain a lot: "It happens all the time. One day when I cannot be late for work, that is when I hit a lot of traffic"; "When I have to fly to California, that's when I get a cold"; "When I have to make an important speech, that's when I get a sore throat"; "When I buy a stock, that's when its price goes down". Do not focus on the things that go wrong in your life. Count the things that go right in your life. I am sure they outnumber the former.

- Allow your hopes and dreams to take you places you never imagined. When you stop dreaming and hoping, you stop living. So dream big no matter how old you are. The joy of anticipation when there is something to look forward to will help keep you young at heart and healthy.

- Do not fear change. If at first you don't succeed, DO NOT try and try the same thing again. Make some changes in your playbook and try a different strategy. Do not hesitate to get help from all the knowledgeable and capable people around you. Most people are glad to offer their knowledge and experience when asked.

- Avoid procrastination. When you think of something important, do it right away or set yourself a reminder so you won't forget. Do not wait for perfect conditions or you could be waiting for the rest of your life and you will never get anything done. When we put something off, time passes and so does opportunity.

- Do not be a "know it all". Be humble and be receptive to new ideas and respect other people's opinions. Listen to everything, then judge and reason for yourself.

- As much as possible, avoid conflicts and confrontations. Just walk away. But if you get into confrontations, arguments and debates, avoid using physical aggression, profanities, ethnic slurs and personal verbal attacks. You can make your point across and win by being calm, reasonable, smart, logical, firm and articulate.

- Always try to maintain a good, cheerful and positive attitude. Be the person that lights up the room as soon as you walk through the door. If you are a customer service representative, salesperson or cashier who deals with customers daily, maintain a pleasant demeanor no matter how you are feeling inside. If you cannot act this way, this type of job is not for you. If you are a cashier, look the customer in the eye and smile when you hand them the change or receipt. This will go a long way.

- Don't hold grudges. Learn to forgive and forget. If you don't let go, the grudge will gnaw at your mind and you will waste precious time and energy thinking of revenge. As long as you hold a grudge, you will feel like a victim that somebody took advantage of. Life is too short. Direct your energy to doing something more productive. When you let go of all the negative feelings gnawing at your insides, the stars will start to align.

- When you talk to people, make occasional eye contact but do not fix your gaze on the person you are talking to. In short, do not eyeball the other person. Excessive staring, especially without blinking, will make you look weird. If you do this a lot, ask yourself why. Do you have an inferiority complex?

Are you depending too much on the other person's facial expression for signs of approval? Why are you staring? Perceptive people do not constantly stare at others. They have the natural insight to sense and recognize facial expressions and body language without having to constantly stare at them. You should know from their facial expression just by glancing at them occasionally and through their body language whether the other person is angry, happy, sad, disappointed, annoyed, hostile, fearful, embarrassed, jealous, proud or confident. Did this ever happen to you? You tell a joke and the person you are talking to misinterprets and thinks you are being sarcastic. Or you continue to goad someone not realizing she is seriously annoyed at you.

- Don't tell others how they should talk to you. Have you ever heard people say, "You shouldn't talk to me that way..." or "If you want to get through me, this is the way you should have said it...." It is not about you, so get over it.

- When driving, get out of the way of faster vehicles that want to pass you. Do not play games by blocking them. It is very dangerous and there is nothing to gain by doing this. Also, never cruise on the passing lane if other lanes are open. If you are driving on a single lane road and a car is tailgating you and wants to pass you, turn on your right directional, slow down gradually and pull over onto the curb if it is safe to do so and let the guy pass you. Maybe he has an emergency or maybe he is just a jerk, but just let it go. Get away and stay far away from any and all that negative energy.

- When you get off trains, buses, subways, boats and planes, do your best to get out of the way by moving to the side so that people behind you who are faster than you may pass. Even if you are handicap and in a wheelchair, do not insist that you have a special right to block and delay the people behind you. Make every effort to move to the side so others may pass. You may be in pain but blocking people will not ease your pain. The powers that BE in the universe will not take your side for wanting other people to suffer with you.

- Take care of Mother Earth. Don't pollute. Recycle. Use trash cans. Don't throw cigarette butts, garbage or anything out of the window of your car.

- Do not keep repeating yourself. Whether in business or in a social gathering, do not repeat the same sentence or story over and over again. Not only is it annoying, but the poor listeners will lose respect for you and another person might even finish the story for you which can be embarrassing.

- Listen. Don't interrupt. Again, whether in business or in a social function, let other people finish their own sentences before talking yourself. Listen to what they are saying, the point they are trying to make, then reply or comment. Do not stray away from the last point the other person made. Again, it is not about you but if it is about you, it is even more prudent to keep quiet and let others talk about you. Do not finish other people's sentences and stories. You will lose friends. Listen so that you can answer the question correctly. For example, if you are a library clerk and a patron asks, "Are there sports magazines on this floor?" Do not reply, "4th floor". Just say, "No" or "None on this floor". Think about it. "4th floor" is not the correct answer to the patron's question. In this particular case, syllogism=stupidity. Don't be stupid, no offense intended.

- Don't use your cell phone in public places. Consider other people's feelings. No one wants to hear your personal conversation and why in the world do you want others to listen to your conversation? If you must use your phone, step away and keep a good distance from other people and talk in an "almost whispering" soft voice. Turn off your phone during business meetings so as not to receive any incoming calls. The caller will not die if he or she does not talk to you at that point in time.

- Turn off the sound of your cell phone when you are in public. Some people do not realize how annoying and inconsiderate they are when their cell phone rings and when it keeps beeping while playing video games or sending emails and text messages. Don't be a moron. Consider other people around you. Living in a democracy does not mean doing whatever you want.

- Do not block streets, doorways, pathways, hallways, aisles,

277

intersections and corridors. I believe that standing in the middle, blocking or impeding other people's access emits such a negative energy that the culprit may become doomed to being a moron for the rest of his or her life. Please get out of the way, move to the side and let others pass. If you think walking in the middle of the street instead of on the sidewalk is a form of civil disobedience or a protest for whatever, stop it! You will only make things worse for yourself. Moreover, do not rush through doors or around corridors and street corners. You can bump into people and cause accidents. Always open doors slowly.

- Make sure to take evening showers. You may get away with just washing yourself in the mornings before your daily activities, but an evening shower is a must. You spend 16 waking hours a day. Can you imagine taking all that dust, filth and grime to bed with you? Ok maybe not grime since you only have a desk job, but I think I've made my point. Add to that, your sweat, drool, dander, the oil that your body excretes and bodily fluids. How do your bed sheets REALLY smell after a day or two? Cleanliness is next to Godliness…so there. While we're at it, always wash your hands after going to the toilet, floss daily, use serving spoons, do not double dip and do not share your soup with anyone.

- Watch television to relax your mind. Watching TV is one of the easiest and cheapest ways to relieve stress, to relax and clear your mind.

- If you have a long daily commute, try to change this by moving closer to your place of work if possible or by finding employment closer to your house. Nothing can cause as much stress as sitting in your car for 4 hours every day in stop and go traffic. You get home late only to get up early to do it all over again. It is not worth the stress, stomach disorders, high blood pressure, anxiety and depression that you will probably suffer by the time you reach retirement age. Even if you commute to and from work by train or bus for distances that are longer than 1 hour each way, imagine all that idle time you lose that could be put to better use, not to mention the money you spend for fuel and train and bus fares. Also, the

probability of accidents is much greater with longer commutes, that's just a given.
- Do not blow or pick your nose, teeth and ears or scratch any part of your body in front of others. Excuse yourself and do these natural but disgusting (to other people) activities in private. Nowadays it is so nonchalant for many uncultured individuals to blow their nose in front of others while sitting at a dinner table. If this is you, listen, IT'S GROSS! Furthermore, do not yawn, burp or fart in front of other people. The gods of the universes put us at the top of the animal kingdom. They will not be happy if we behave no different from animals.

The following are other minor rules of life that I faithfully follow which do not need much explanation:
- Don't keep your appointments waiting. Be there first.
- Offer a firm handshake.
- Walk fast and take wide steps. Good for your health.
- Watch your posture, stand up straight and keep your head up.
- Always park far away from the entrances of malls and shopping centers where there are fewer cars and more parking spaces. Walk a longer distance. It's healthy for you. And you'll avoid nicks, scratches, dings and dents.
- Do not cross your arms when talking to people.
- Don't call in sick if you're not really sick.
- If you cannot afford to lose, don't gamble.
- Do not cut in front of any line.

Conclusion

Why not make life easy? Take care of your health, try to simplify everything in your life, avoid stress whenever you can, use the gifts that God gave you, keep your hopes and dreams alive, don't dwell on past mistakes, do not envy successful people, don't hold grudges, spend leisure time with your loved ones, be as kind and as generous to others as you can, don't take unnecessary risks, keep your body, mind and spirit healthy and always try to do the right thing---everything else will fall into place. Let the poem by Max Ehrmann shape the rest of your life.

Desiderata – author's interpretation

Written by Max Ehrmann in the 1920s –

I
Go placidly amid the noise and the haste,
and remember what peace there may be in silence.

As far as possible, without surrender,
be on good terms with all persons.
Speak your truth quietly and clearly;
and listen to others,
even to the dull and the ignorant;
they too have their story.

II

Avoid loud and aggressive persons;
they are vexatious to the spirit.

If you compare yourself with others,
you may become vain or bitter,
for always there will be greater and lesser persons than yourself.
Enjoy your achievements as well as your plans.

III

Keep interested in your own career, however humble;
it is a real possession in the changing fortunes of time.

Exercise caution in your business affairs,
for the world is full of trickery.
But let this not blind you to what virtue there is;
many persons strive for high ideals,
and everywhere life is full of heroism.

IV

Be yourself. Especially do not feign affection.
Neither be cynical about love,
for in the face of all aridity and disenchantment,
it is as perennial as the grass.

V

Take kindly the counsel of the years,
gracefully surrendering the things of youth.
Nurture strength of spirit to shield you in sudden misfortune.
But do not distress yourself with dark imaginings.
Many fears are born of fatigue and loneliness.

Beyond a wholesome discipline,
be gentle with yourself.

VI

You are a child of the universe
no less than the trees and the stars;
you have a right to be here.
And whether or not it is clear to you,
no doubt the universe is unfolding as it should.

VII

Therefore be at peace with God,
whatever you conceive Him to be.
And whatever your labors and aspirations,
in the noisy confusion of life,
keep peace in your soul.

VIII

With all its sham, drudgery, and broken dreams,
it is still a beautiful world.
Be cheerful. Strive to be happy.

The following is my short interpretation of the poem. For sure, my thoughts about what it means might be different from those of anyone else. If you have a thought you would like to share, please visit my website: http://Arthur V. Prosper.com/

I
It is OK to do your own thing. Listen to other people's opinions and ideas but judge and reason for yourself.

II
Stay away from all people that emit negative energy. Stand on your own personal achievements. There is no need to strive towards a goal in trying to match other people's success.

III
Concentrate on your own career. It is a possession that no one can steal away from you. But be cautious that you do not fall victim to frauds and scams throughout your life. But remember that in general most people around you are good, honest and kind and willing to lend a hand.

IV
Be truthful to your emotions. Do not fake your emotions when it comes to giving love and receiving love. For no matter how many times you lose in love, love is everlasting it will forever grow in your lifetime.

V
Forgive yourself for past mistakes. Learn from the past and let go of the past. Let go of "what might have been", "what could have been". Hopefully, you have grown older and wiser.

VI
The author of this poem and I agree that we exist but we do not know why. We only know that we have a right to exist and though we can control our own existence, our behavior and attitude, we have very little control of what goes on around us and in the universe.

VII

Let God take control of your destiny. You can always try to do the right thing but you may not always be rewarded with the right outcome. Be at peace with your mind, body and spirit and calmly and joyfully accept your destiny.

VIII

We live in this majestic wonderland. Out of all the known planets in this particular universe, how did it happen that we just happened to exist in this marvelous world surrounded by wastelands that are the neighboring planets around our solar system? Is there another fantastic livable location, another world as grand as ours in a galaxy somewhere within our universe or in another universe somewhere out of the billions of universes out there? Maybe. But right now, this is the only world we know, so take care of it and…be happy, healthy, simple, well-balanced and rich!

****

If this book helped you, your positive Amazon review would be much appreciated.

If you have comments or questions, visit author's website at: http://didosphere.com/

****

SUPPLEMENTAL DISCLAIMER

The information contained in this book is provided to you "AS IS" and does not constitute legal or financial advice. All sample forms are for educational purposes only. We make no claims, promises or guarantees about the accuracy, completeness, or any specific result from the use of the contents or adequacy of the information contained in this book. Information contained in this book should not be used as substitute for obtaining financial and tax advice from a competent and licensed financial advisor and/or legal advice from an attorney licensed or authorized to practice in your jurisdiction. Medical or health information written in this book must not be misconstrued as medical advice. Consult your doctor or other healthcare provider before acting on any information provided in this book. Narratives in this book are based on true events.

No warranties are made regarding the suitability of this book. This book contains an accumulation of information based on the personal experience of the author. Prior results do not guarantee a similar outcome. The author and publisher does not guarantee the accuracy, completeness, efficacy and timeliness of the information provided herein. The information may no longer be current at the time of publication of this book. The reader should seek the advice of a licensed professional before acting on any information provided herein.

Various advice in this book do not take into account your objectives, financial situation or needs. Before acting on any advice you should consider the appropriateness of the advice and its applicability to your current situation. Any products mentioned in this book may not be appropriate for you. Product Disclosure Statements for those products must be requested and reviewed before making any decisions. We make no claims, promises or guarantees about the accuracy, completeness, or any specific result from the use of the contents or adequacy of the information contained in this book. The author and publisher, their affiliates, parents, subsidiaries, assigns, officers, directors, shareholders, employees, representatives, agents and servants assume no responsibility to any person who relies on information contained herein and disclaim all liability in respect to such information.

****

Made in the USA
Columbia, SC
07 December 2018